Mark Nohl
Photographs of New Mexico

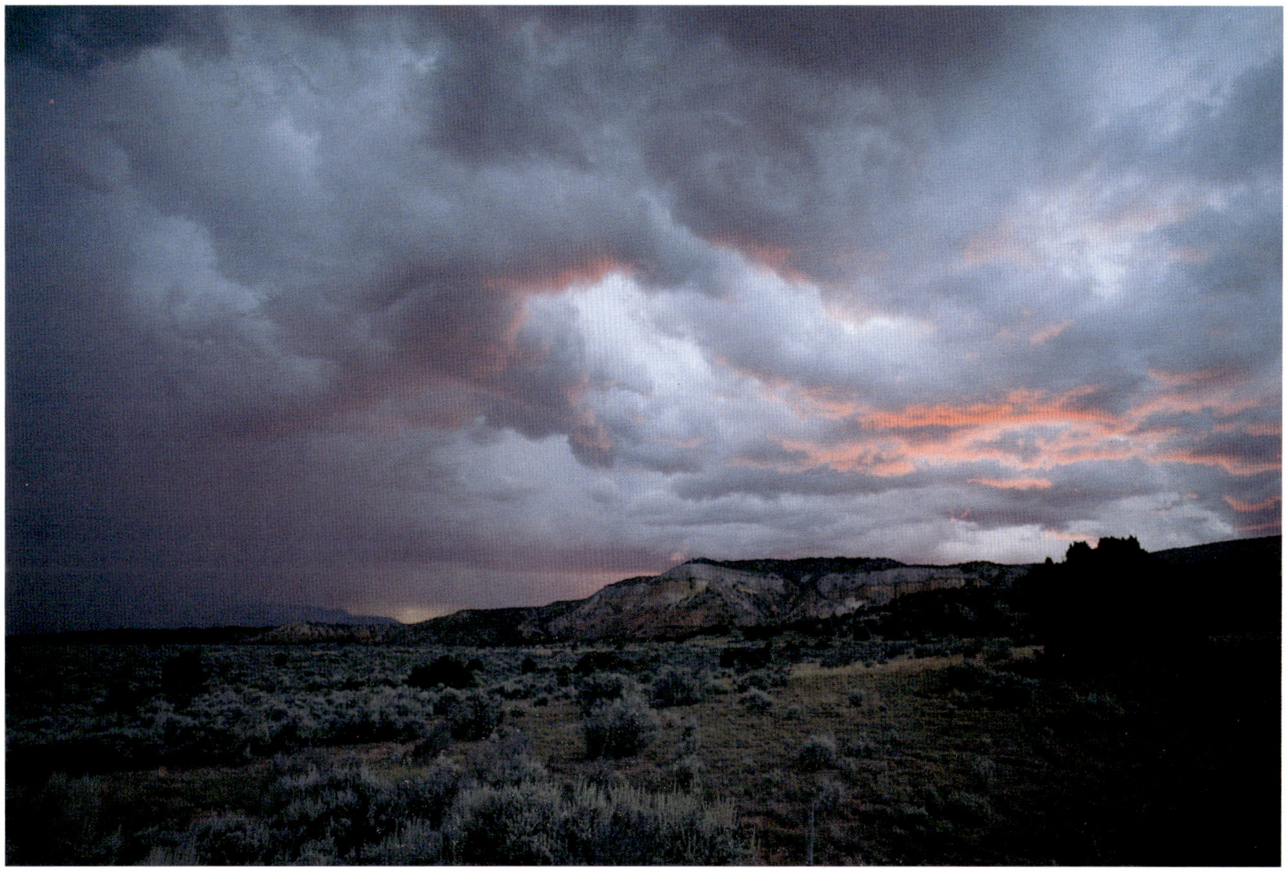

"To see the world in a grain of sand
And heaven in a flower,
Hold Infinity in the palm of your hand,
And eternity in an hour."

William Blake

THUNDERSTORM MESA DE LAS VIEJAS

To my beautiful wife and partner Deborah who has put up with me since high school.

To my son Colin for the love and illumination he brings to my life.

My parents Catherine and Albert and my brother Keeton.

And, of course, the New Mexico landscape and all the

colorful and generous people who are passing through it.

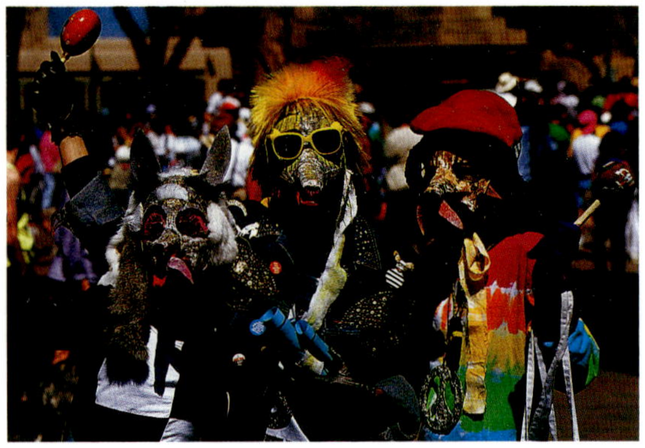

DOG DAY AFTERNOON

Revelers don zany animal costumes in celebration of All Species Day in Santa Fe, where the event is held in conjunction with the global Earth Day.

Mark Nohl
Photographs of New Mexico

New Mexico Magazine is a division of the
New Mexico State Department of Tourism

Authors: N. Scott Momaday,
Conroy Chino, Arnold Vigil, Mark L. Gardner
Editor: Arnold Vigil
Copy Editors: Emily Drabanski, Tera Killip
Designer: Bette Brodsky
Photo Coordinator: Joy Stickney
Publisher: John McMahon
Associate Publisher: Ethel Hess

Library of Congress
Catalog Card Number: 96-072248
ISBN: 0-937206-50-4

Table of Contents

Preface

I don't know how old I was at the time, but one of my earliest memories is sitting on the studio floor of Santa Fe artist Tamotzu and being engulfed by the smell of woodcut ink. My mother belonged to a modern dance/exercise group comprised of the wives of many Santa Fe artists. The group was headed by the late Jacques Cartier, who became famous as the fire dancer who torched Zozobra every September for decades.

I often found myself in one studio or another. This enkindled in me a burning desire to be an artist. Throughout high school I used an old Contax camera to take photographs from which I would attempt oil paintings. I later studied art at the University of New Mexico.

But after three years of trying to paint in the studio I got stir crazy and began to feel lonely and out of touch with the world around me. At this point my roommate talked me into taking a photojournalism class.

That was it – photography. It was the right blend of technology, art and reality. Photography still posed all of the same philosophical questions as other art forms but it also seemed to offer more answers. I've often called it the five-dimensional medium. Height, width, depth, time – which photographer Cartier Bresson has shown us so well – and photography's fifth dimension – believability. Within a week I switched to the Fine Art Photography program.

One of my first photo tasks was assigned by Beaumont Newhall, an unparalleled pioneer of photography and founder of the Museum of Modern Art's Department of Photography. He told me to take photographs like Ansel Adams, Edward Weston or Minor White. I couldn't do the assignment and fell back on the written word to explain why.

I rationalized that "as man begins to understand photography we realize that photographs are 'equivalents,' as Alfred Stieglitz put it. They are not just superficial records, something is going on in a photograph that has nothing to do with the objects that are depicted. Something is seemingly overlaid upon these objects by the photographer."

This was my dissatisfaction with trying to copy the photographs of Weston or any other photographer. I could copy the subject but not the man. This reminded me of something I read by the naturalist Loren Eiseley called the secret of life. "You cannot describe how the body you inhabit functions," Eiseley wrote, "or picture or control the flights and spinning, the dance of molecules that compose it, or why they choose to dance into that particular pattern which is you."

So, along with my written explanation I included a few of my own photographs done in the spirit, but not the emulation of these photographers.

Horses roam the rural countryside near Cuba, NM, along the western foothills of the Jémez Mountains. The area has multicultural roots as both the McCoy (Anglo) and Atencio (Spanish) families initially settled here around 1879. There is no doubt that the Anasazi also roamed through here for centuries prior as the great structures of Chaco Canyon lie just to the west and many modern pueblos built by their Puebloan descendants are situated east through the mountains and to the north-east and southeast.

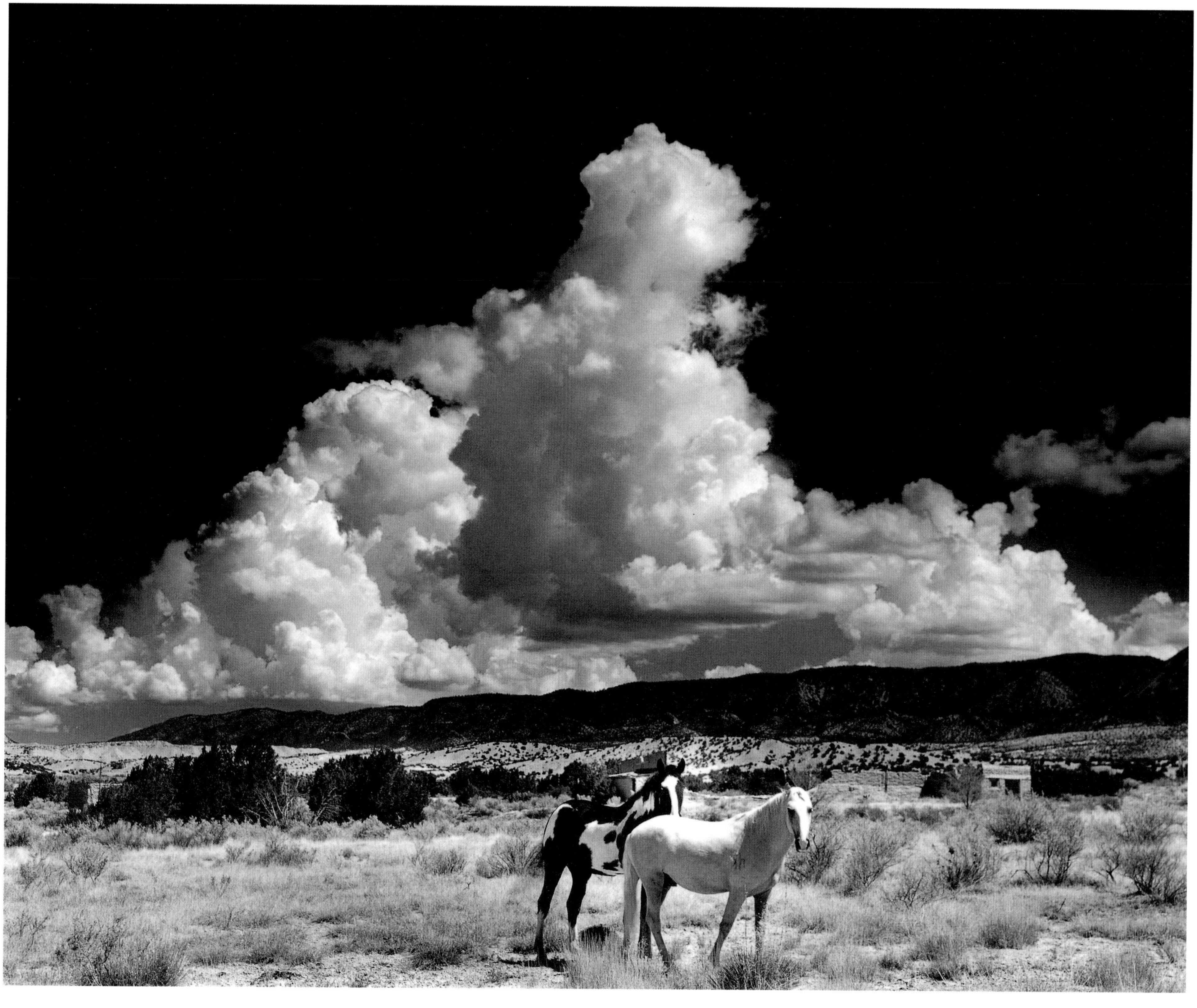

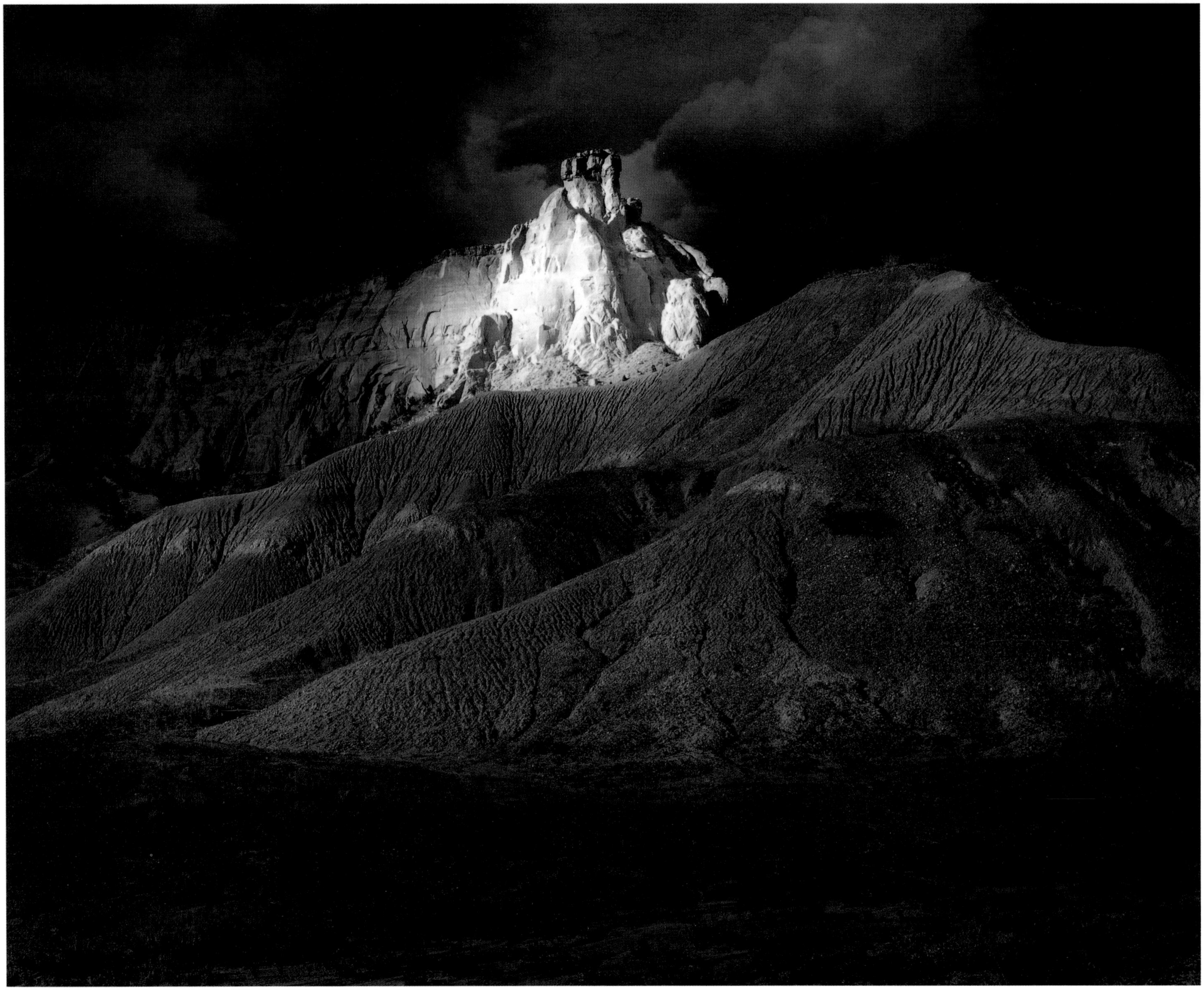

This is a way of saying we are each unique and the only act we have to follow is our own. We must identify our own gifts and insights and use them to improve the world around us. Edward Weston once said, "My work has vitality because I have done my part in revealing to others the living world about them... ."

There is a sense of truth in photographs, right or wrong, that no other medium can depict. A painter friend and I once had a discussion as to why it was so difficult for people, often artists, to accept photography as an art form. He set down his beer and said to me, "That's just the point – photography may be the ultimate art form – it can be too revealing, and that's scary."

After college, I became the first staff photographer for the New Mexico Department of Tourism. I traveled New Mexico's innumerable dirt roads to fill up the department's stock photo file.

New Mexico has long been nicknamed the place "where the Southwest began." Here, I can wander through the ruins of the "ancient ones," the Anasazi. I can climb into an alpine forest or hike the Chihuahuan Desert. I can brand cattle, see a Buffalo Dance or watch the metamorphosis as the Indian culture is forced to integrate into contemporary western society. I can sit peacefully and watch the moon set over Ship Rock and contemplate New Mexico's and the world's many new beginnings.

During World War II, about 500 yards from where I now live, my mother, holding my infant brother, stood at dawn to witness the first nuclear flash from a test bomb detonated at Trinity Site, about 221 miles to the south. Some believed the blast would set off a chain reaction and destroy the world. My mother was able to anticipate the explosions because at the time she was a secretary who coordinated Counter Intelligence Corps agents following physicist Robert Oppenheimer as he worked on the first atomic bomb in Los Alamos.

DARK STORM CLOUDS CREATE A GLOOMY BACKDROP FOR THIS MAJESTIC ERODING PEAK NEAR GHOST RANCH, NM (OPPOSITE). THE RENOWNED PAINTER GEORGIA O'KEEFFE FOUND THE SURREALISM OF THIS AREA IRRESISTIBLE. SHE LIVED THE LATER YEARS OF HER LIFE NEARBY IN RELATIVE SECLUSION AND FEATURED MANY OF THE SURROUNDING LANDSCAPES IN HER COLORFUL PAINTINGS.

On my assignments, I continually encounter people attempting to understand the meaning of their very existence, a perpetual struggle for many. The mission churches, the kivas, the scientific labs at Los Alamos all testify to this struggle, exemplifying man's need for meaning. The psychologist Erich Fromm philosophized that at a certain point in evolution the animal sidestepped nature and man emerged – life became aware of itself.

But self-awareness often times leads to self-importance and causes some to use it as a license to take indiscriminately from the world around us. There are few more aware than a landscape photographer of the constant evidence of man. Fromm also advises that self-awareness is at the root of all man's psychological problems. If this is so – it can also be the source of our greatest opportunity.

There is no greater symbol of man's self-awareness than the camera, which my son calls a "happy machine." This leaves little more to be said about photography's potential. The camera is an invaluable tool and photography a wonderful medium for exploring ourselves and the world around us.

–Mark Nohl

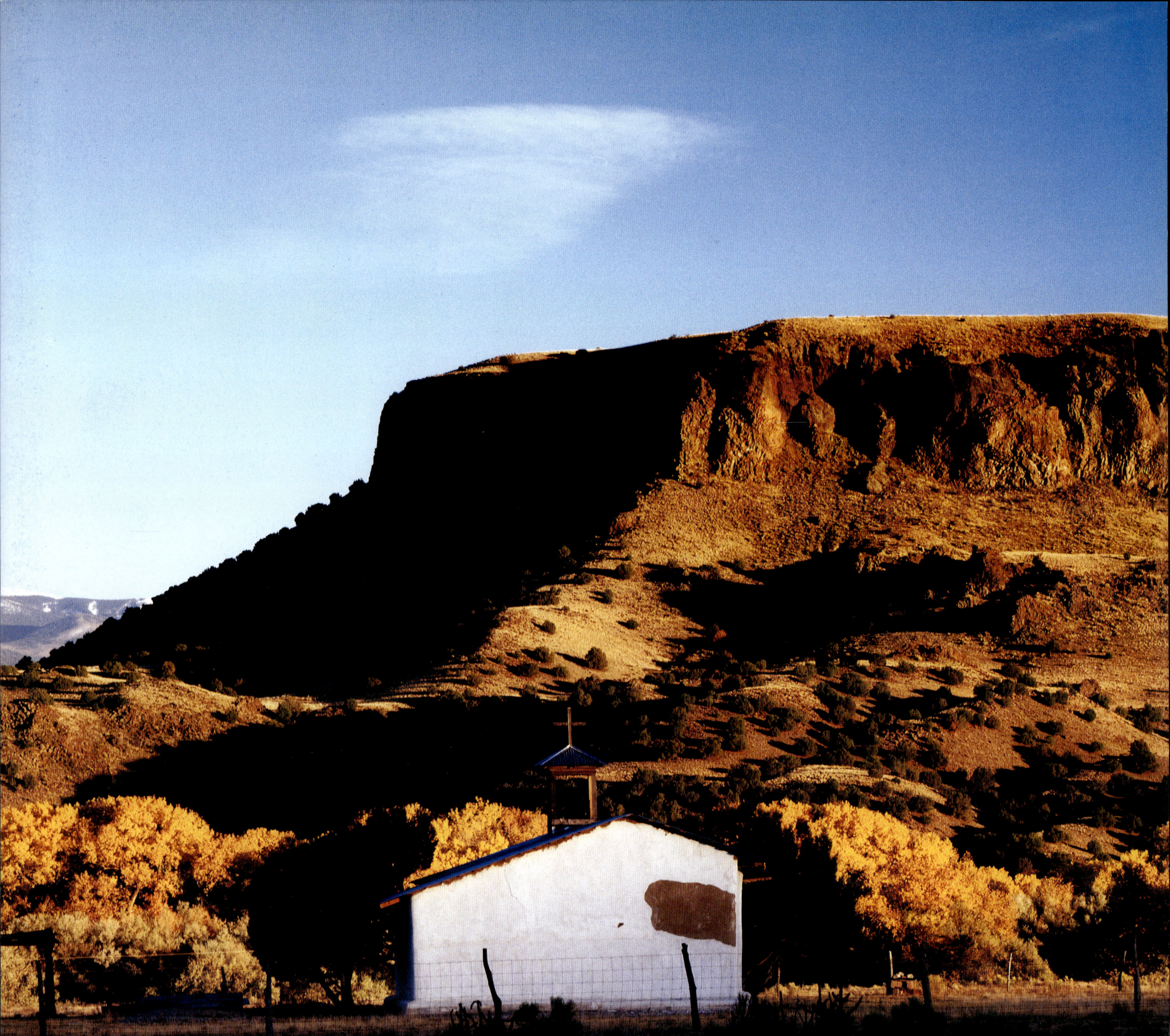

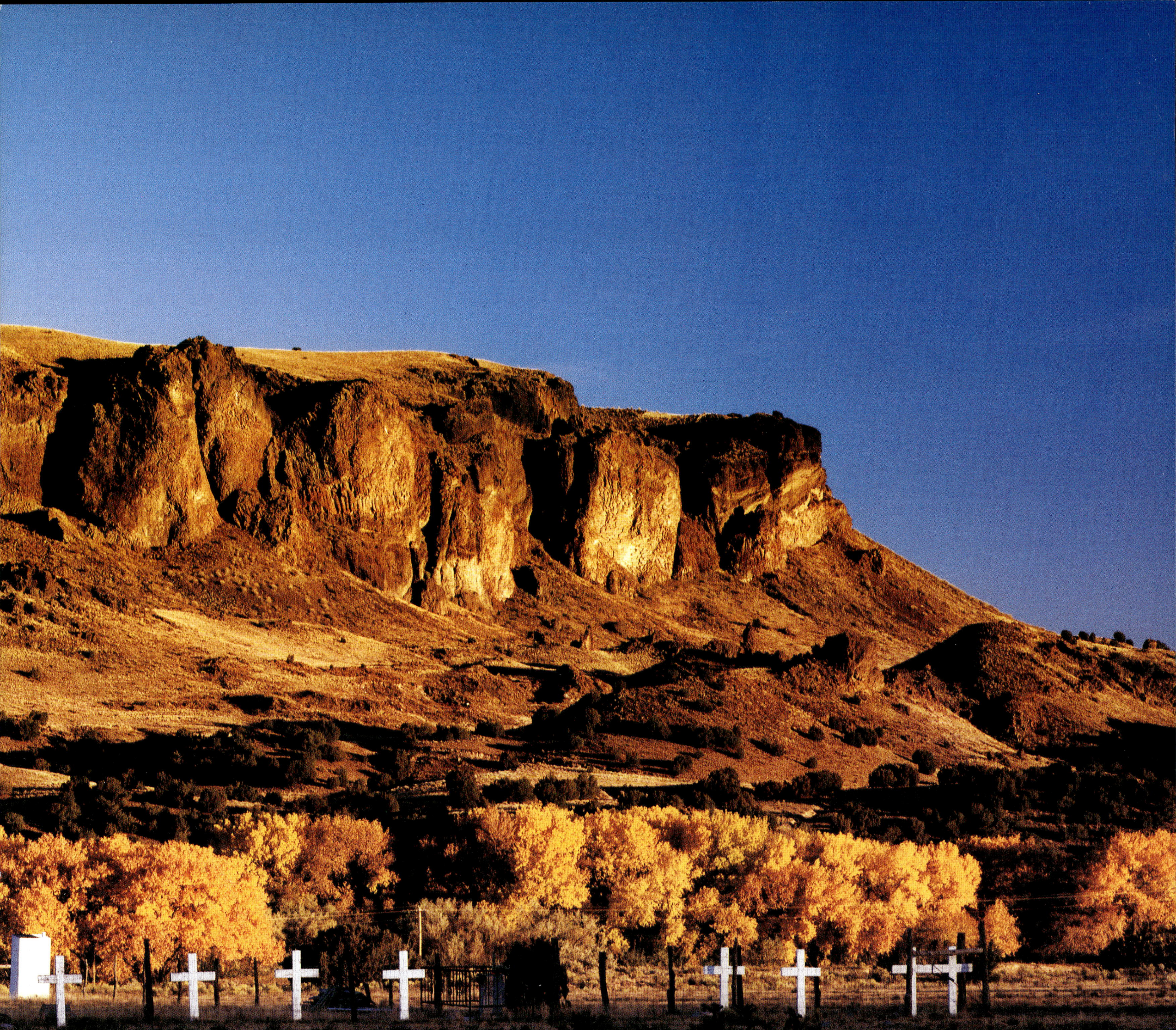

Black Mesa looms mightily in Native American legend just as it does over Capilla de la Sagrada Familia (Chapel of the Sacred Family) south of Española (previous page). The Mountain is called *Toonyopeeng ya* (very spotted mountains) in the Tewa language and Indians believe the mound and another nearby bluff have supernatural powers. Black Mesa sits next to the Río Grande within the San Ildefonso Pueblo boundary and is off limits to visitors. Warriors from the pueblo used the natural strategic characteristics of the mountain to thwart three unsuccessful assaults by soldiers of Gen. Diego de Vargas, who was forced to lay siege on the Indians during the reconquest of New Mexico 13 years after the Pueblo Revolt of 1680.

Soy Nuevo Méxicano

An Introduction by N. Scott Momaday

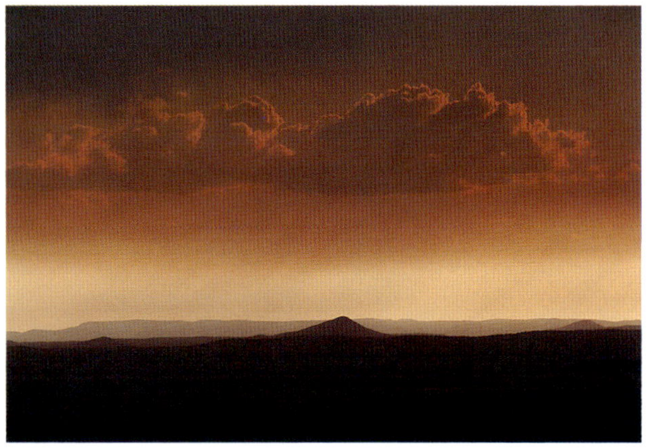

MANY ARTISTS, WRITERS, PHOTOGRAPHERS AND OTHERWISE CREATIVE SOULS — SOME FAMOUS, SOME NOT — HAVE MARVELED AT THIS PANORAMIC VIEW FROM NOVELIST D.H. LAWRENCE'S RANCH IN TAOS. THE BEAUTIFUL LANDSCAPES AND DISTINCT PEOPLE OF NEW MEXICO QUICKLY CHARMED LAWRENCE AND HE WROTE THAT THE STATE "CHANGED HIM FOREVER."

S*oy Nuevo Méxicano*. I am a New Mexican because I want to be. It is a matter of the will, at last. I was born elsewhere, but like many, many others, I have adopted, and have been adopted by, *La Tierra del Encanto*. I can imagine that when Francisco Vázquez de Coronado entered into this landscape, when he camped along the Río Grande at present Bernalillo and beheld at sunset the southern end of the Sangre de Cristos, he said to himself, "*Soy Nuevo Méxicano*." Countless others have said so, surely, and the declaration has been an act of faith, a sacred testimony, a definition of the self.

I came to New Mexico when I was a year old, and I grew up in this landscape. In time, I came to identify with it. It was always a world accessible to my imagination. In time, it became my home. I have traveled over much of the world, and I have settled here and there for weeks and months — Europe, Russia, Central Asia, the Arctic, for 20 years in California. But I have never doubted that New Mexico was my home. There is a homing instinct, I suppose, a spiritual gravity, a conviction that one is where he ought to be, that governs here. *Soy Nuevo Méxicano*.

I want here to invoke the memory of four men and one woman whose lives are impressed deeply upon the soil of New Mexico and who reflect for me the particular spirit of *La Tierra del Encanto*. There is a crucial relation between a person and a place, I believe. This is a sacred equation. When I enter into a particular landscape, I want to see it in terms of some historical perspective, to appropriate it into my experience as others before me have appropriated it into theirs.

At Lawrence Ranch, for example, I can imagine, "This is where D.H. Lawrence stood on a bright New Mexican morning and looked out over the Río Grande Gorge." Or at Lincoln, I can say to myself, "This is where Henry McCarty, alias Billy the Kid, made one of the most famous escapes in American history." Such associations serve to validate, even consecrate the land. History plus land equals story; and where words and names touch upon place, there is the sacred.

Padre Martínez

I first encountered Padre Martínez in the pages of Willa Cather's *Death Comes for the Archbishop*:

> *At the moment of the Elevation the dark priest seemed to give his whole force, his swarthy body and all its blood, to that lifting-up. Rightly guided, the Bishop reflected, this Mexican might have been a great man. He had an altogether compelling personality, a disturbing, mysterious, magnetic power.*

Antonio Jóse Martínez was born in Abiquiú at the end of the 18th century. At 20 he married and sired a daughter, but soon thereafter his wife and child died. Although illiterate, he decided to become a priest and he entered a seminary in Mexico, where he was encouraged for the first time to develop the extraordinary powers of his mind. He became a brilliant scholar and was ordained after six years of study. In 1826 he was appointed pastor to the parish of Taos. In 1856 he resigned his post on grounds of old age and infirmity. Thereafter, serious disputes arose between Padre Martínez and his successor, Rev. Demaso Taladrid.

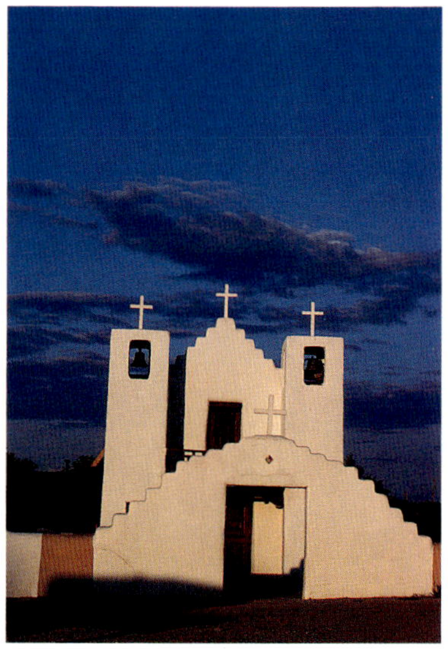

Though officially retired, Padre Martínez continued to conduct Mass, and he officiated over the affairs of the parish as it pleased him to do so. At last there came about a rupture that the Church could not tolerate. Padre Martínez was suspended from the performance of all priestly functions. Notwithstanding, he continued in his posture of a priest and a revolutionary, and, indeed, went so far as to set up an independent church. Bishop Lamy was constrained to pronounce upon the dark priest of Taos the sentence of excommunication.

Willa Cather neglects to mention what are surely the most important accomplishments of this man, the true measures of his genius. Padre Martínez was passionately dedicated to learning, and he spared no effort to advance the cause of education in his parish. To this end he opened a school in which he was the principal instructor.

Determined that his parishioners should be literate, he founded a printing office. He printed his own school books and he published a newspaper, *El Crepusculo* – the first newspaper, printed on the first press, in New Mexico.

Of his home he made a kind of monastery to which the best young men of the time and place came to study and formulate ideas. Padre Martínez made of Taos, in the first half of the 19th century, a center of intellectual activity. It is difficult to account for such men; they happen upon us, and they are the pillars of our civilization.

For a winter and a spring I lived at Taos. The mountains loom above the village. The air is sparkling, and magpies flutter among the bare branches. A broad plain extends westward to Tres Piedras and Tierra Amarilla, deeply divided by the Río Grande. From the mountains on the east, the Lawrence Ranch above San Cristóbal in particular, you can see farther than you have ever seen. In the spring, the old streets of Taos turn to mud. The last great hacienda in northern New Mexico is the Hacienda Martínez, south and west of the Taos Plaza. This was the home of Padre Martínez, built by his father about the time of the Lewis and Clark expedition. It has been restored to its original splendor, and it is one of the glories of the Southwest. Taos, too, has a compelling personality, a disturbing, mysterious, magnetic power.

Francisco Tosa and Fray Angélico Chávez

Francisco Tosa was a friend of my youth. He was my neighbor when I lived at Jémez Pueblo in the late 1940s and early 1950s. He was a striking figure, erect, agile, with all the dignity of an Indian elder. It was impossible to tell his age. He was old, but he seemed in his prime. He had long, white hair and dark, weathered skin. His face was remarkably beautiful, like a sculpture made by a great artist. And he was definitively gracious. He herded sheep. In the mornings, when I passed by his corrals on my way to school, he would greet me with boisterous good will, "*¡Buenos días! ¡Muy bonita día!*" In my autobiographical narrative, *The Names*, I wrote:

> *Now as I look back on that long landscape of the Jémez Valley, it seems to me that I have seen much of the world. And I have been glad to see it, glad beyond the telling. But what I see now is this: If I should hear at evening the wagons on the river road and the voices of children playing in the cornfields, or if in the sunrise I should see the long shadows running out to the west and the cliffs flaring up in the light ascending, or if riding out on an afternoon cool with rain I should see in the middle distance the old man Francisco with his flock, standing deep in the colors and patterns of the plain, it would again be all that I could hold in my heart.*

Fray Angélico Chávez was priest and postmaster at Jémez Pueblo when I was a boy. Some of his books

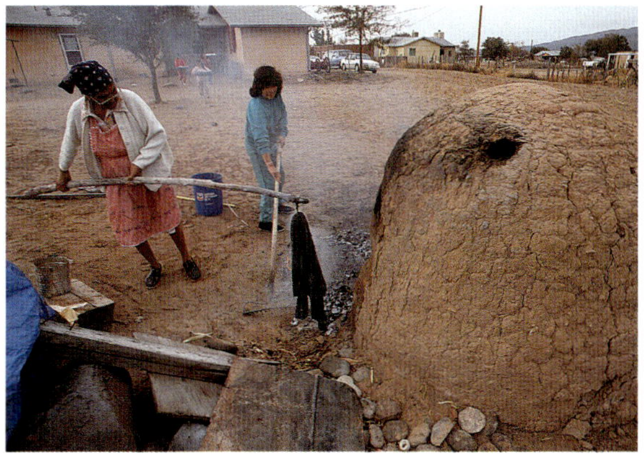

ABOVE – AS PART OF SAN DIEGO FEAST DAY AT JÉMEZ PUEBLO, JUANITA TOLEDO, LEFT, AND SANDY SEONIA PREPARE BREAD IN A WOOD-FIRED *HORNO*. HERE, THEY REMOVE HOT COALS FROM THE ADOBE OVEN AFTER THE TEMPERATURE INSIDE REACHED THE OPTIMUM LEVEL FOR BAKING.

LOWER OPPOSITE – THE MORNING LIGHT CASTS A MAGICAL GLOW ON THE SYMMETRICAL SAN GERÓNIMO CHURCH, WHICH REPLACED TWO OTHERS OF THE SAME NAME AT TAOS PUEBLO. THE FIRST WAS DESTROYED BY INDIANS IN THE 1680 PUEBLO REVOLT AND THE SECOND BY U.S. SOLDIERS DURING THE 1847 TAOS REBELLION.

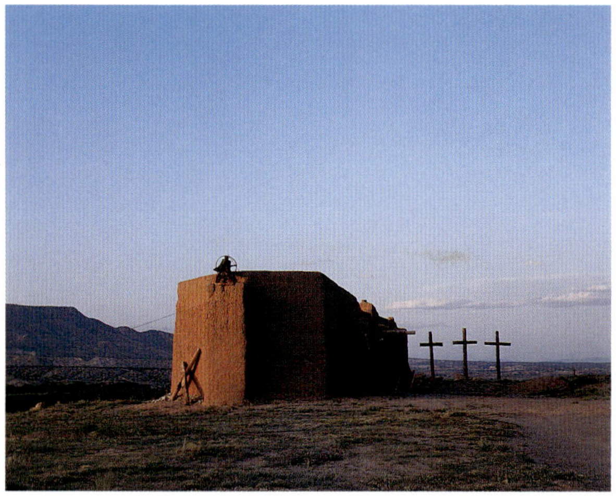

THE AGED ADOBE WALLS OF A HILLTOP *MORADA* IN ABIQUIÚ ADD TO THE PEACE AND SERENITY OF THE RURAL SURROUNDINGS. SUCH *MORADAS* ARE FOUND THROUGHOUT NORTHERN NEW MEXICO AND ARE USED BY DIFFERENT SECTS OF SECRETIVE *PENITENTE* BROTHERHOODS WHO MEET INSIDE TO PRAY AND PLAN FOR THEIR COMMUNITIES.

were in my home, and he was a literary giant to me. When I summoned the courage, I went to talk to him about writing, for I was beginning to try my wings. We sat in the tiny post office, next to the rectory, and we conversed like old, somber men of letters, on the subject of poetry. He indulged me. And he gave me good advice. Years later, he married me to my sweetheart in Cristo Rey Church in Santa Fe.

Fray Angélico, like Padre Martínez, maintained a delicate position in the Church, for there was something of the intellectual renegade in him. But he was definitively a man of God. Moreover, he was as native a New Mexican as was the old man Francisco. He wrote a biography of Padre Martínez, and he wrote a book on Spanish family names in New Mexico. He was born at Wagon Mound, and he died in Santa Fe. From birth to death, he was a man who defined for us the inheritance of Spain and the conquistadors, and the old settlements in our mountains.

Georgia O'Keeffe

On a clear, crisp winter afternoon in the early '70s, I called upon Georgia O'Keeffe. She came to the door in a black suit, a stiff, white collar, and a demeanor that was at once gracious and austere. She showed me her recent paintings. They were of rocks. She showed me her window boxes full of stones that she had collected from the arroyos nearby. She asked me about my work, my ideas on education, politics, art. She could not find the key to her liquor pantry and ended up taking the pantry doors off at the hinges with a screwdriver, so that I could have refreshment. Of course, I fell in love with her.

We shared luncheons of wine and cheese, she and I. Once I gave her an unusual and beautiful stone I had found. And I wrote a poem, which I dedicated to her, entitled "Forms of the Earth at Abiquiú":

I imagine the time of our meeting
There among the forms of the earth at Abiquiú,
And other times that followed from the one —
An easy conjugation of stories,
And late luncheons of wine and cheese.
All around there were beautiful objects,
Clean and precise in their beauty, like bone.
Indeed, bone: a snake in the filaments of bone,
The skulls of cows and sheep;
And the many smooth stones in the window,
In the flat winter light, were beautiful.
I wanted to feel the sun in the stone —
The ashen, far-flung winter sun.
And then, in those days, too,
I made you the gift of a small, brown stone,
And you described it with the tips of your fingers
And knew at once that it was beautiful —
At once, accordingly you knew,
As you knew the forms of the earth at Abiquiú:
That time involves them, and they bear away,
Beautiful, various, remote,
In failing light, and the coming of cold.

Georgia O'Keeffe loved the light of northern New Mexico. Speaking of Abiquiú, where she lived when I met her, she said, "It is simply the place I love best in the world." As painters, we had a meeting of the minds. When we spoke of the light, the New Mexican light, we shared a kind of gratitude and reverence. I think of the Pedernal and the cliffs above Abiquiú, the skies full of billowing clouds, and the colors of the earth there, which are not like the colors of the earth elsewhere.

Billy the Kid

Henry McCarty, alias Billy the Kid, passed from history into legend on April 28, 1881, when he escaped from the Lincoln County Courthouse and rode off, in the direction of Fort Stanton, to live the last days of his life in the only freedom that he could know. He was a hunted man – a boy, really – who was bound to pay the price of his misdeeds. There is no way to defend him. He was a killer, and he was shot down by a man of the law. We know little enough about him, except the notable facts: He was involved in the infamous Lincoln County War; he was among those who killed Sheriff Brady in an ambush and was convicted on that account. He was sentenced to be hanged. While imprisoned in the Lincoln County Courthouse, he staged an extraordinary escape, killing his two guards, and riding off to his doom and into legend.

Like the story of Padre Martínez, the story of Billy the Kid is generally told in two dimensions. He was an outlaw, and he was extremely dangerous. There is another side. He was extremely well-liked among those who knew him. He inspired deep loyalty among his friends, especially his Spanish acquaintances. He had buck teeth, and he liked to demonstrate, to children especially, that he could take a larger bite from a pie than anyone else.

But there is even more to Billy the Kid. In an ironic sense his legend has become a kind of New Mexican icon, a curious personification of the land, and of the people who came to settle here in the latter half of the 19th century. Billy the Kid weaves the disparate cultural elements of New Mexico together in a way. He was probably of Irish descent, born in New York City, about 1860. He came with his parents to Kansas, where his father died. Billy, his mother and his brother Joe came to Santa Fe, where his mother married a man named Antrim. The family moved to Silver City. There Henry got into trouble with the law and ran away. From that time on, he was a fugitive. His career as an outlaw was short. He was killed by Pat Garrett, sheriff of Lincoln County, when he was in his early 20s.

Billy the Kid also interests me because he roamed the landscape of New Mexico from Silver City and Mesilla to Santa Fe and Fort Sumner. He probably knew the landscape of New Mexico as well as anyone of his time did. If you place a ruler diagonally across the lower half of a map of New Mexico and draw a straight line from Mesilla, on the lower Río Grande, to Fort Sumner, on the Pecos River, your line will extend northeastward across the Organ Mountains to the White Sands National Monument, through Ruidoso, San Patricio and Lincoln, and across the vast plain bisected by the Pecos to Fort Sumner.

In a building that still stands on the Mesilla Plaza across from the station on the Butterfield Stage line that ran from St. Louis to Los Angeles, Billy the Kid was sentenced to be hanged. He was taken to Lincoln, where the sentence was to be carried out on Friday the 13th, May 1881. He escaped from the Lincoln County Courthouse on April 28, 1881.

From that day, Billy the Kid had less than three months to live, and he lived on the run. I like to think he visited San Patricio again, a village that was one of his favorite places, established by Irish soldiers who mustered out of the Army in 1866 and built a church dedicated to St. Patrick, San Patricio. That Irish-New Mexican equation must have appealed to Billy, to the McCarty and the *El Chivato* in him. In his last days he stayed with sheepherders in their camps and stole into Fort Sumner to dance with pretty women, or so I imagine. It was there that Pat Garrett surprised him on the night of July 14, 1881, and shot him dead.

History plus land equals story. Billy the Kid must be comprehended, in his place in the landscape, in his place among the people, to achieve a real understanding of New Mexico, *Nuevo México*.

Old Fort Sumner is gone. There are only a few historical markers, a few reconstructed walls, a small museum and even smaller cemetery, where Billy was buried. It is a somber place, a place for pilgrimage. In the early 1860s the Apaches and the Navajos, raided and pillaged by Kit Carson and starved into submission, were forced to make the "Long Walk," a distance of some 300 miles to the Bosque Redondo, the site of Fort Sumner. One night in 1865, the Apaches escaped en masse, surely one of the truly remarkable military actions in our history. In 1868, the Navajos were allowed to return to their homeland. Yet this remains a sacred place, consecrated with blood and sacrifice.

Soy Nuevo Méxicano. I live in this landscape, which is truly a landscape of enchantment. I have known it virtually all my life. I would not live elsewhere, given my choice. I have lived in other places, and I have delighted in those landscapes. The earth is rich with places that are equal to the imagination. New Mexico is one of the few places that exceed the imagination. *Soy Nuevo Méxicano.*

N. Scott Momaday
Santa Fe, 1996

Mark Nohl

Photographs of New Mexico

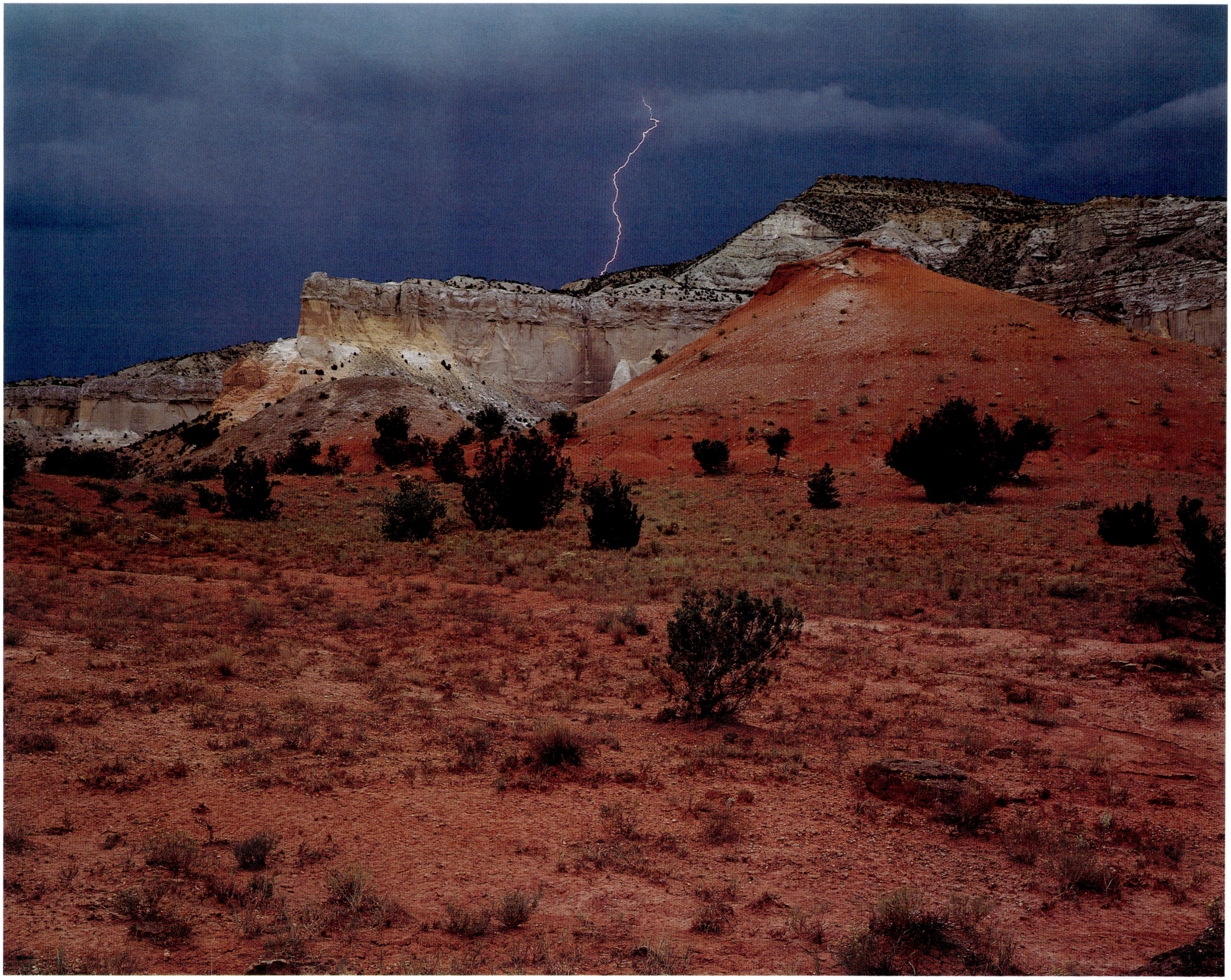

Lightning bolt at Ghost Ranch

A lightning bolt from the heavens pierces a dark stormy sky to strike the top of a steep mesa at Ghost Ranch.

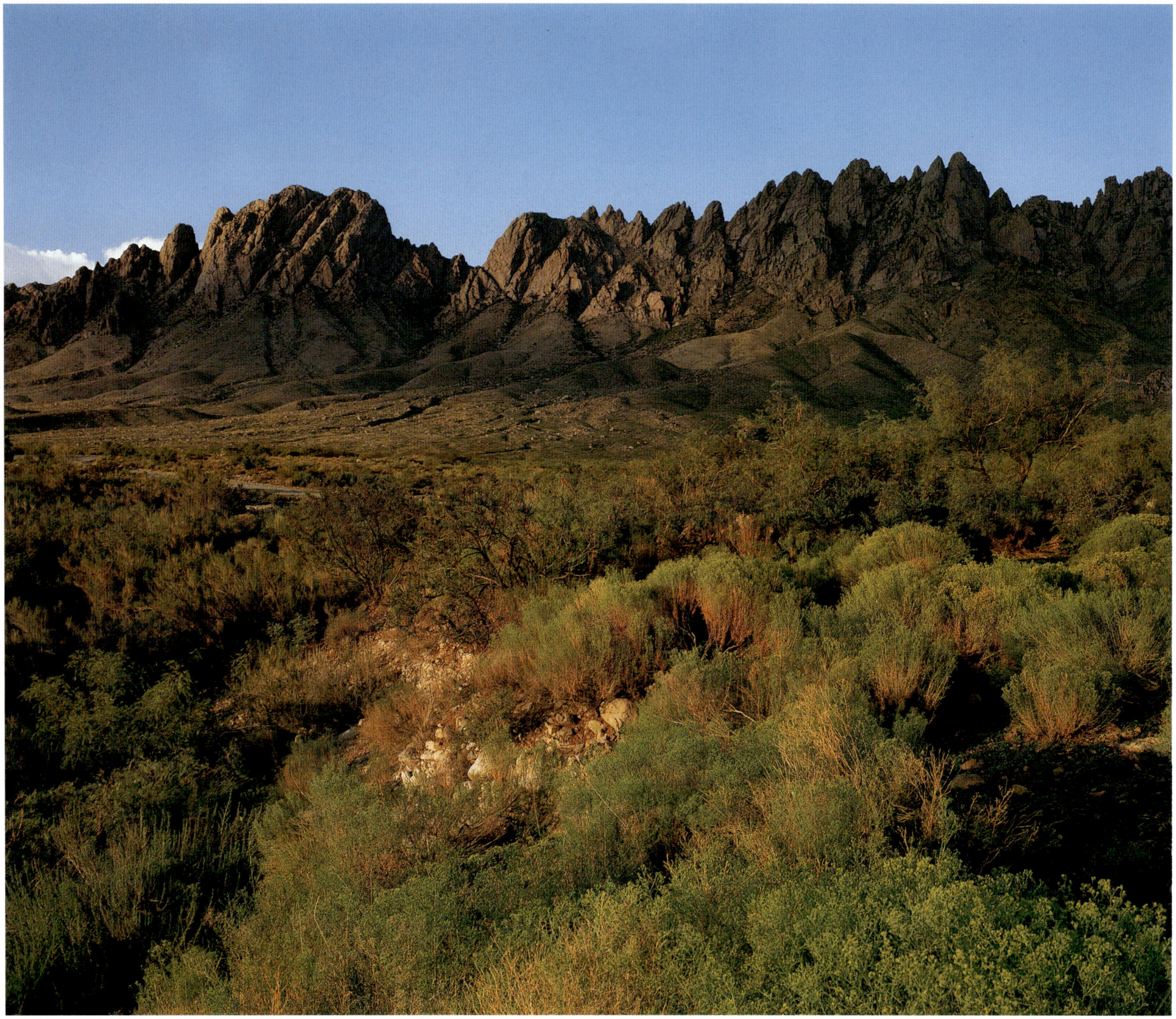

Organ Mountains

An unexpected verdant display of drought-resistant vegetation colors the Chihuahuan Desert floor in front of the grandiose Organ Mountains.

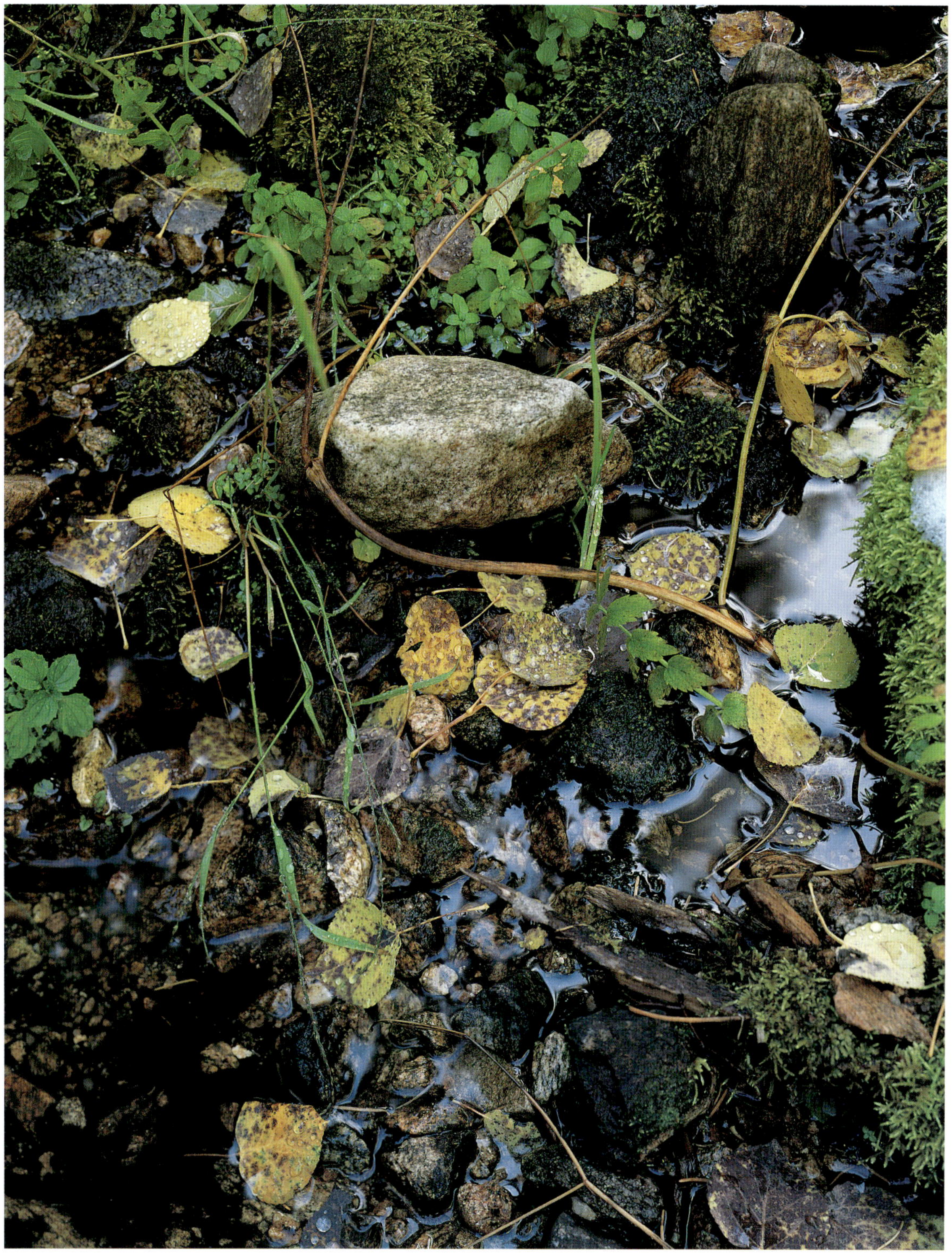

Big Tesuque Rock

Lush mountain foliage in the Big Tesuque Creek near Santa Fe dispells myths of New Mexico being solely a desert state.

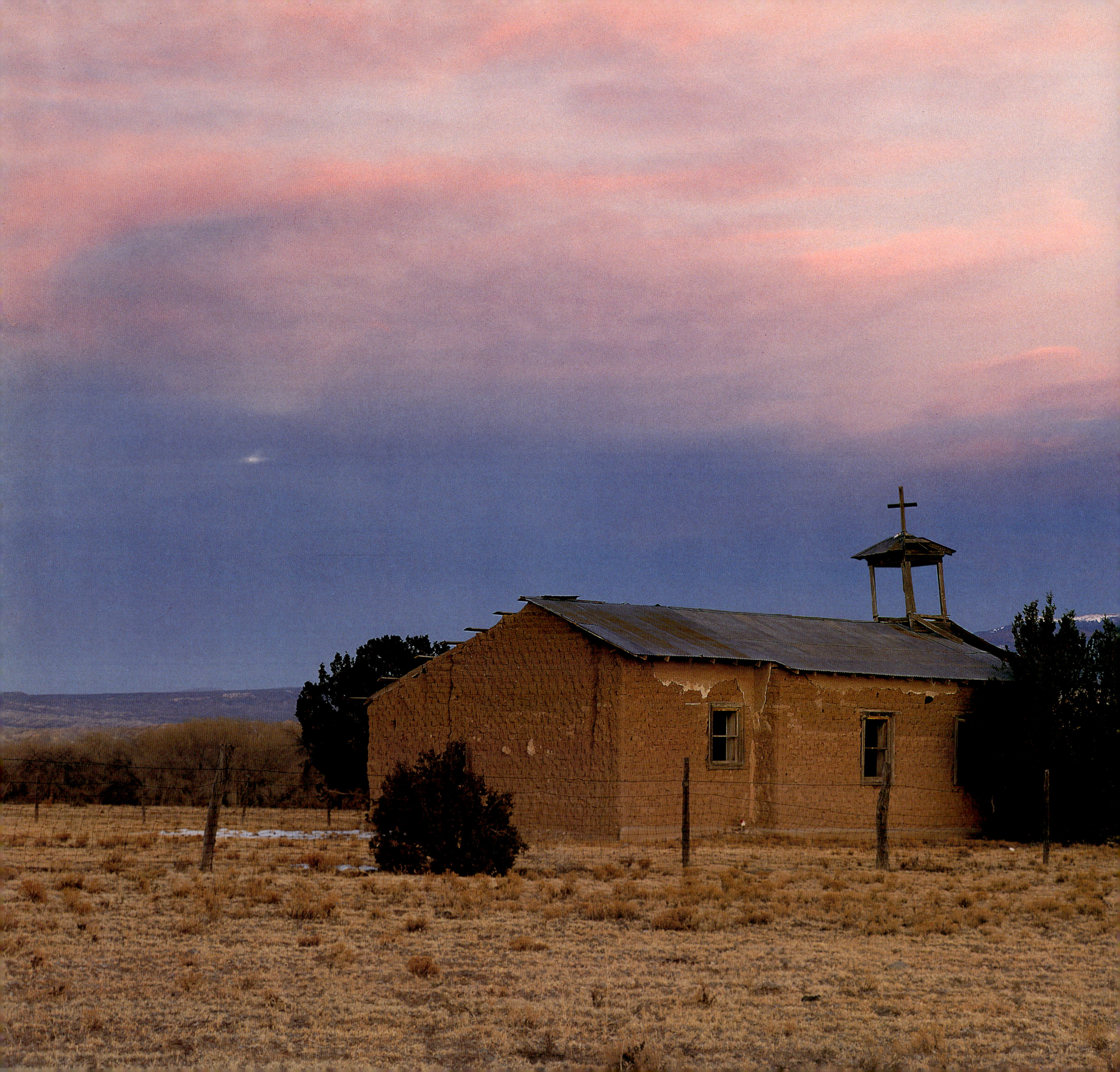

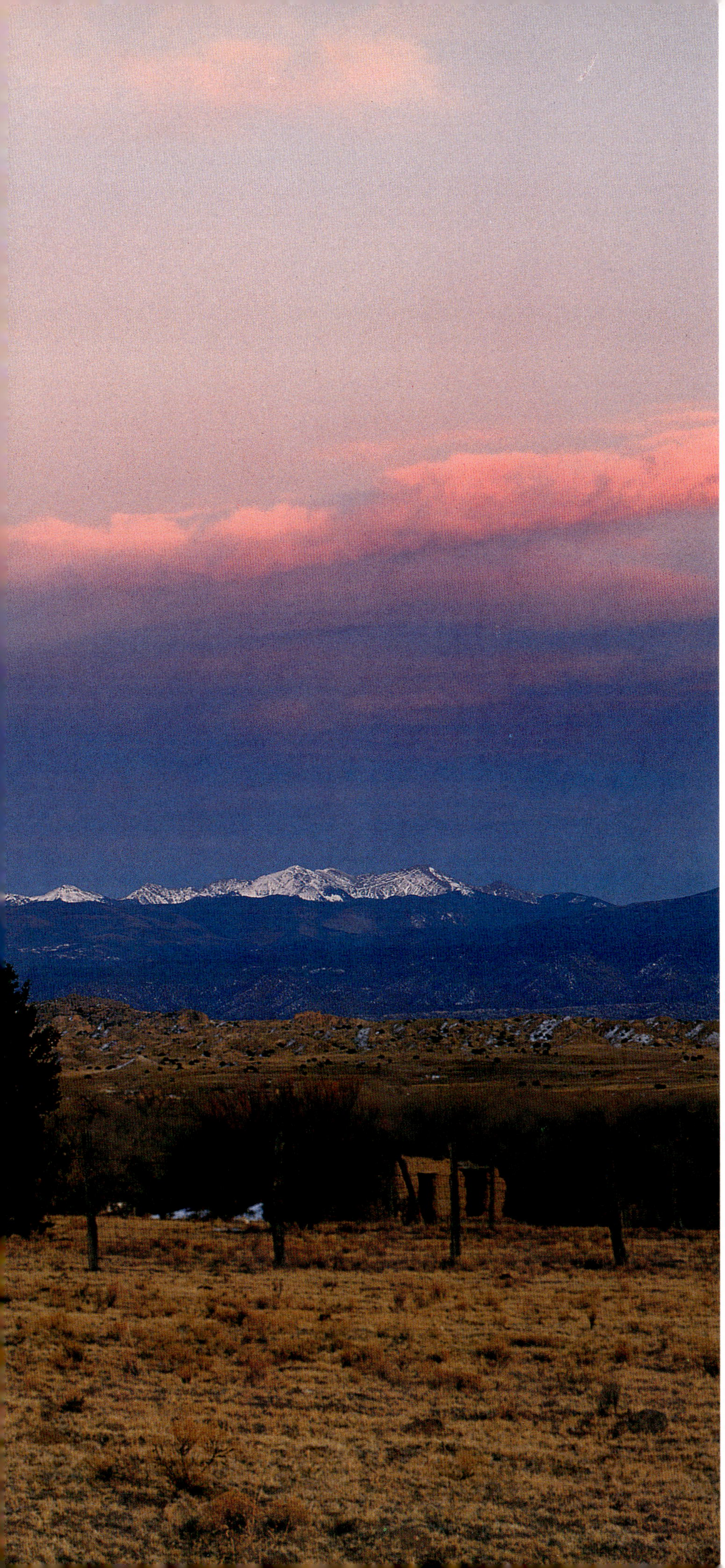

The Truchas Peaks loom over the Capilla de la Sagrada Familia (Chapel of the Sacred Family) in the peaceful light of early morning. This small chapel south of Española along NM 30 near the Río Grande sits between San Ildefonso Pueblo to the east and Santa Clara Pueblo to the west.

Many families living in remote areas of the state built their own places of worship because they were so far removed from the larger established churches. Often times priests and other church authorities would travel on a weekly or monthly basis to some of these small chapels to conduct special services for the area's residents.

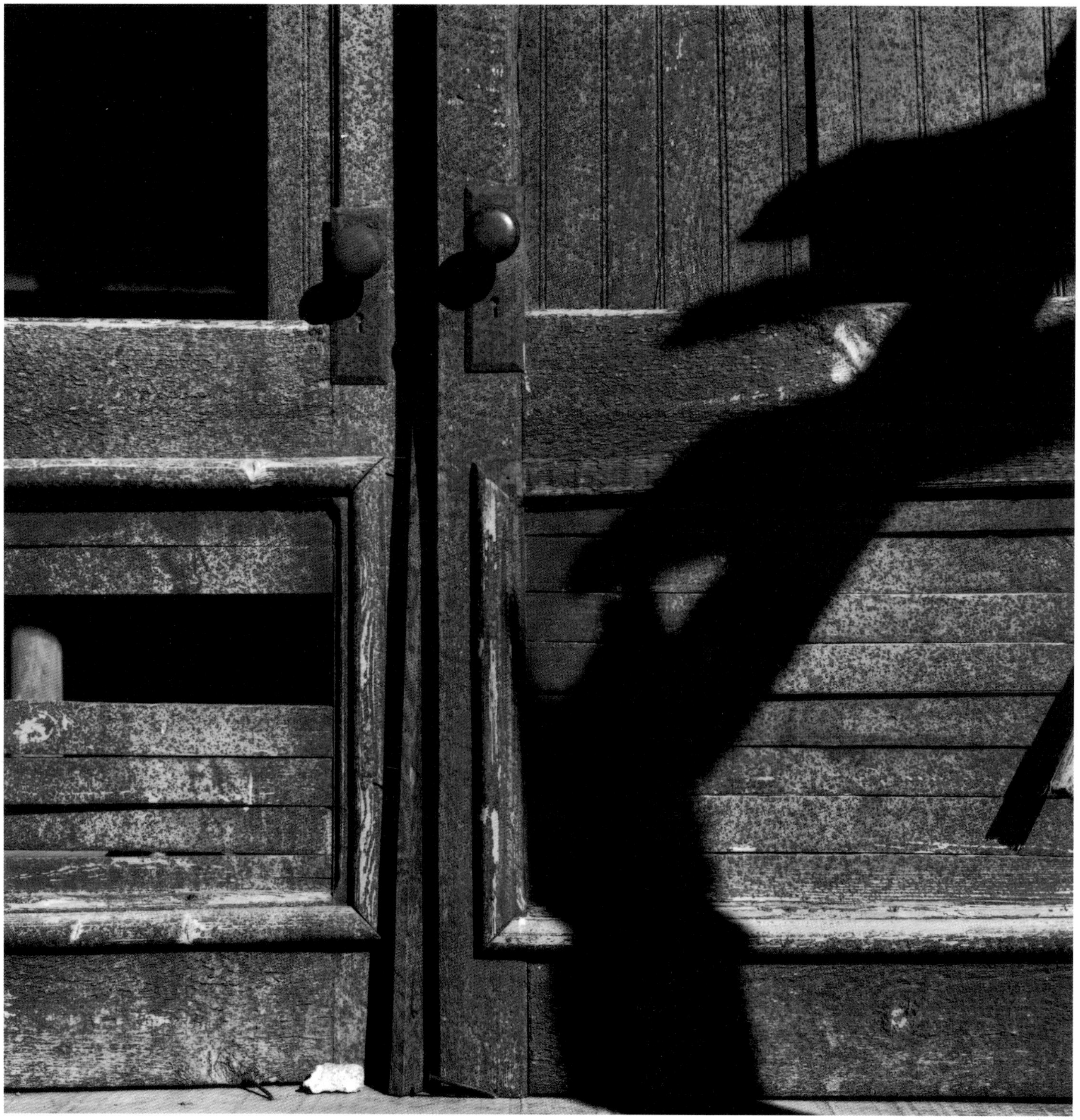

Doorway to the Past

Still standing after surviving a rough-and-tumble era, these weathered doors in the ghost town of Mogollón near Silver City could tell a story or two about those who passed through.

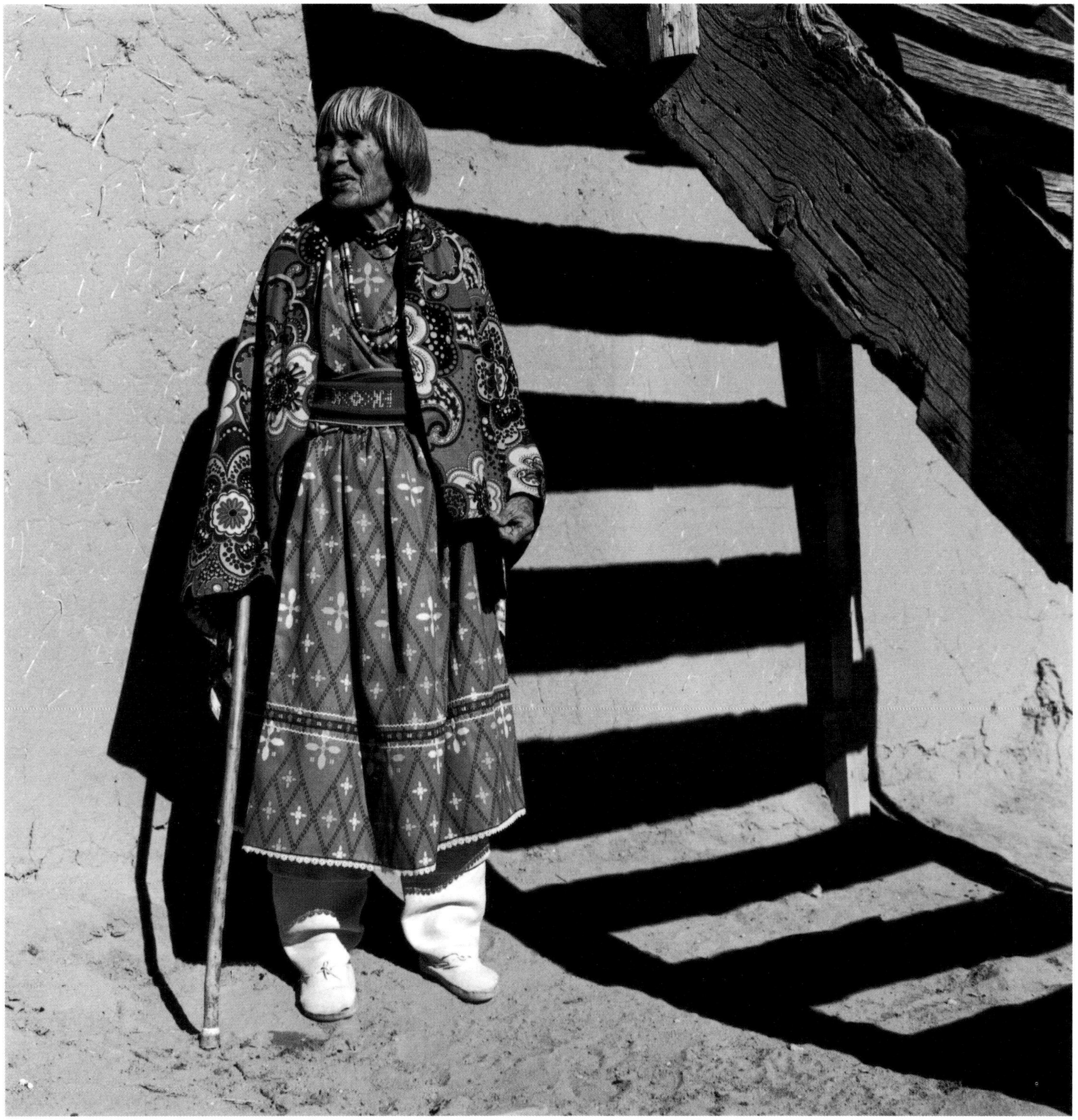

A New Mexico Treasure

The late María Martínez brought global fame to herself and San Ildefonso Pueblo with her magnificent black pottery. She often admitted to being amazed by the high prices people would pay for her work.

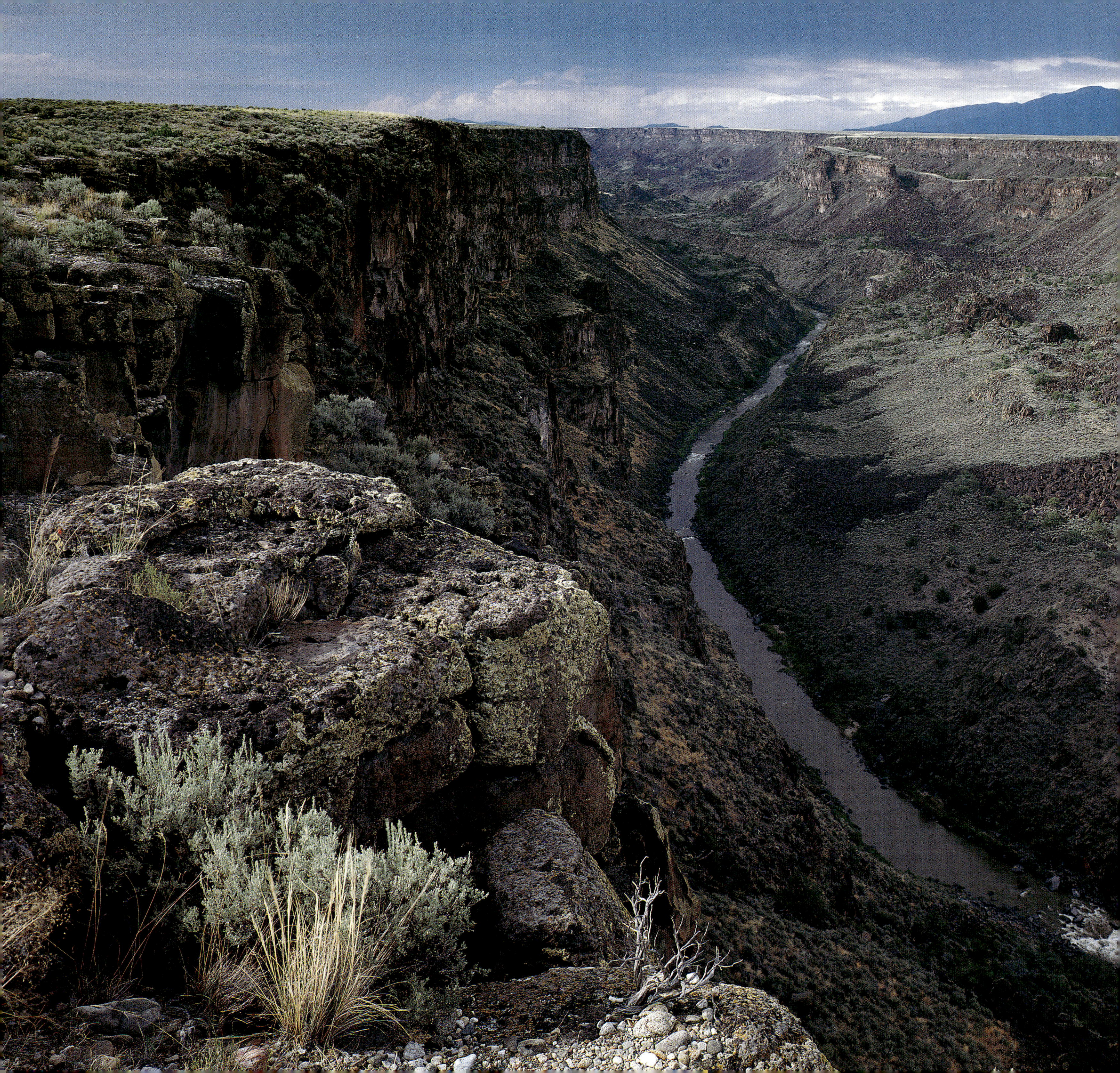

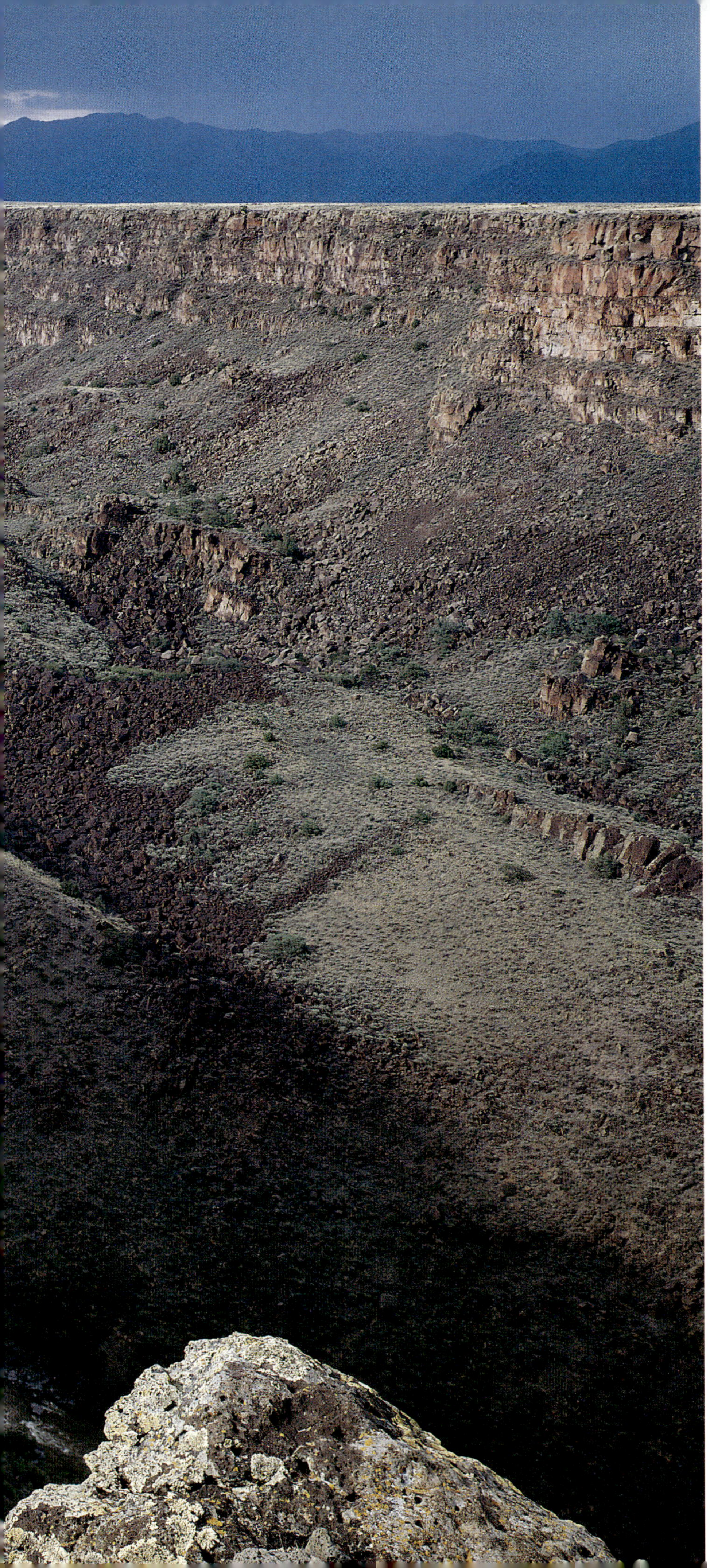

The Río Grande slices through the steep Río Grande Gorge west of Taos. The river journeys from its headwaters in southern Colorado to a final destination in the Gulf of Mexico. After the Río Grande leaves New Mexico it serves as the entire southern Texas/Mexico border.

A study of *Matachines* dancers, clockwise, left to right – Rudy, Skullface and La Malinche. There are multiple variations of the colorful *Matachines* dance in many small villages and even in some Indian pueblos throughout New Mexico. Although its origins are obscure, many believe the Spanish learned the basic tenets of the "good versus evil" dance from the Moors in the 8th century. The dance naturally evolved and incorporated New World characters, including La Malinche, who symbolizes "good" and was the Indian interpreter and mistress of Spanish conquerer Hernán Córtes, as well as the wife of the legendary Aztec ruler Montezuma.

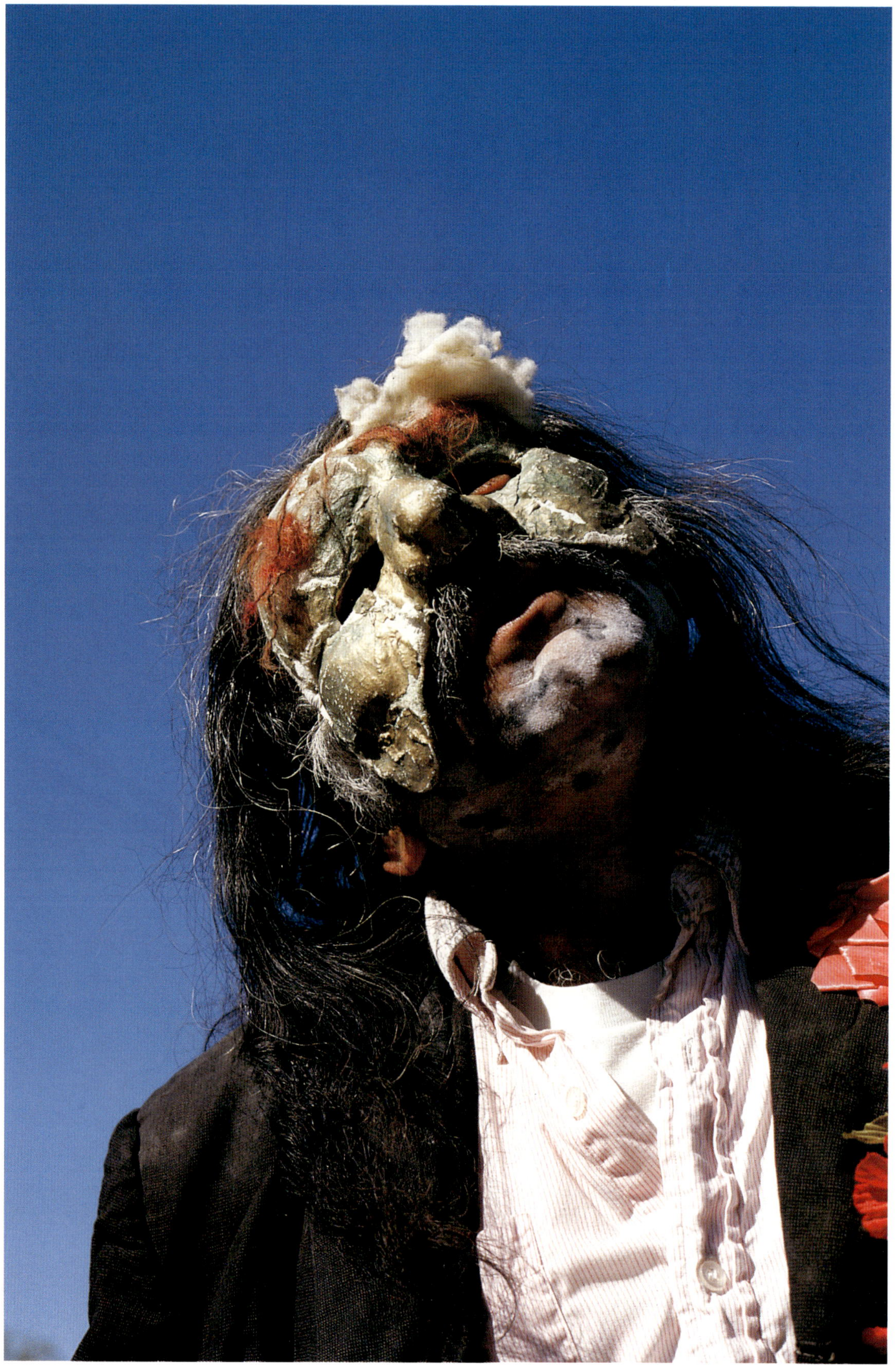

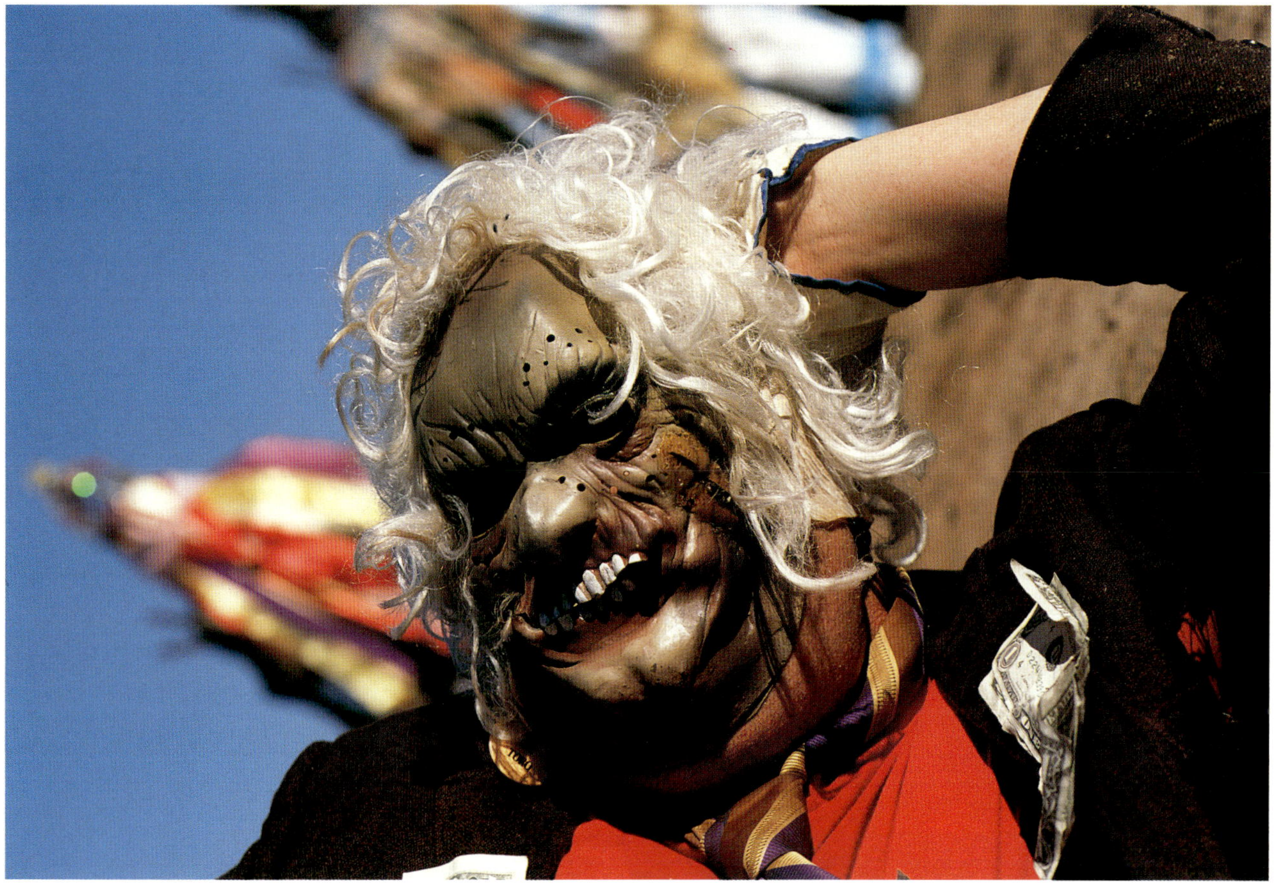

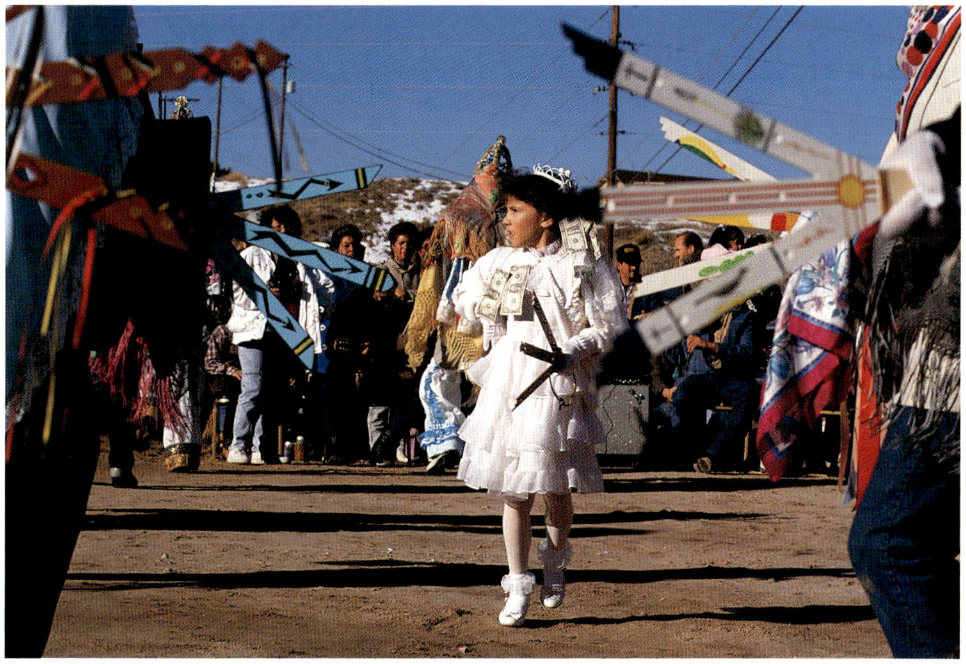

Also included in the dance troupe, which usually totals a dozen masked characters save La Malinche, is the leader El Monarca who symbolizes Montezuma and is Christianized during the course of the dance; the masked El Toro who symbolizes "evil"; los abuelos (the grandfathers), who threaten the village children with whips, provide comedy and challenge and conquer El Toro; and the colorful *Matachines* dancers who constantly surround the other characters as the drama builds and climaxes between El Monarca, La Malinche and El Toro.

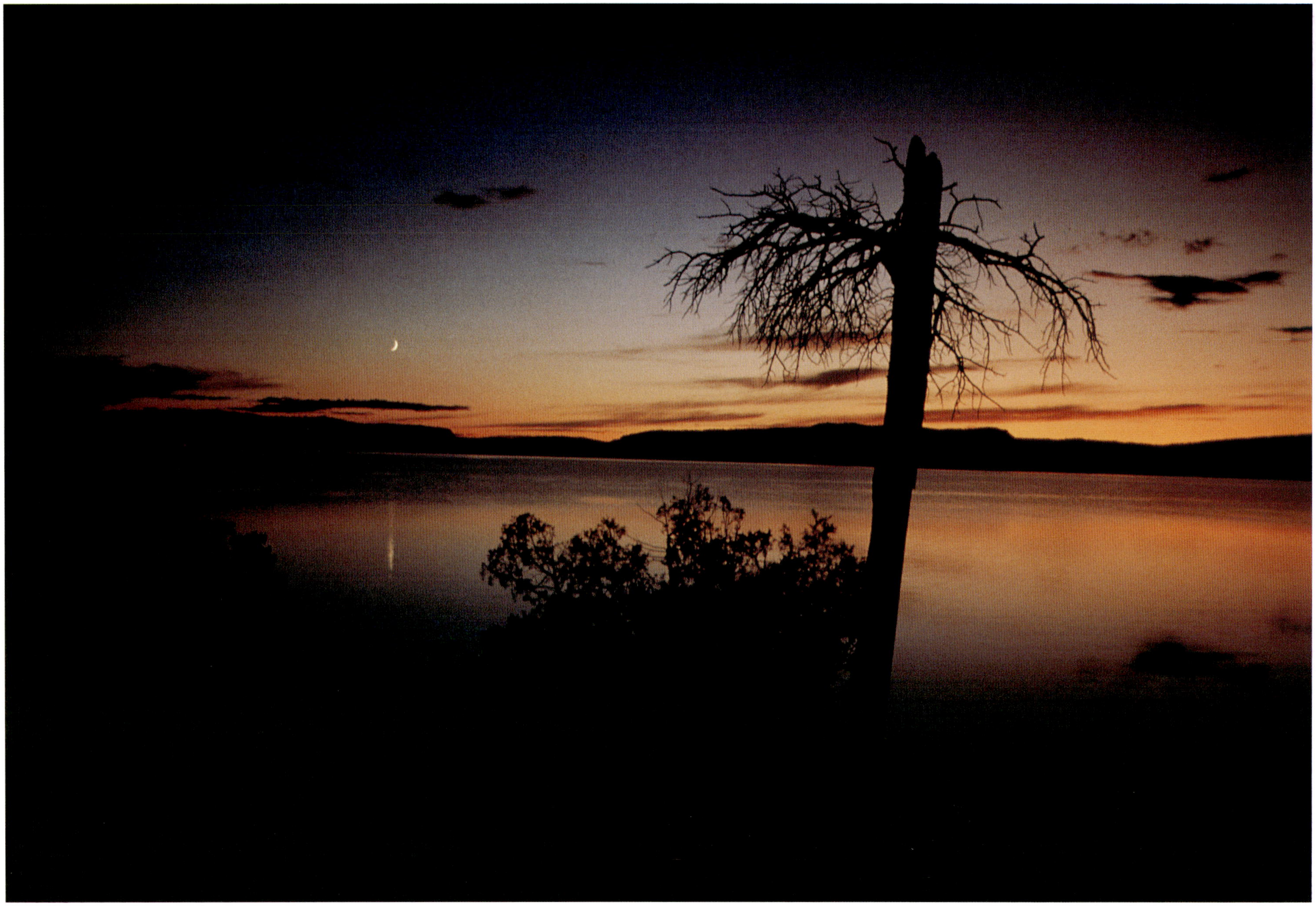

Moonset Heron Lake

Before darkness wins out over the waning day, the evening twilight at Heron Lake accentuates waterside silhouettes and a descending crescent moon.

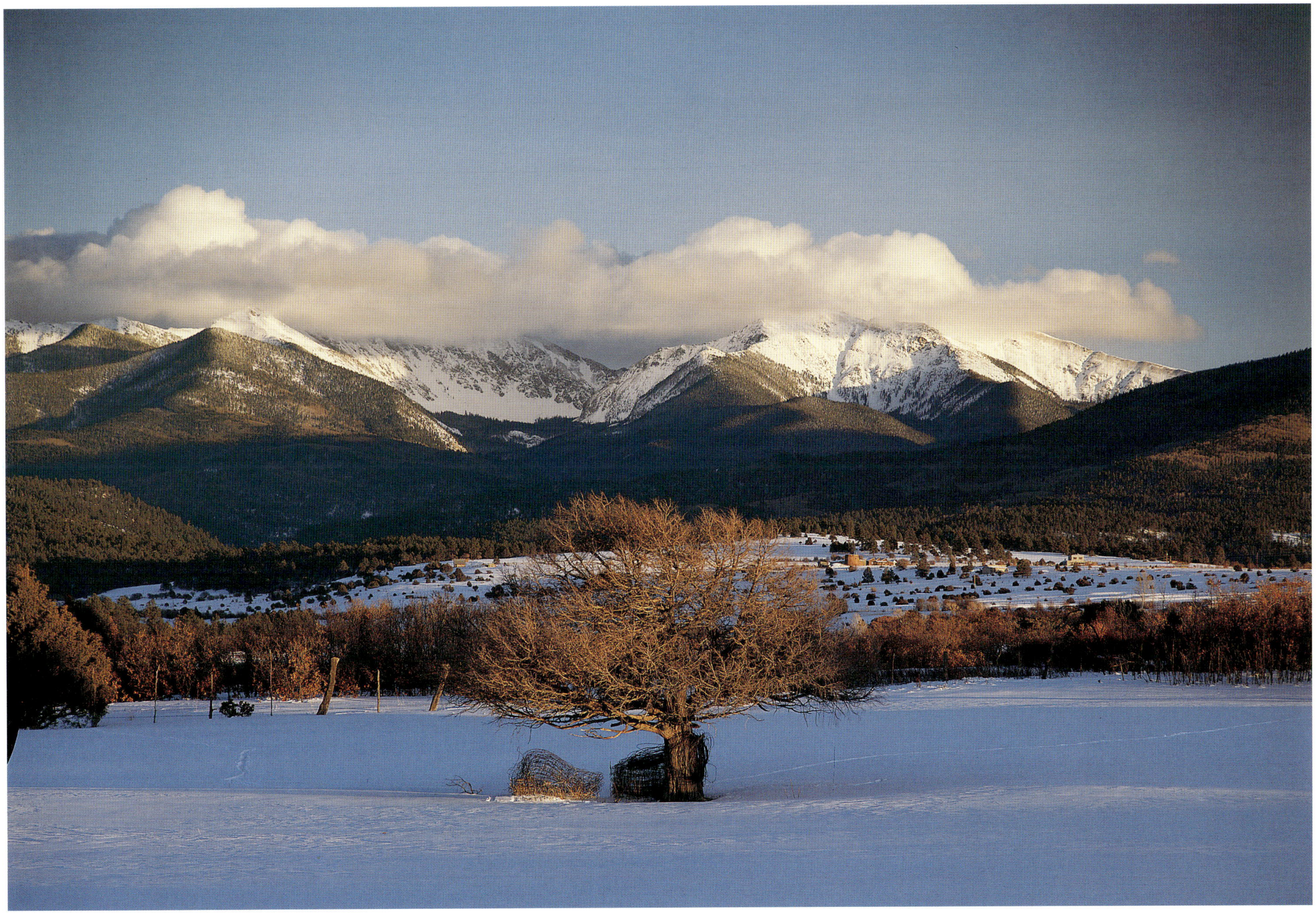

Sunset Truchas Tree

Dormant fields bask in the last warming sunrays of the day while winter storm clouds gather over the towering Truchas Peaks.

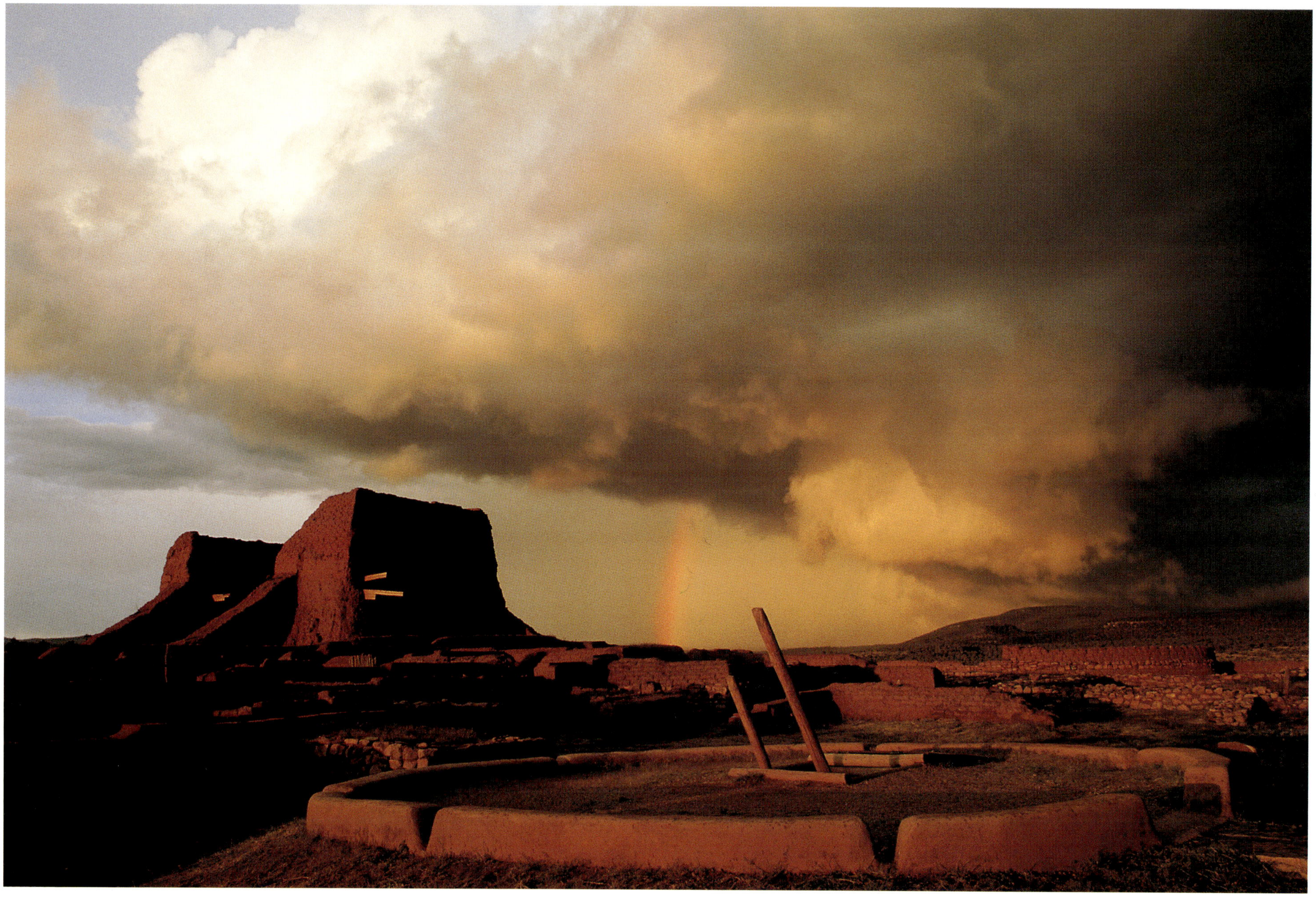

GROUNDED IN TIME

A LATE-AFTERNOON THUNDERSTORM BUILDS OVER THE HISTORIC GROUNDS OF PECOS PUEBLO NATIONAL MONUMENT. WARRIORS FROM THIS RUINED PUEBLO ALLIED WITH SPANISH SOLDIERS WHO WERE ON A MISSION TO RE-CONQUER NEW MEXICO 13 YEARS AFTER THE PUEBLO REVOLT OF 1680.

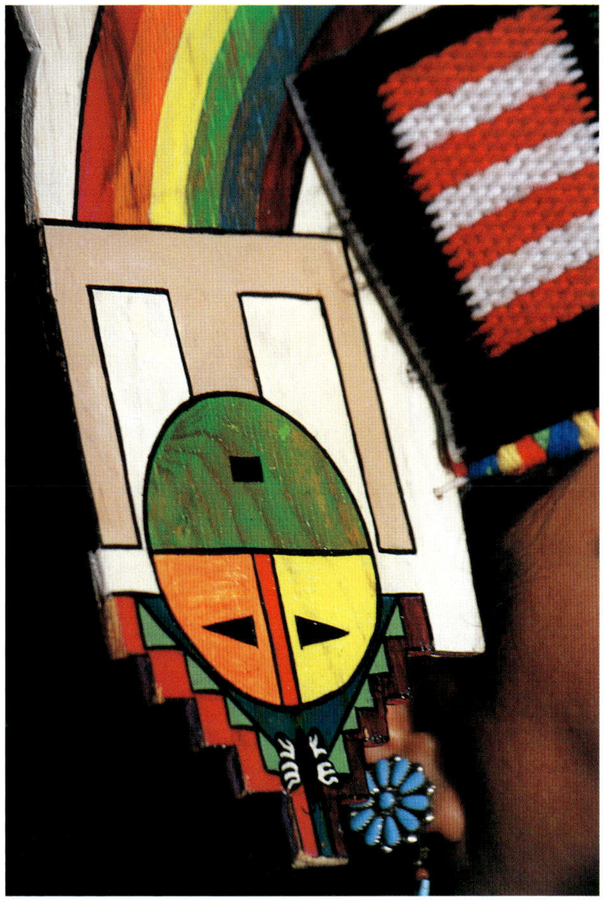

New Mexico's various Native American tribes have multitudes of designs that they consider sacred. Some of these designs are portrayed on a variety of objects, including jewelry, pottery, paintings and this headdress worn by a woman at Acoma Pueblo.

The First New Mexicans: *The Way We See It*

by

Conroy Chino

History defines a people. Whether it is written or spoken, it shapes, molds, and refines one's perception and self-image. But often history is taught and told through the eyes of those who dominate. That version of history can't always be trusted. That's why it is essential for native people to tell their own. All historical events have repercussions somewhere, someplace. They always define contemporary times.

I remember as a young boy listening to my great-grandfather tell me about a battle at Acoma hundreds of years ago. He spoke with a tone of pride in his voice recalling the valiant effort by "The People," *Ah-cu-meh-Hanu*, in the fight against an attacking regiment of Spanish soldiers, *Kush-tyu-da*. He described how the Acoma men maneuvered strategically from the cliff top and hurled rocks at the enemy below. The stones were no match against weapons of steel, including a small cannon. During the day, the Spanish soldiers had the upper hand, but at night Acoma warriors would descend from the cliff top village and even the score. They hurled balls of mud filled with wasps at the soldiers. While the enemy fought off the angry insects, the warriors would aim their arrows at the men in armor.

The battle lasted for days. By the end of the eighth day, the Spanish began running out of food and water. They thought they could outlast the Acoma warriors since there was no apparent source of water on the mesa top. They were unaware of the large, natural cisterns filled with water from rain and snow.

Finally, the Spanish grew weary. Tired, hungry and

thirsty, they called to the mesa top and begged for a peaceful end to the battle. The Acoma warriors, also weary of fighting and watching too many of their people get killed, met with the soldiers and negotiated. It was recorded in symbols and figures etched into a section of sandstone wall blackened by cannon fire. The petroglyph showed an Acoma warrior facing a Spanish soldier on horseback. They held poles that crossed between them, a symbol of peace.

That battle was never recorded in history books, much like other events that happened in the thousand-year-old history of a village called Haaku, where the people defined themselves as always being prepared, ready, but maybe not for the strangers arriving from the south.

I wonder what it was like to stand at the edge of the mesa on a hot summer day in 1540 and look out over the valley, past the cedar trees, the shrub grasses and the corn fields, past the huge monumental rock formations, to a shimmering movement off in the distance.

No doubt, the men and women peered and wondered, strained and questioned about the approaching figures, except for the shiny reflection off something they were wearing. The strangers rode on the backs of large animals. The Acoma had never seen that before. The women probably uttered the word that usually expresses fear, *e-me-ee*, but the men stood firm and unafraid. They felt secure, protected from enemies and predators by the sheer walls of sandstone. Legend told them they had been living here since time immemorial.

But that all changed the day the men in armor appeared. The soldiers came from Zuni pueblo, one of the fabled Seven Golden Cities of Cíbola. They arrived in Acoma valley, searching for "the kingdom of the Acus." They actually were searching for another rich Aztec or Inca kingdom.

There's no record of what was said at this first historic meeting. What is known is that by the time the men in armor left, the people of Haaku had made peaceful offerings of turkeys, bread, deerskins, piñon nuts and corn. There's no record of what they received in return.

Spanish conquistadors discovered there was no gold in New Mexico . . . just an abundance of land, labor and idle souls. Over an 80-year period, they raided fields, taxing and taking, while missionaries raided kivas, trying to eradicate ancient beliefs and ceremonial practices. By 1680, there was no other choice except to revolt. Pueblo leaders like Popé of San Juan, Tupatú of Picurís, Catiti of Santo Domingo and Malacati of Cochití and numerous others collaborated and carried out the most successful uprising in this country.

Pueblo historians say the Revolt of 1680 is significant in New Mexico Indian history because it ensured the survival of ancient cultures, religion, land and language. Other historians say it was the first successful battle for independence in what was to become the United States. Yet, despite its significance, the Pueblo Revolt rarely gets mentioned in textbooks because it was a defeat suffered by the Spanish, and therefore, insignificant in American history. To native people, it's an event that doesn't get celebrated, only remembered.

Now, some 300 years after the Spanish conquistadors, and after the U.S. government replaced Mexican rule, New Mexico tribes still battle many powerful forces. In 1996, they are struggling to deal with the influence of western values, modern culture, technology and the pressure to assimilate into American society. Most significant is the impact on language.

English has now become the dominant language in many homes. It's happening in my own household, my own family, around my mother's table, in my kiva, at our

A ROOM WITH A VIEW! THIS SOLAR-POWERED CAVE AT TSANKAWI RUINS JUST MIGHT HAVE BEEN CONSIDERED LUXURY LIVING DURING THE TIME ANASAZI INDIANS CALLED THE DWELLING SITE THEIR HOME BETWEEN A.D. 1400 AND THE LATE 1500S.

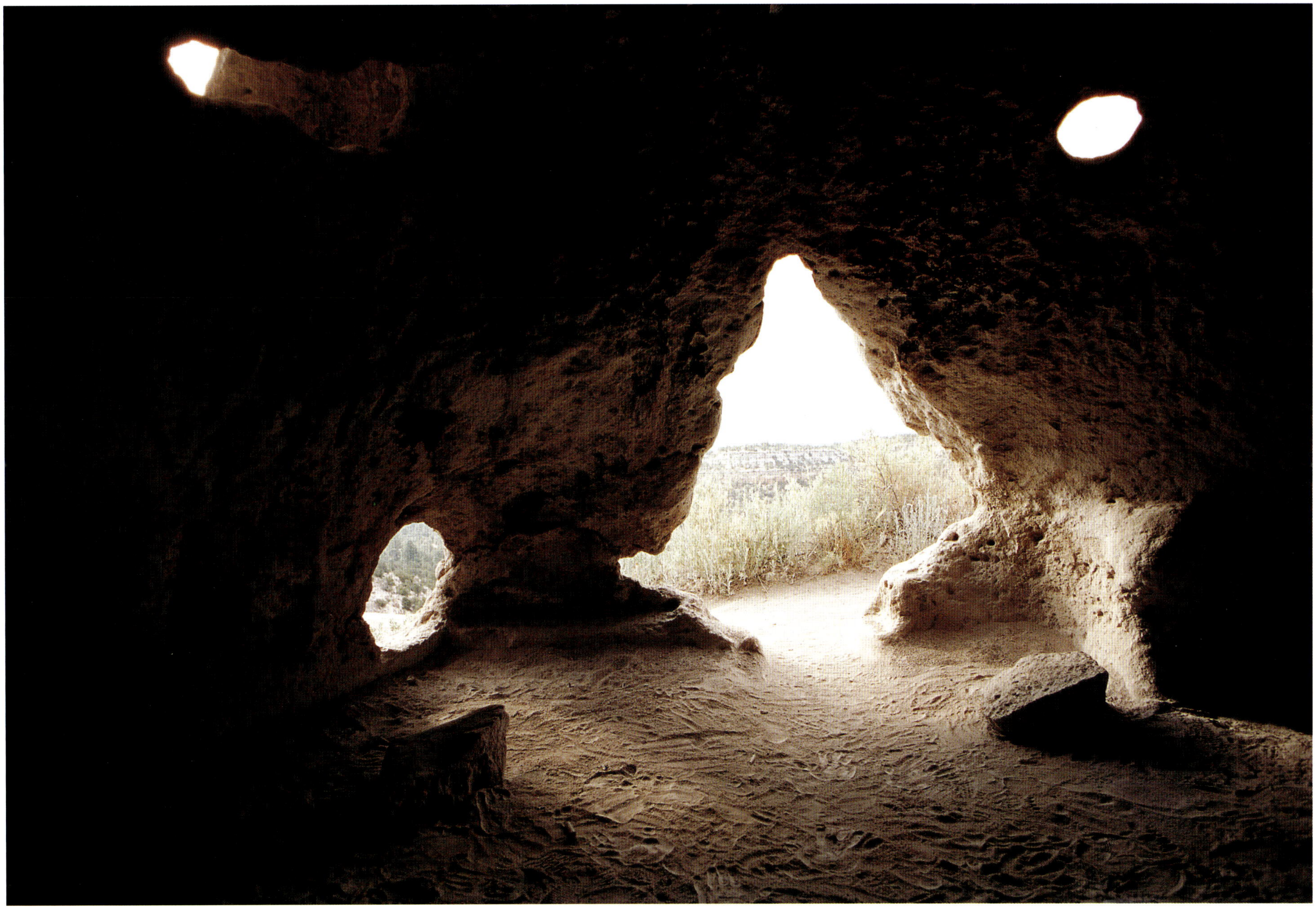

plaza, children speaking less and less Acoma – the cornerstone of religious beliefs, song and ritual. Experts say in 50 years, less than 5 percent of Acoma people will barely be able to utter complete sentences in Acoma. Today, only the adults speak the language. They are no longer teaching the next generation.

Historians say that trend may have started when the Santa Fe Railway took working men from Acoma to faraway places like Barstow in the California desert. They left farming and herding sheep to repair locomotives and lay new tracks. The railroad company set up so called "Indian camps" and allowed the men to send for their families. When they arrived, parents quickly learned that in a cash economy, English was the ticket to a better job, a better home, a better way of life. They learned there were more rewards from speaking English than Acoma. Parents spoke to each other in Acoma, but not to the children. Now, grandparents bemoan the fact that the language is dying, and children no longer speak "Indian."

There's been another powerful influence that's exerted pressure to abandon culture and tradition. It has affected our self-image and our self-worth. It has bombarded reservation households for years, influencing what we eat, drink, wear and drive. Television has done more to change attitudes and values than any other single influence in contemporary native history.

For many growing up in isolated communities, TV became the little window to the world beyond the reservation boundaries, to a world where life was always so much better. It took us to faraway places, introduced us to a whole different culture, and exposed us to a lifestyle unknown to our parents and grandparents. All that, without ever leaving our sun-baked homes.

But, television did something else. Saturday night movies, grade B westerns and prime time sitcoms twisted our image and reinforced the perception that we were nothing more than a people relegated to the frontier past. For us, the images, the portrayals were just too absurd, too unreal, too removed and simply offensive. Unfortunately, television burned such a deep lasting, distorted image in the minds of so many that we are barely recovering.

Despite the distortions and influence of high tech, or the fact that we have no written history, we are a people who know who we are and where we came from. Much of that identity is based on a connection with the land and all living forces. In the Acoma world view, life forces are invoked, summoned through intense prayer, song and dance. Through ritual and ceremony, all of humanity is celebrated. Prayers are for life, the continuance of life through rainfall.

We are a people intensely connected to the land and fiercely dedicated to preserving our culture, religion and language, but we are not a people out of touch with the rest of the world. We have TVs, drive cars, and wear polyester. We love Kentucky Fried Chicken and Pepsi and we can't program our VCRs. We are also a people struggling to survive, struggling to understand the actions of state and federal governments when it comes to contemporary and controversial issues like Indian gaming and religious freedom.

Acoma people, like other tribes, have always believed we are the caretakers of the earth, that she is a living being, much like ourselves, that we are rooted to the land and by being rooted we know who we are. We know we exist by looking out over the landscape, the rain clouds, the rolling hills, the cedar trees, the flesh colored sandstone cliffs. We see the earth enduring, and so will we. That is our history.

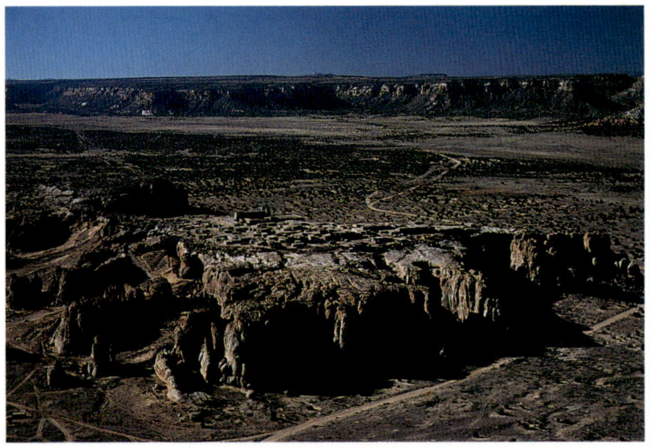

ACOMA PUEBLO RESTS UPON A TOWERING MESA IN WESTERN NEW MEXICO NEAR GRANTS. MANY OF ITS RESIDENTS HAVE SHUNNED MODERN CONVENIENCES AND CHOOSE TO LIVE IN THE MANNER OF THEIR ANCESTORS. FOR CENTURIES, THE ONLY WAY TO THE PUEBLO FROM THE BOTTOM WAS A STONE STAIRCASE. IT WASN'T UNTIL THE 1950S THAT A ROAD WAS BUILT TO THE TOP; IT WAS CONSTRUCTED BY A MOVIE COMPANY SHOOTING AT THE ANCIENT SITE.

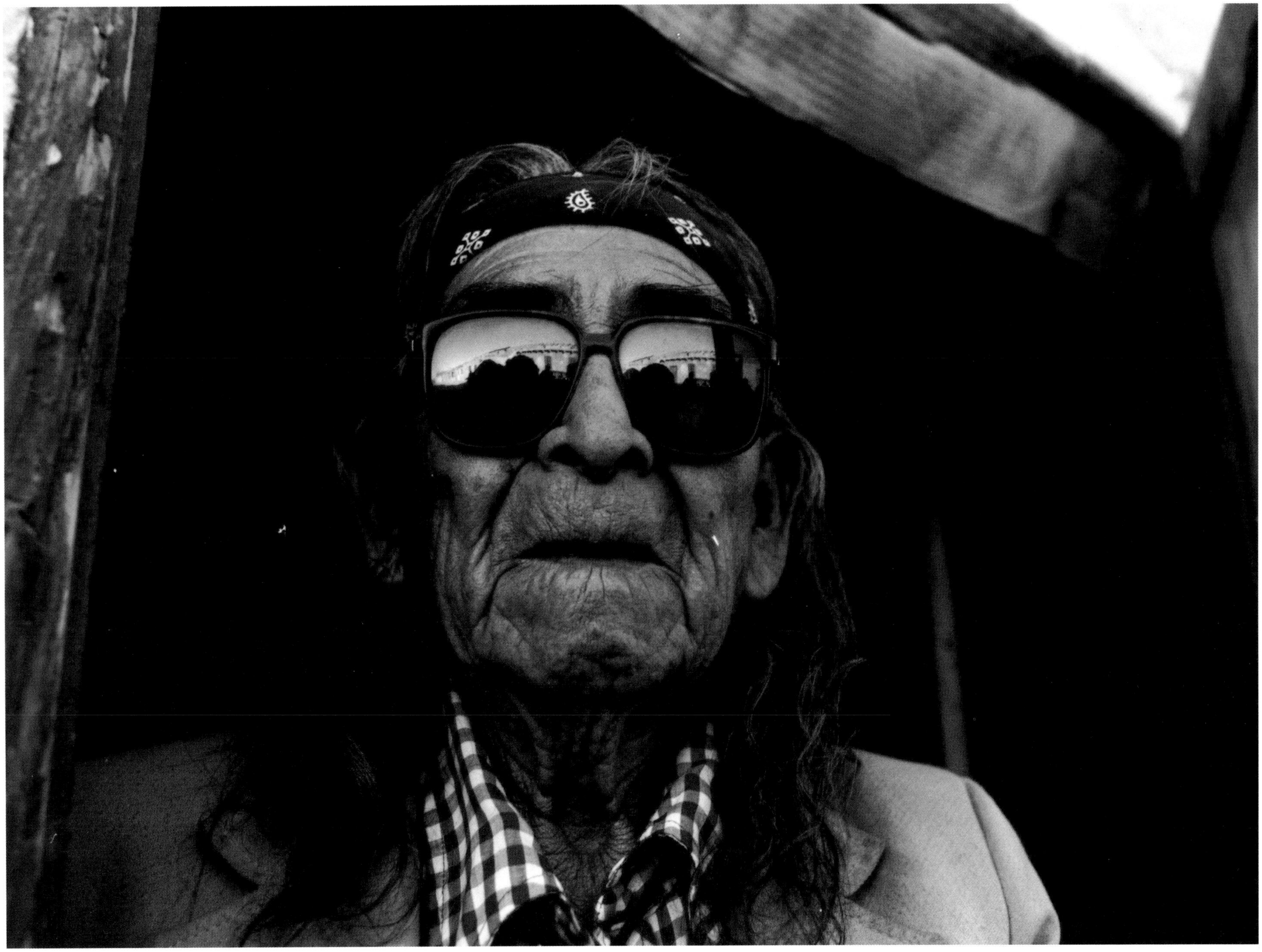

Get With It, Baby!

J Ray of Acoma Pueblo sports a headband and sunglasses while dressed in clothes quite in line with the American mainstream. Despite J Ray's appearance, Acoma, also known as "Sky City," is one of the more traditional pueblos of New Mexico.

Many centuries ago,
a Native American artisan
living in the once-thriving
Tsankawi Ruins (pronounced
sank-ah-WEE) east of Los
Alamos carved this face with
headdress into the soft,
porous volcanic tuff
characteristic of the
Pajarito Plateau.

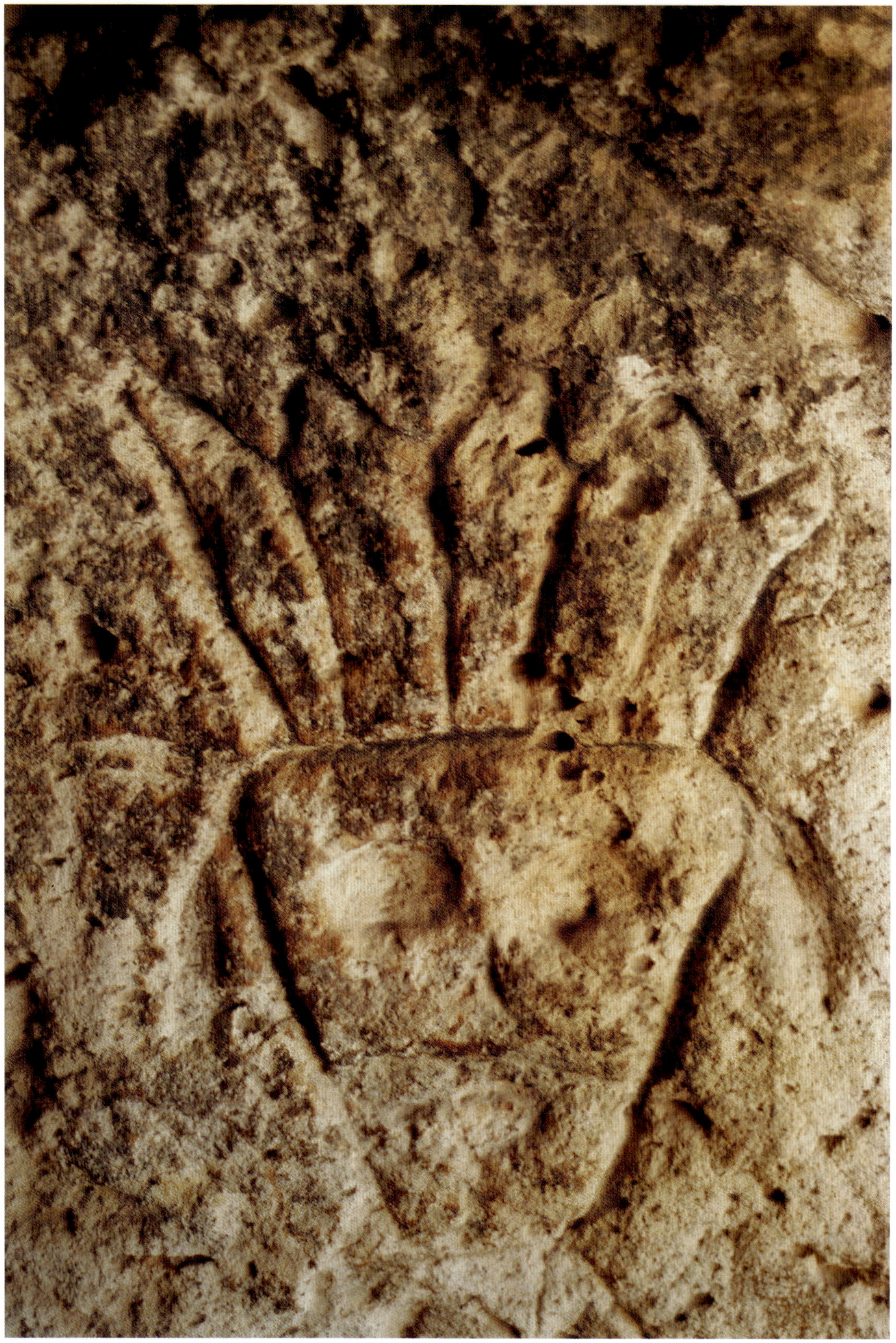

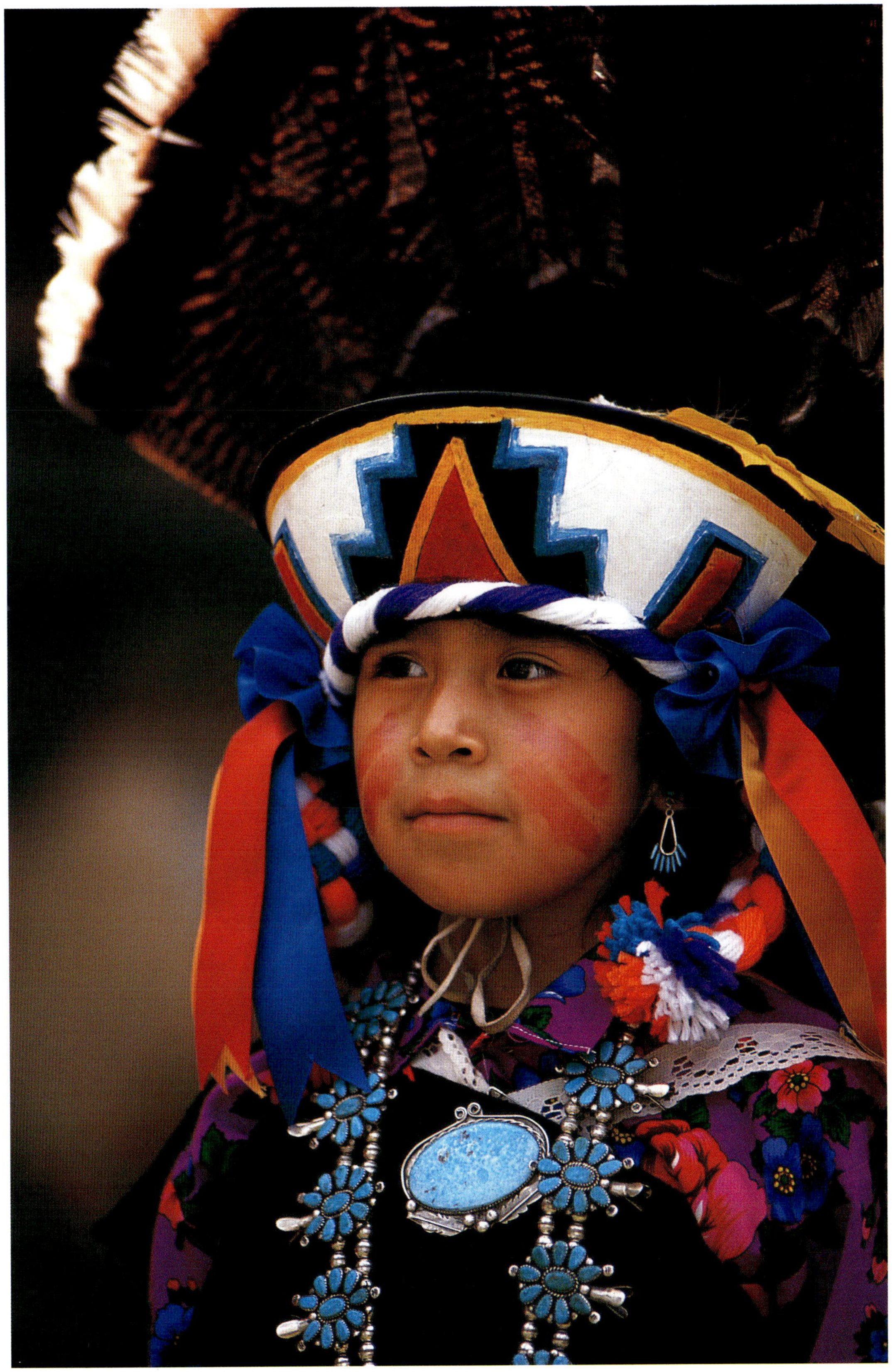

Zuni Pueblo Turkey dancer Kinsey Eddakie wears a traditional squash blossom necklace and turquoise pendant at the Santa Fe Indian Market. Zuni jewelry makers have become world-renowned for their craft.

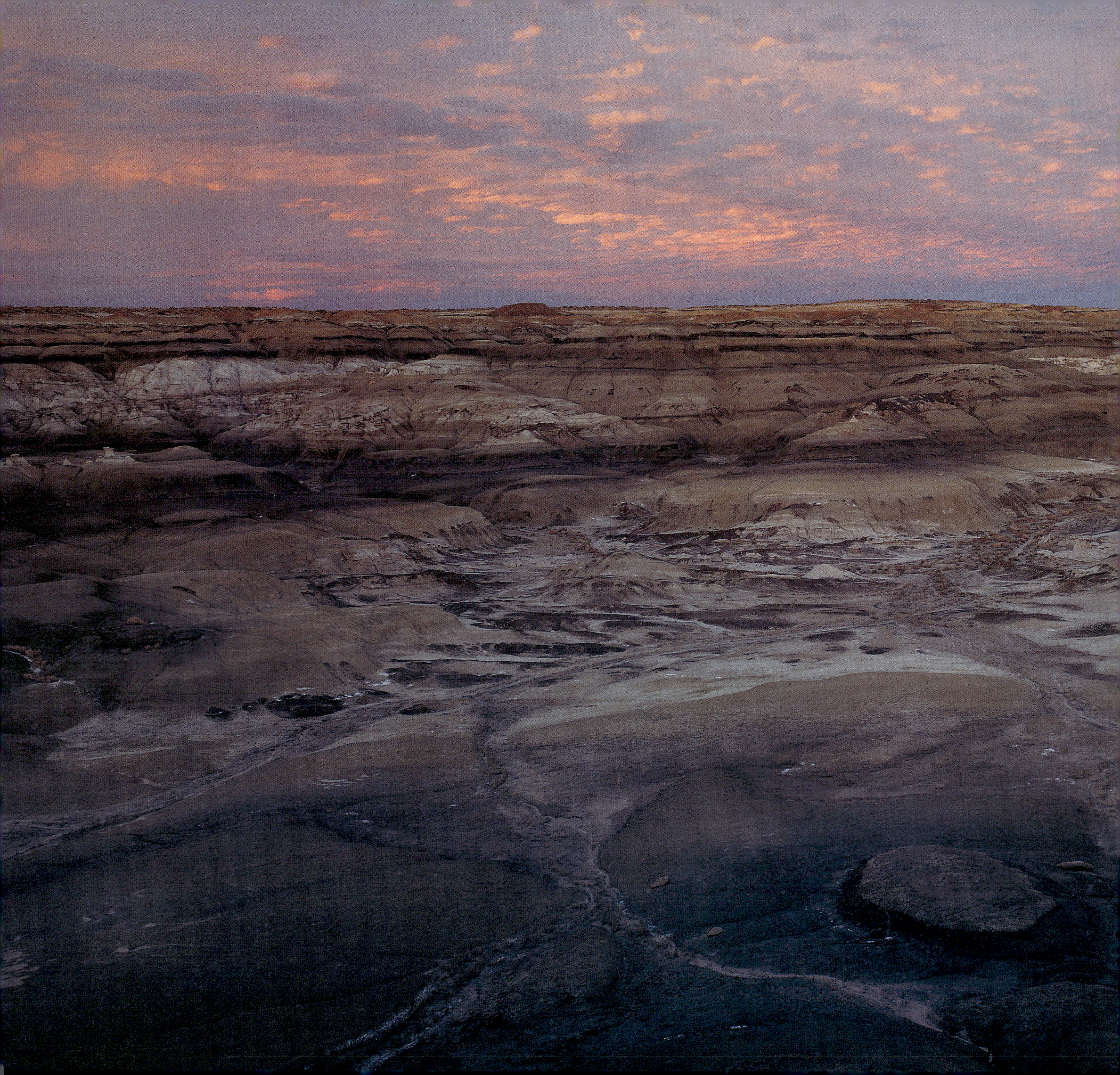

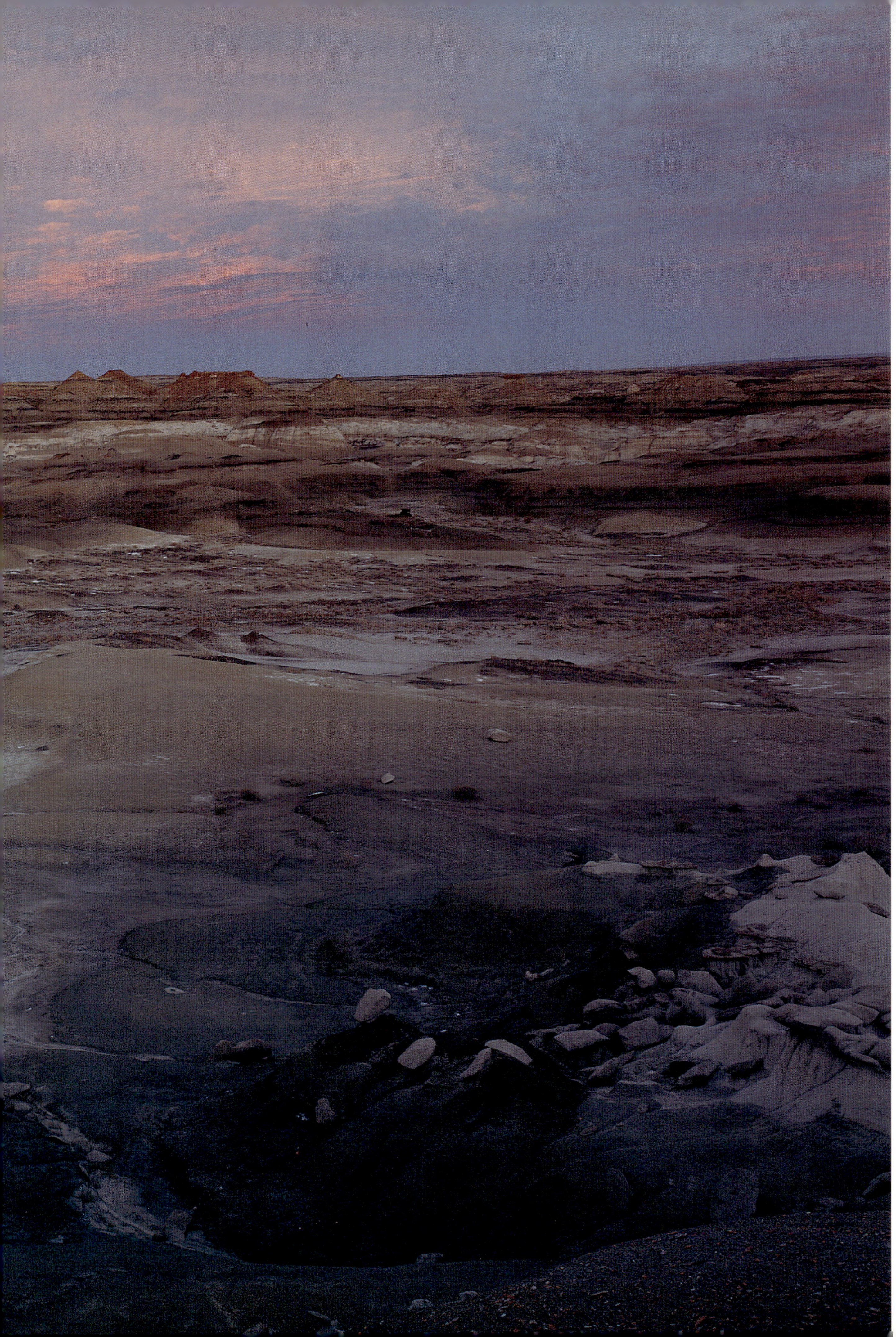

Twilight grips the weird, barren landscape of the Bisti Badlands Wilderness in northwestern New Mexico. Bisti is an approximation of a Navajo word for badlands.

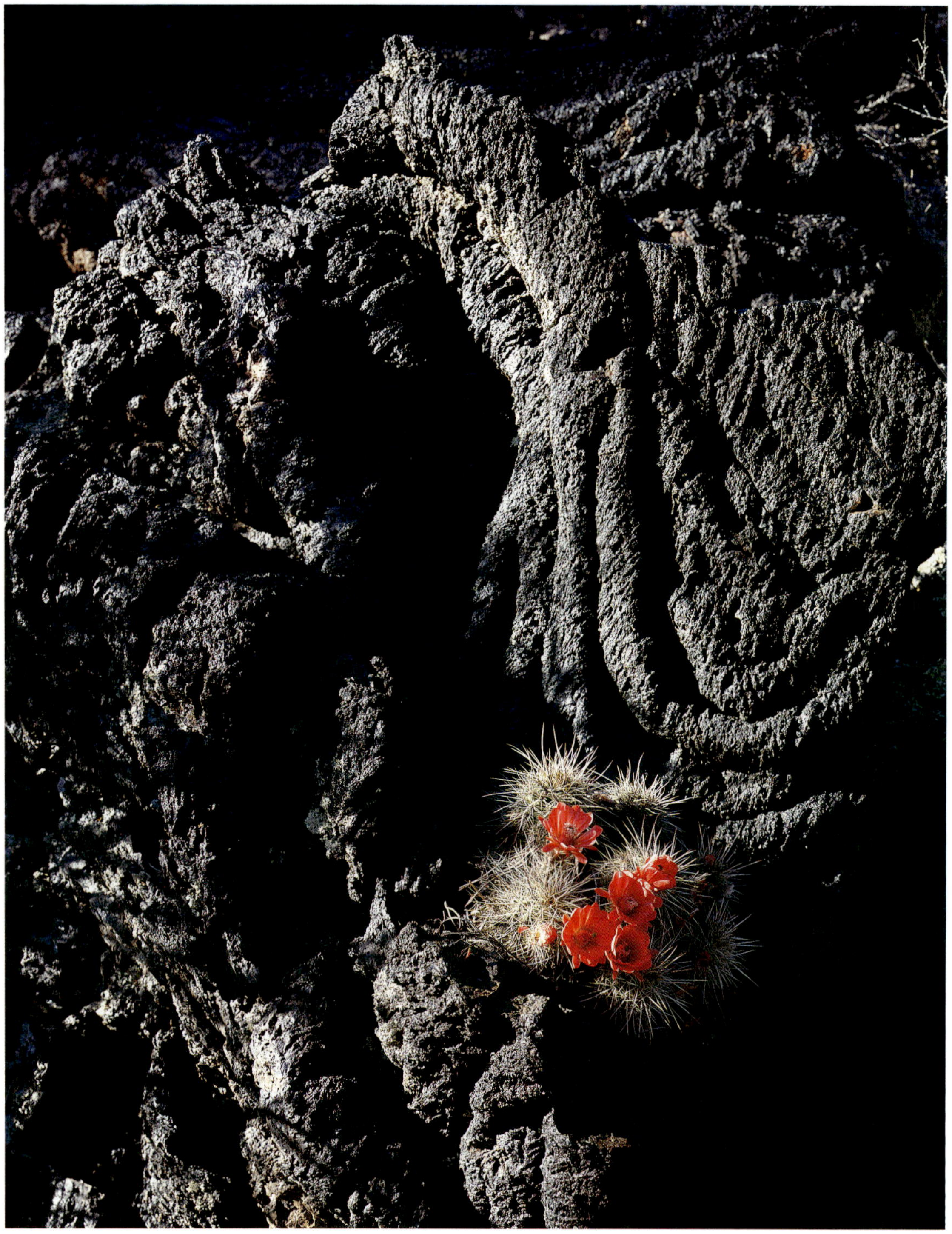

Perseverance

A hardy cactus plant blooms on a lava flow at El Malpais National Monument. Malpais in Spanish means badlands, but in New Mexico it usually refers to lands marred by lava.

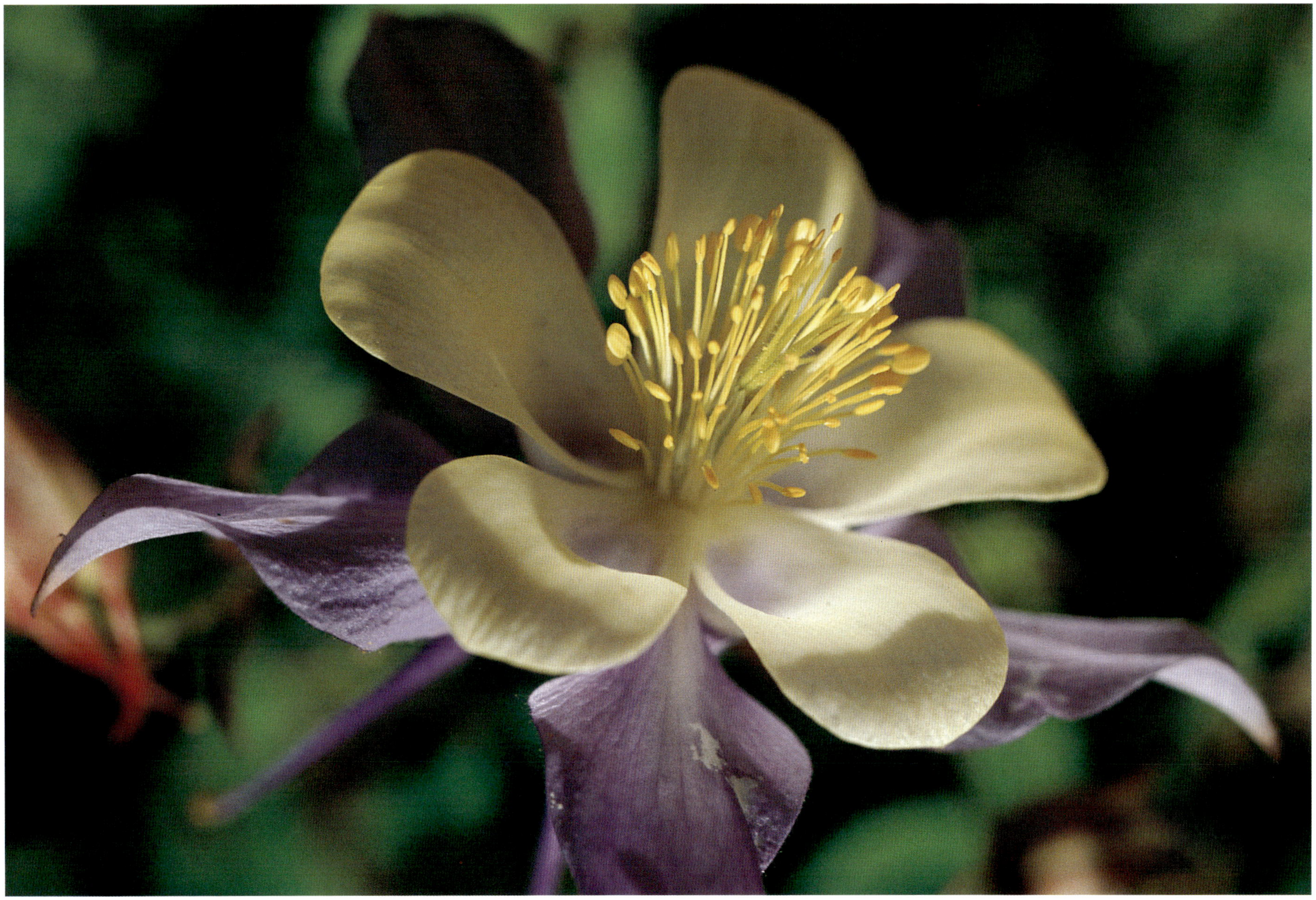

LIFE'S LITTLE PLEASURES

COLORFUL WILDFLOWERS ABOUND IN THE LAND OF ENCHANTMENT. THIS YELLOW BLOOM IN THE ZUNI MOUNTAINS IS TYPICAL OF THE NATURAL BEAUTY OF NEW MEXICO.

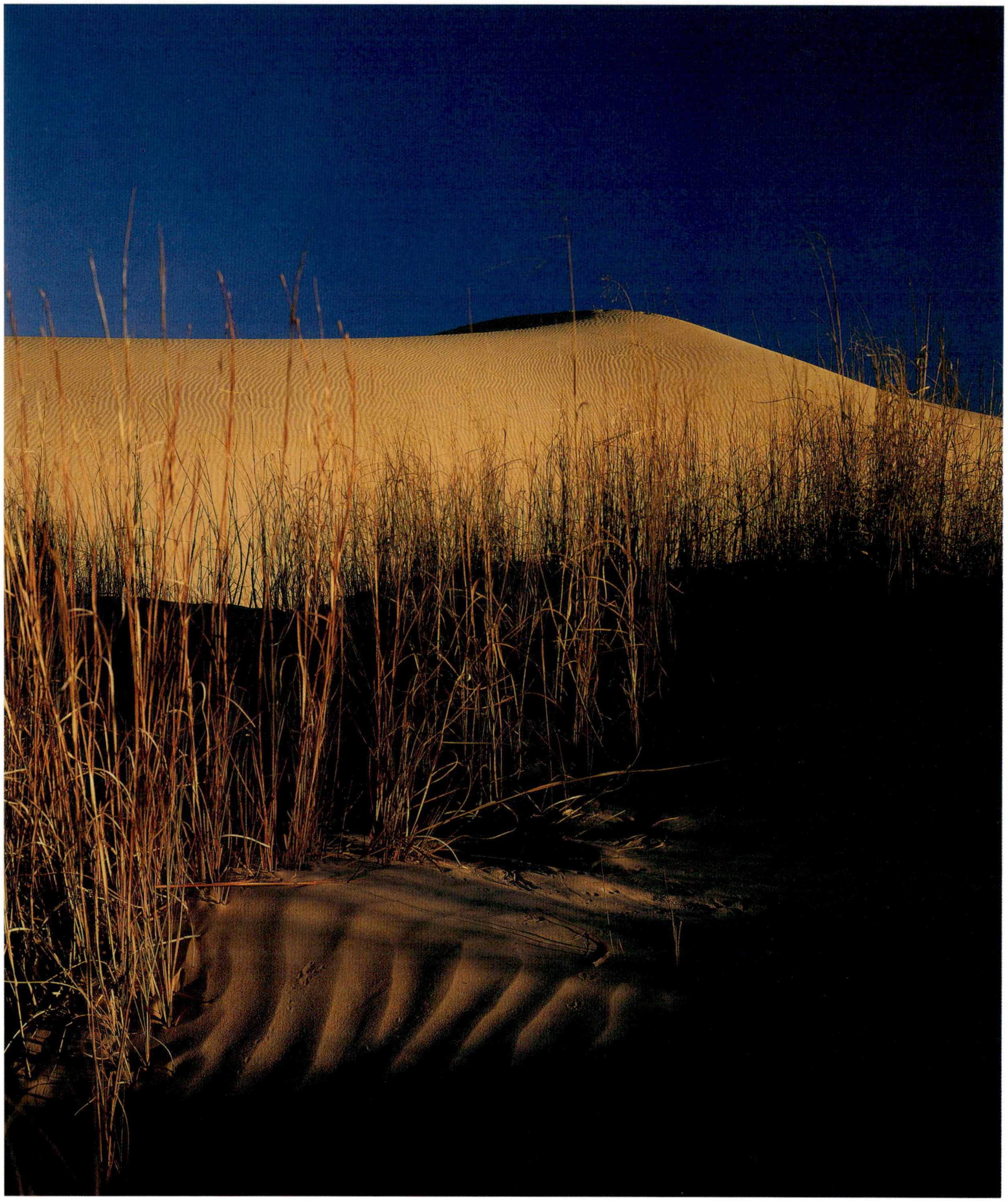

BARREN BEAUTY

THE LITTLE-BROTHER VERSION OF THE SAHARA DESERT MANIFESTS IN SOUTHEASTERN NEW MEXICO AT MESCALERO SANDS, NAMED FOR THE NOMADIC APACHE INDIANS WHO USED TO ROAM THROUGH HERE.

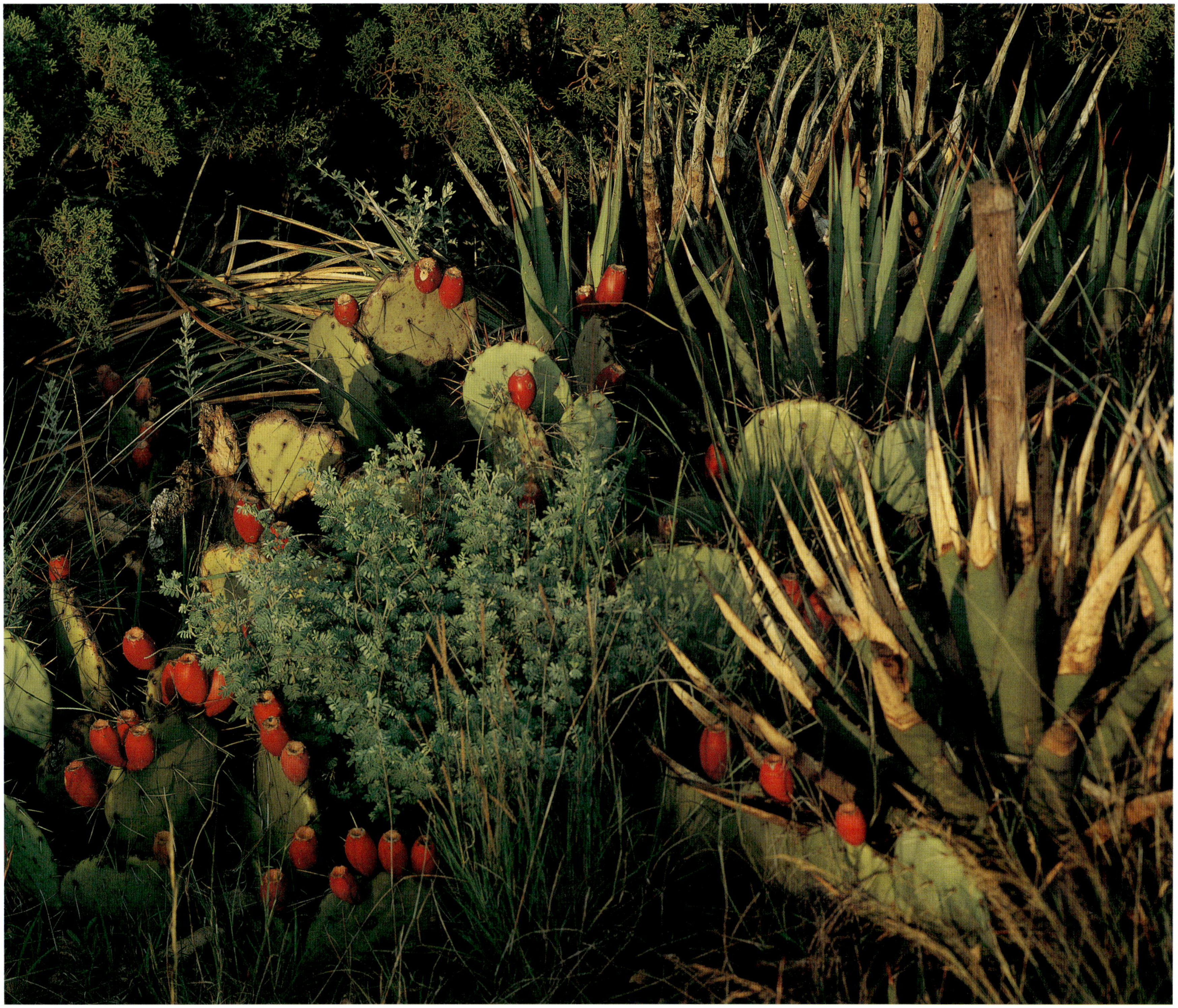

Desert Delight

A smattering of ripe, red prickly pears add color to the cacti and other indigenous flora of the Chihuahuan Desert within Carlsbad Caverns National Park near the Texas border.

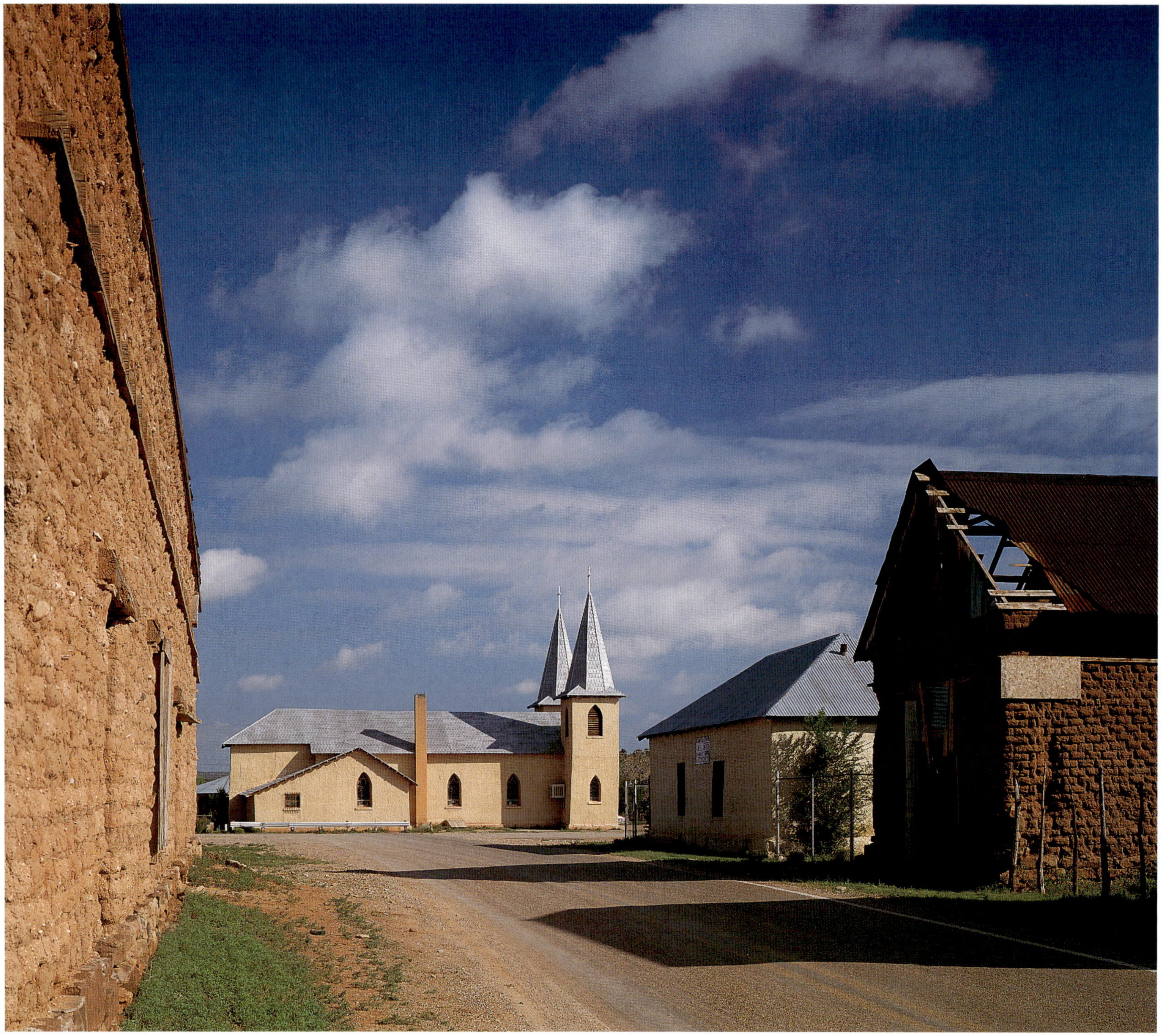

Dimensions

Dilapidating adobe walls and deteriorating rooftops on a side street in Antón Chico remind that this community settled in 1822 is one of the oldest in Guadalupe County.

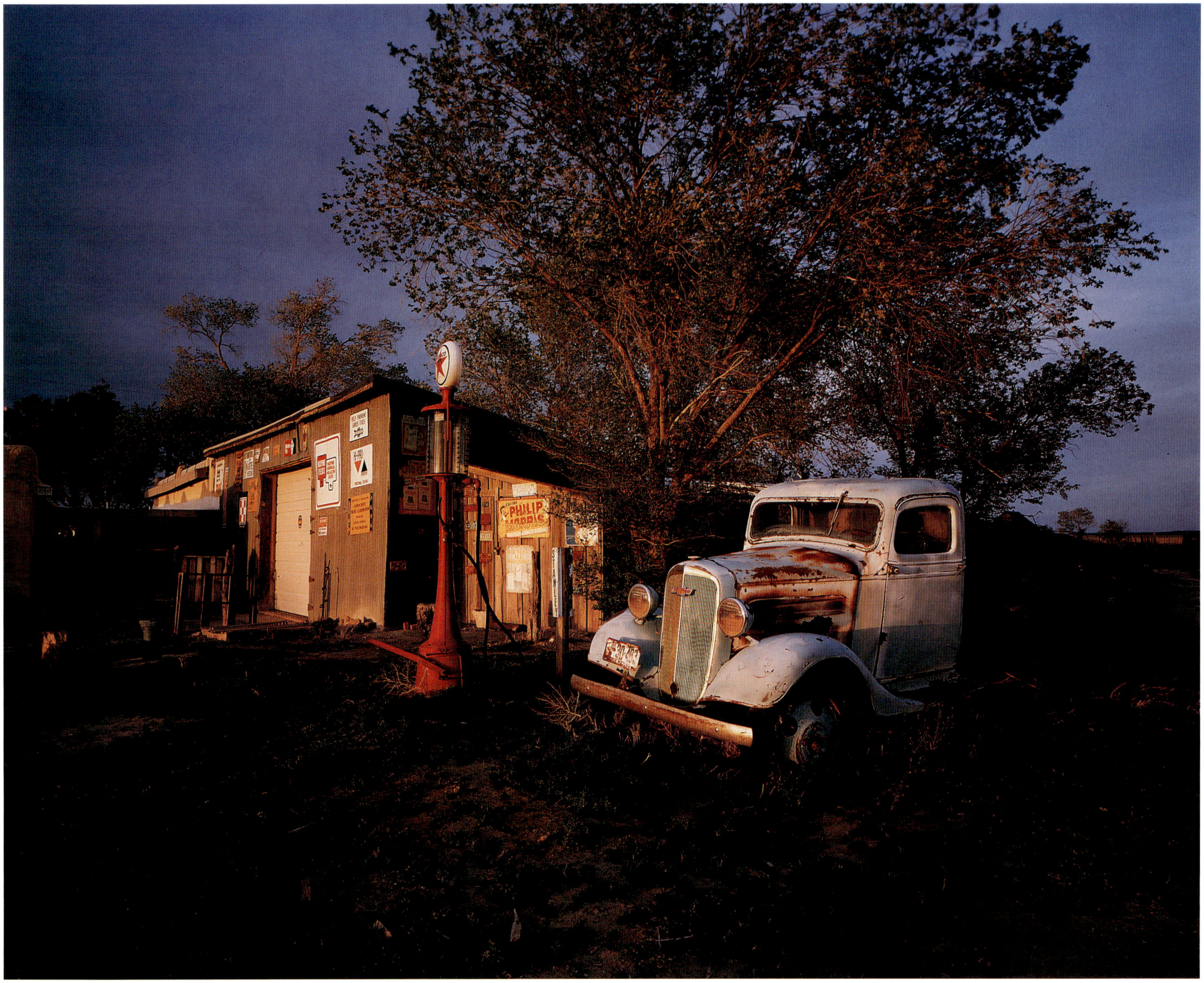

Another Place, Another Time

Seeming like the set of a silent movie, these vestiges from a bygone era at a Stanley garage roar of the early technological inventions that changed New Mexico and the world forever.

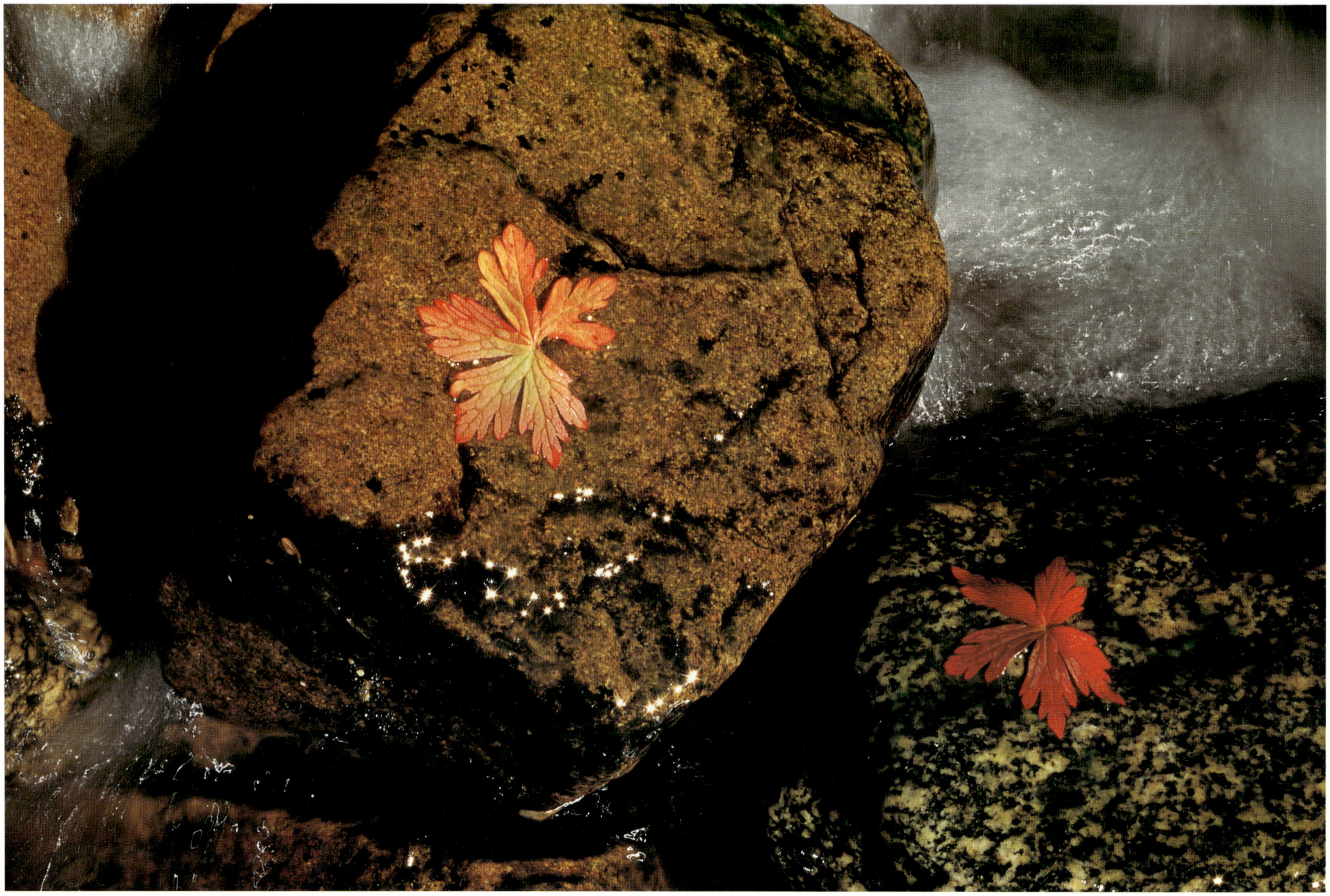

Cycles

Colorful autumn leaves dot these fallen granite boulders on the Big Tesuque Creek east of Santa Fe, signaling winter's near arrival to the Sangre de Cristo Mountains.

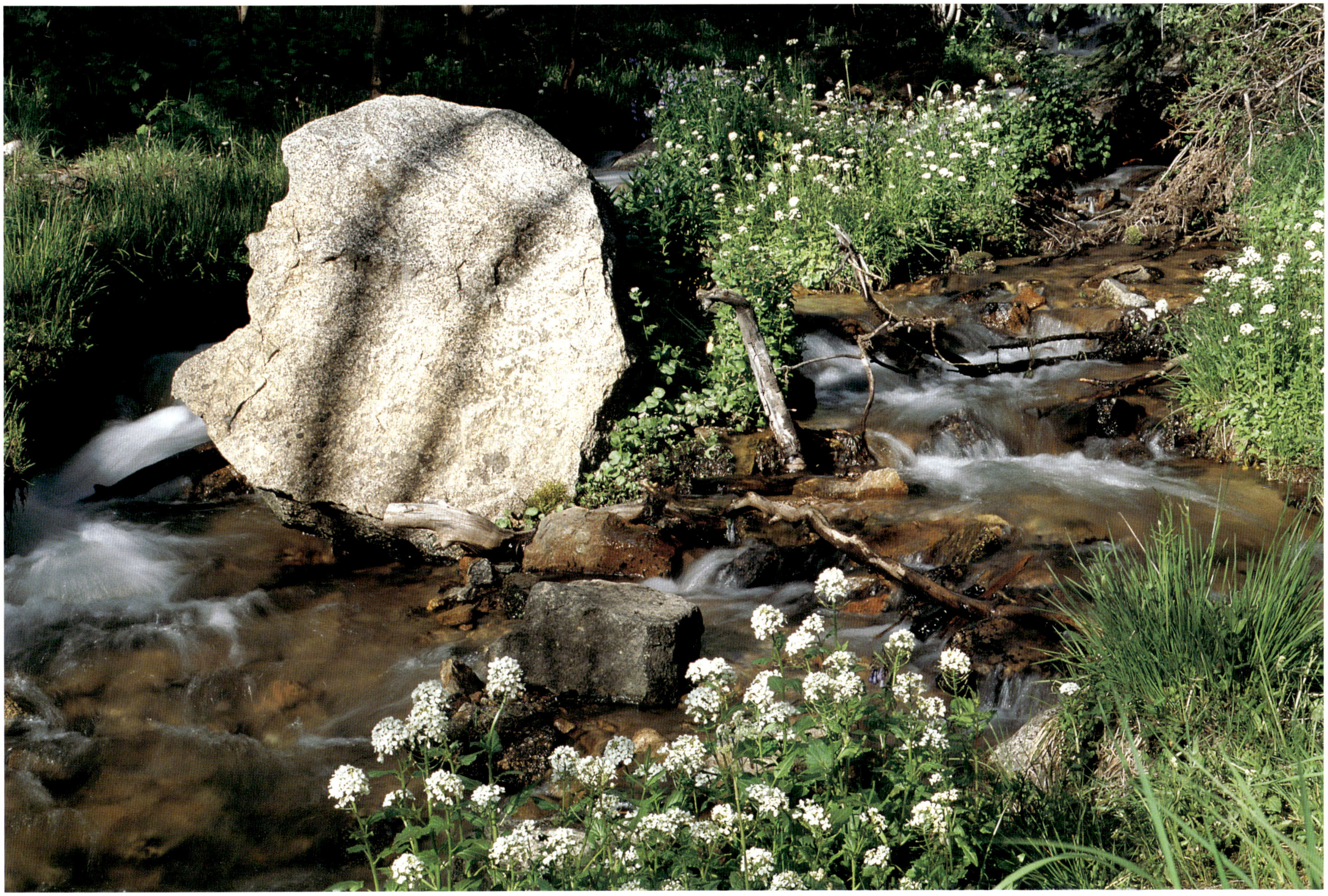

Spring Delight

Blooming wildflowers and the sight of rushing water on the Big Tesuque Creek in the Santa Fe National Forest create a delightful springtime mountain setting.

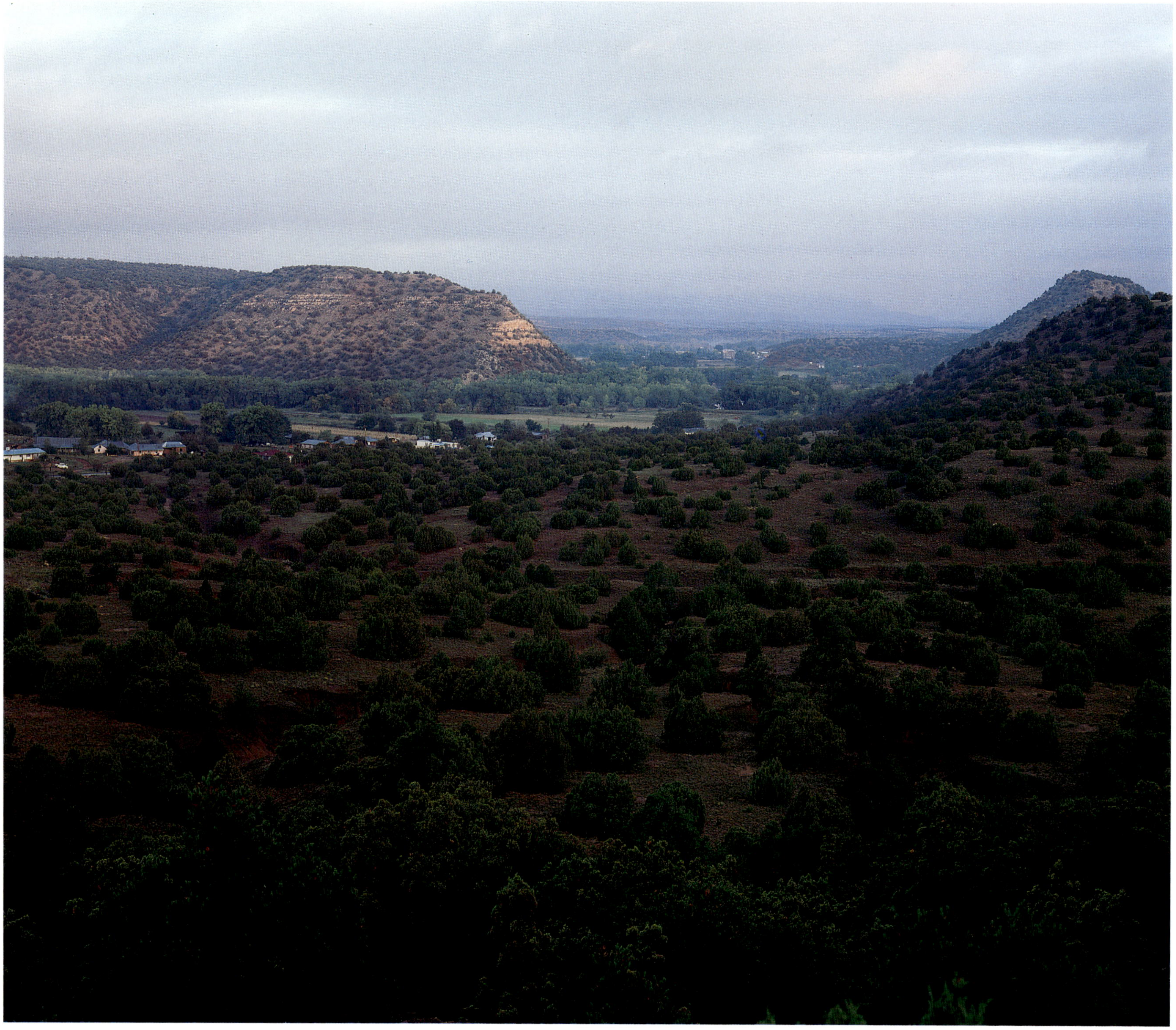

A Separate Reality

The subtle morning light creates an ethereal setting on this classic piñon and juniper studded hillside overlooking the upper reaches of Pecos Village in San Miguel County.

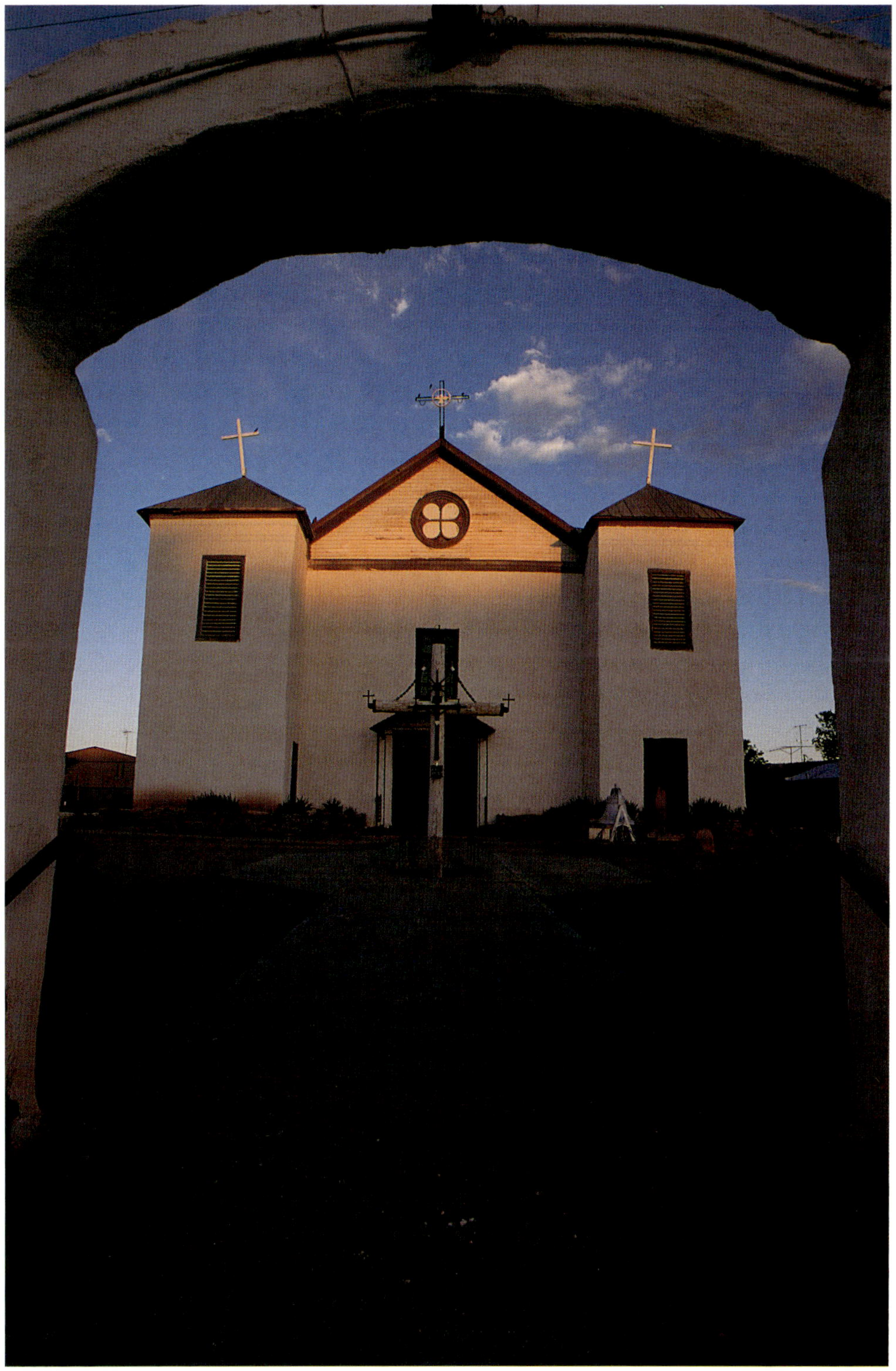

MONUMENT OF HOPE

The historic church in San Miguel del Bado has been catching rays from sunsets since 1805, the year historians believe *genízaros* (Christianized Indians) erected it on land granted from the Spanish governor.

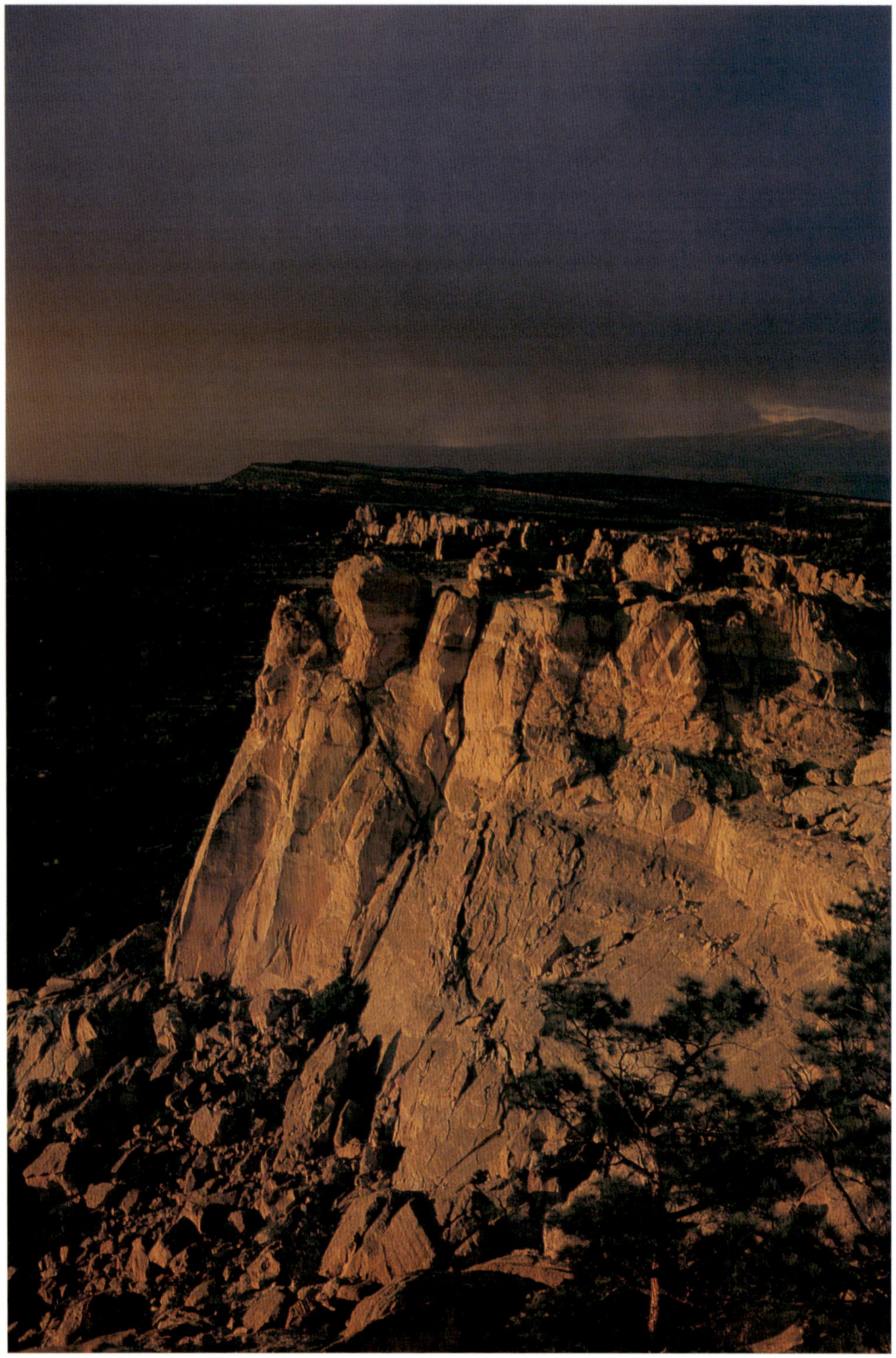

Fiery Flurry

A late-afternoon storm joins the setting sun to color a row of raging craggy cliffs formed from the overlook at El Malpais National Monument to the base of 11,301-foot Mount Taylor.

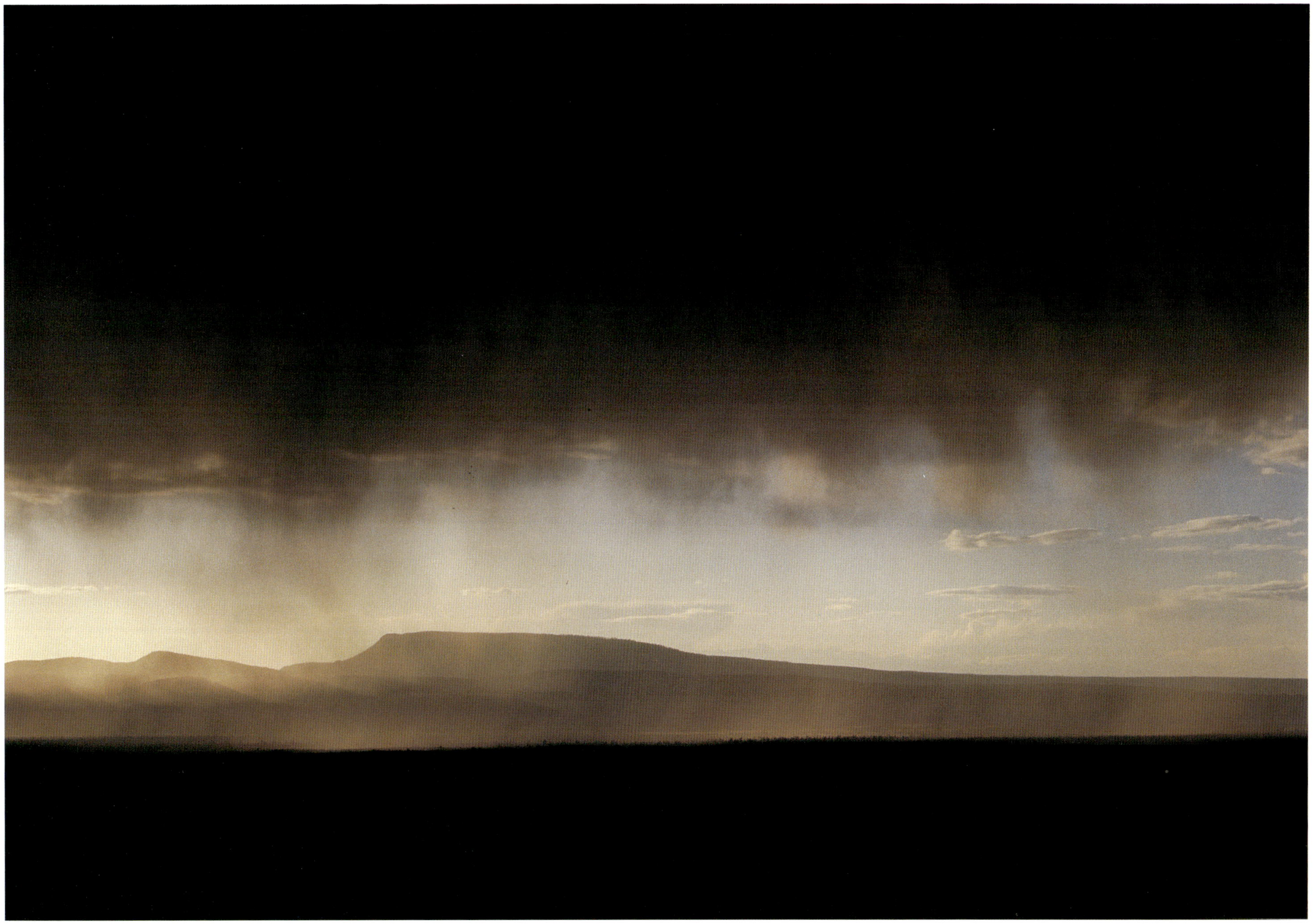

Vision of Creation

Rainstorms pound the ancient lava flows of El Malpais National Monument, creating a steamy setting that possibly resembles the area's fiery creation from volcanic activity millions of years ago.

Below right — Boulders line this long settled lava tube at El Malpais National Monument. Far right — Steve Fischer of the Bureau of Land Management shows a piece of a pot dropped by robbers of an archaeological site at El Malpais. Right — Archaeologists say that taking even one potsherd from a site is damaging, especially when thousands of people over time do it. It's a federal offense to be in possession of illegally obtained artifacts from federally administered lands and many private lands.

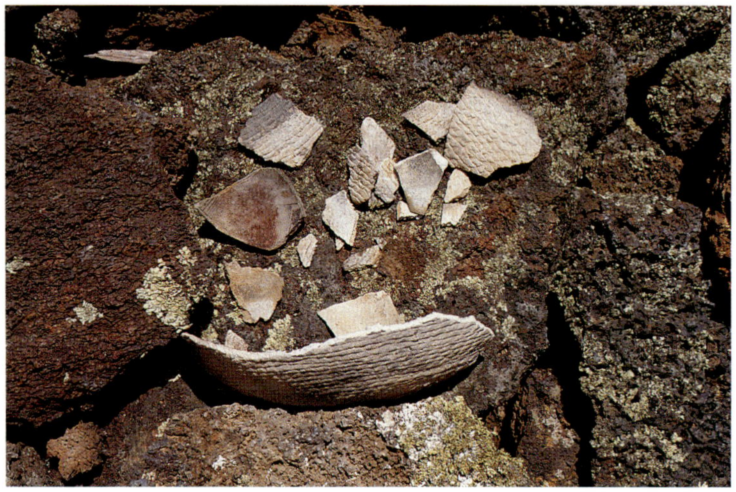

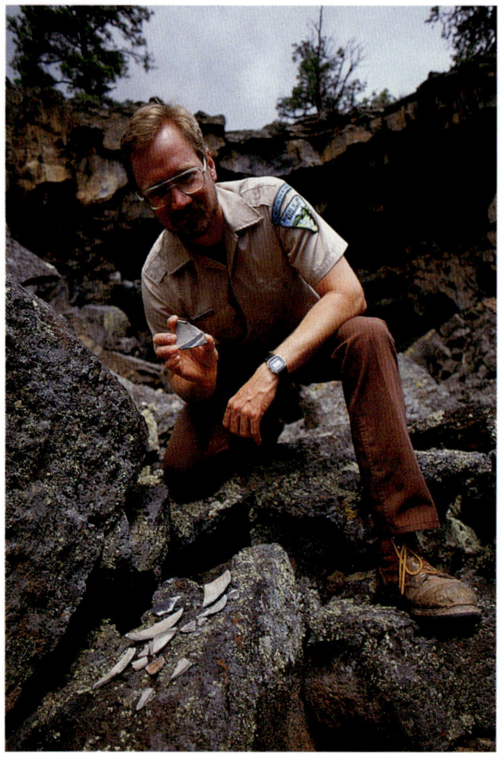

El Malpais National Monument and an adjoining conservation area were established in 1987. The 115,000-acre preserve in northwest New Mexico contains many valuable geological and archaeological sites in an area where Native American presence is known to be

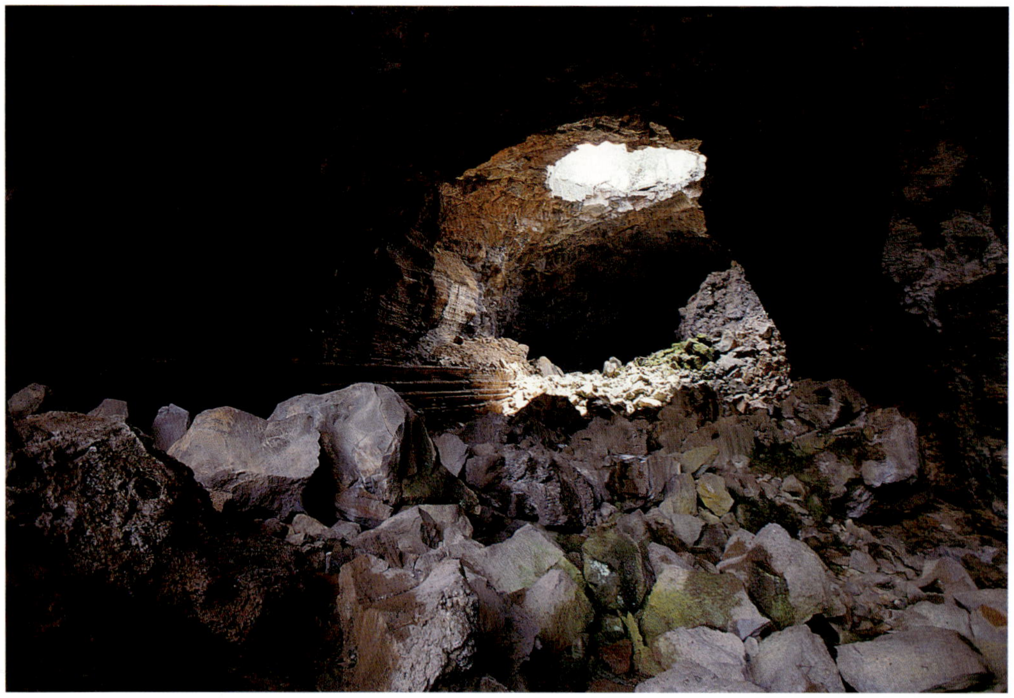

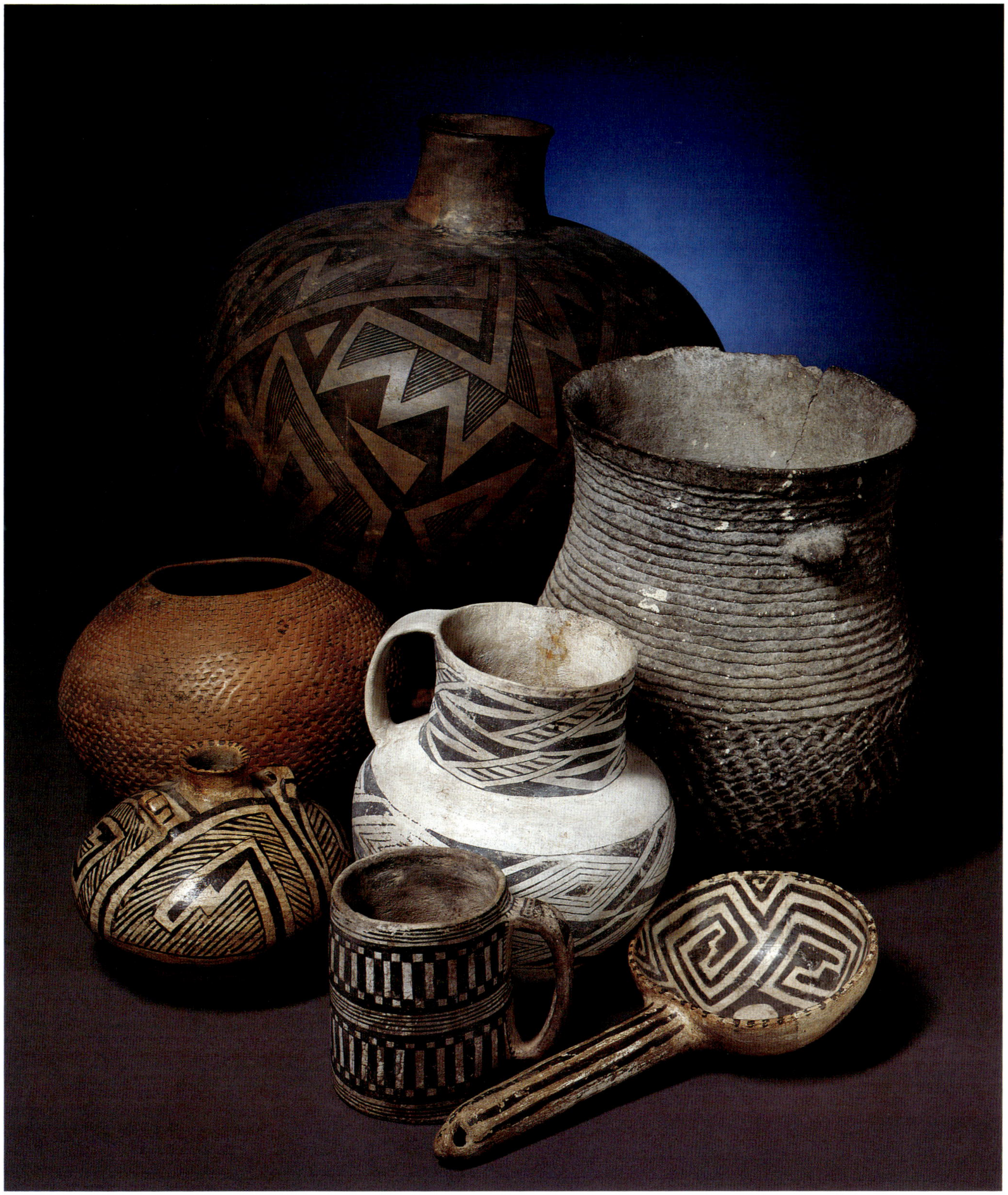

LONG ESTABLISHED. ARCHAEOLOGISTS ESTIMATE THAT 90 PERCENT OF ALL KNOWN SITES HAVE BEEN LOOTED. ANOTHER ANCIENT SITE, CHACO CANYON NATIONAL HISTORICAL PARK, SITS TO THE NORTH NEAR THE NAVAJO NATION INDIAN RESERVATION, WHILE THE CONTEMPORARY ACOMA AND LAGUNA PUEBLOS SIT NEARBY.

ACOMA RESIDENTS BELIEVE THEIR PEOPLE HAVE LIVED IN THE OLD MESA-TOP VILLAGE SINCE A.D. 600, WHICH WOULD MAKE IT THE MOST CONTINUALLY INHABITED COMMUNITY IN THE UNITED STATES. HOWEVER, SOME ARCHAEOLOGISTS DISPUTE THE ACOMA CLAIMS AND THEY CAN ONLY SCIENTIFICALLY CONFIRM OCCUPATION BACK TO A.D. 1150.

LEFT — ANCIENT POTS REST SAFELY IN STORAGE AT THE SCHOOL OF AMERICAN RESEARCH IN SANTA FE, WHICH HAS CONDUCTED NUMEROUS ARCHAEOLOGICAL DIGS IN THE SOUTHWEST SINCE ITS FOUNDING IN THE EARLY 1900S.

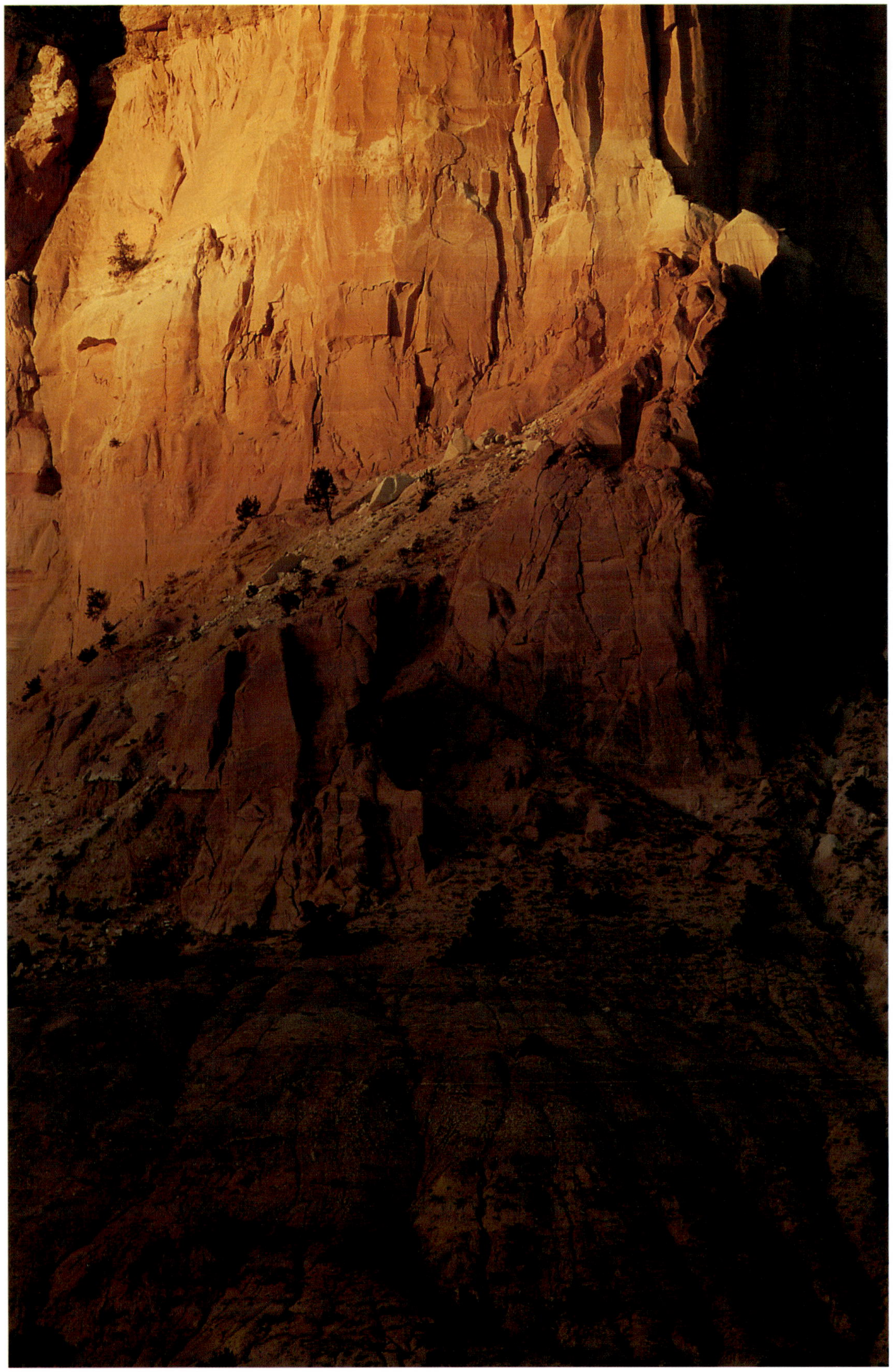

The light at sunset colors these bluffs at Ghost Ranch near Abiquiú. These and other multilayered bluffs in the area have enabled scientists to trace many major geological periods in New Mexico's dynamic past.

The fiery colors of fall manifest upon these trees and bushes on the valley floor of Big Canyon in the rugged Guadalupe Mountains near the Texas/New Mexico border.

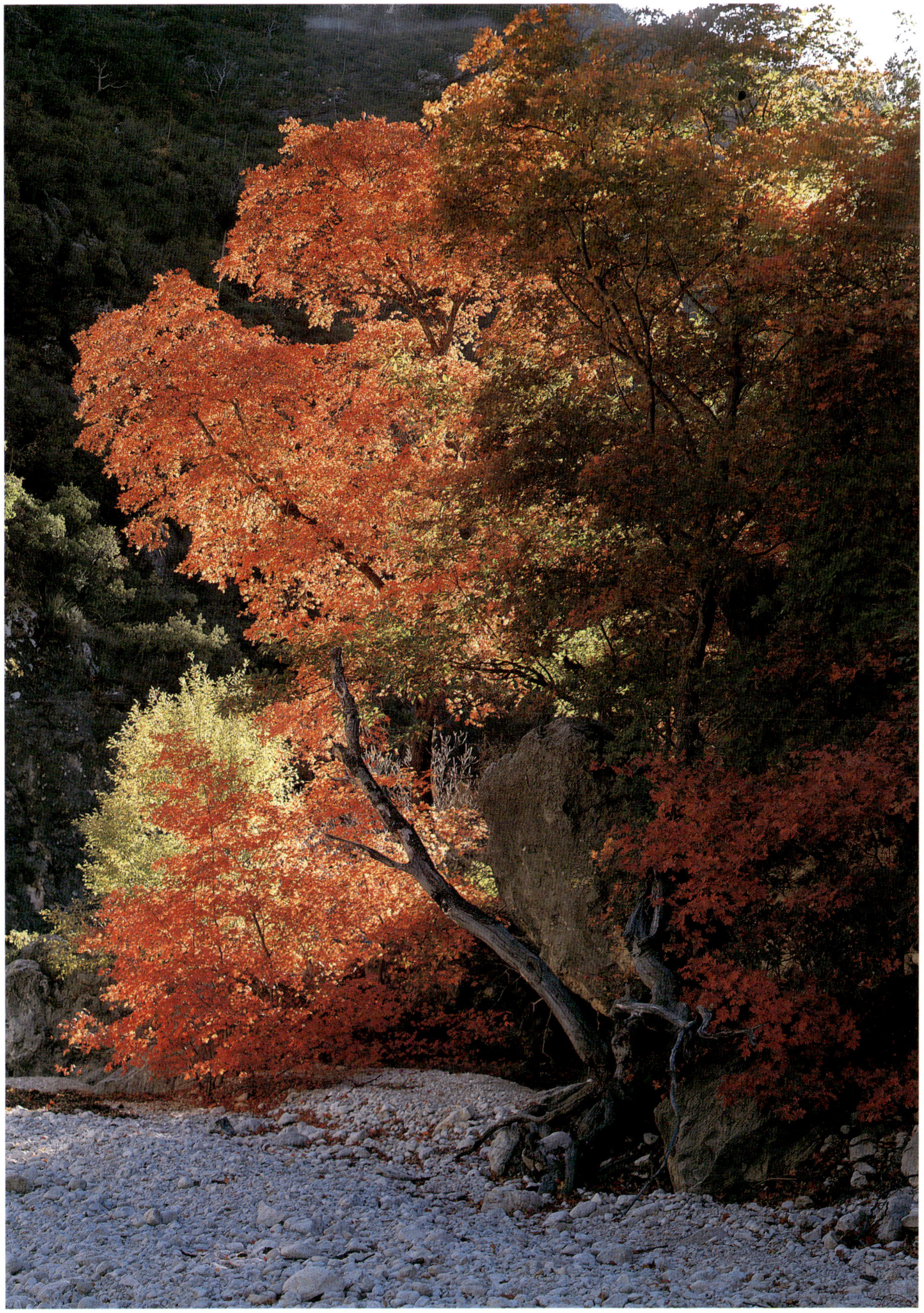

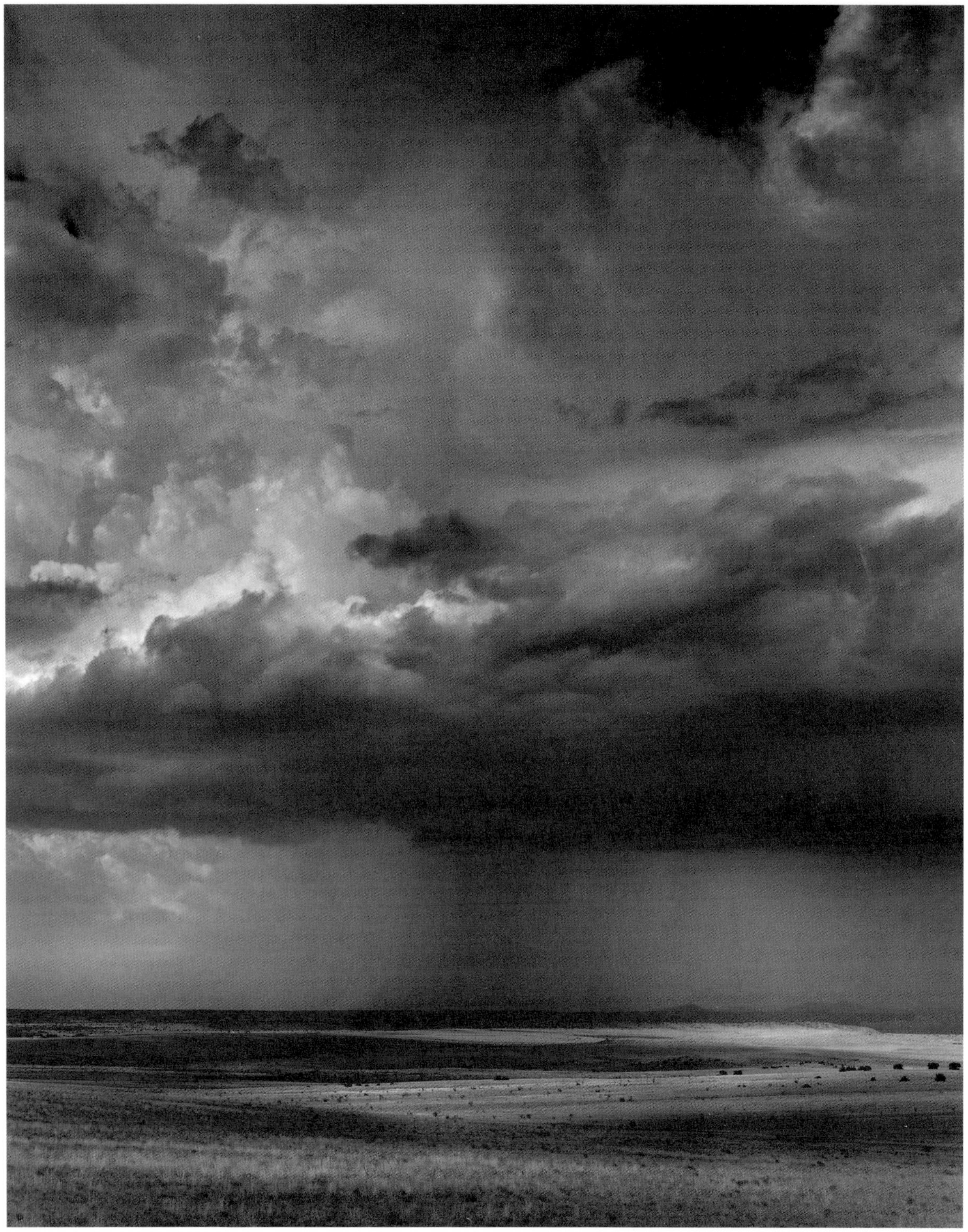

Thunder on the Horizon

Dark rain clouds develop over the expansive Galisteo Basin south of Santa Fe,
where any moisture from the sky is rejoiced by all living things.

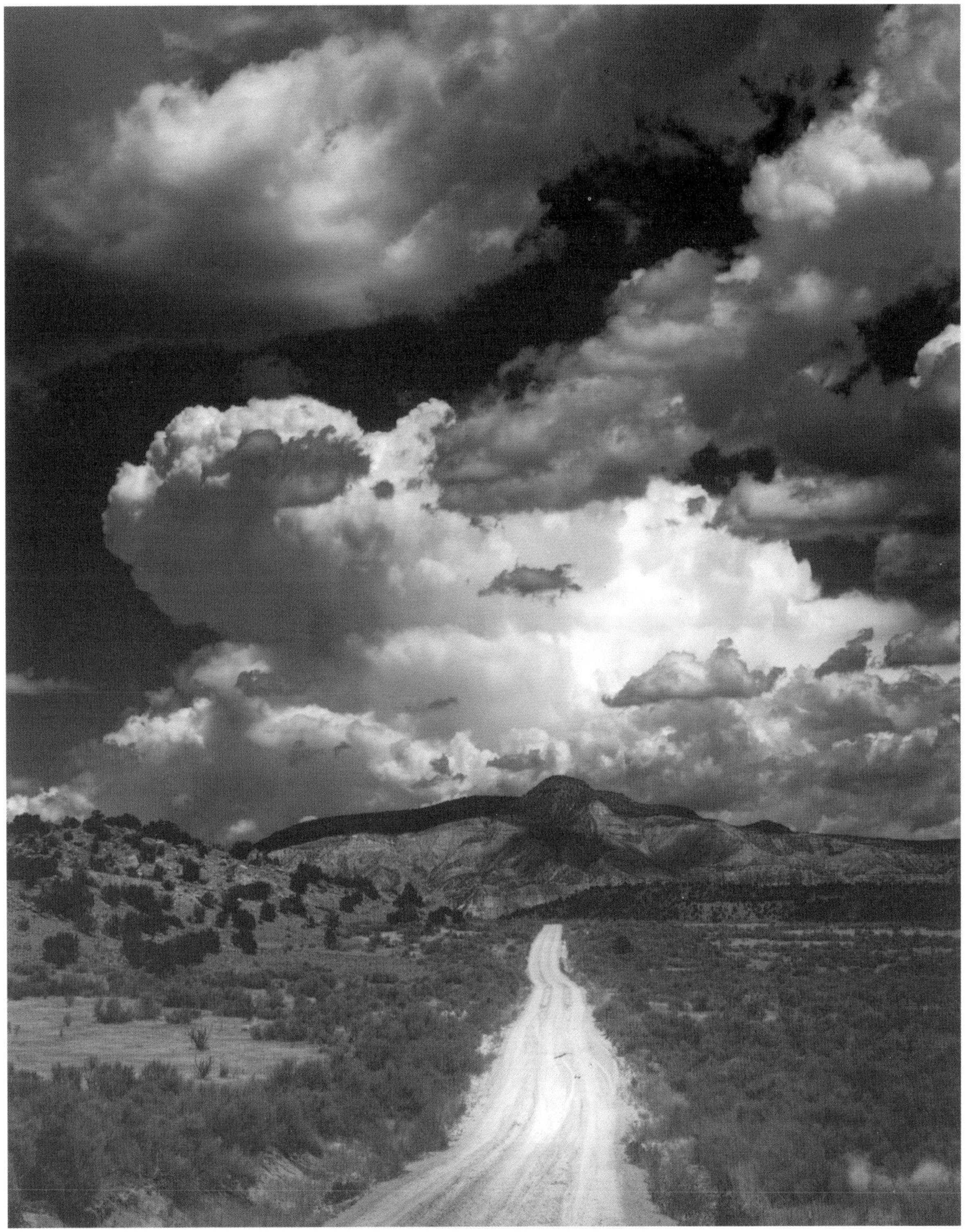

Road to Heaven

Underneath a magnificent cloudy sky, Mesa de las Viejas near Abiquiú beckons adventurous travelers to this lonely dirt road leading to the nearby Chama River.

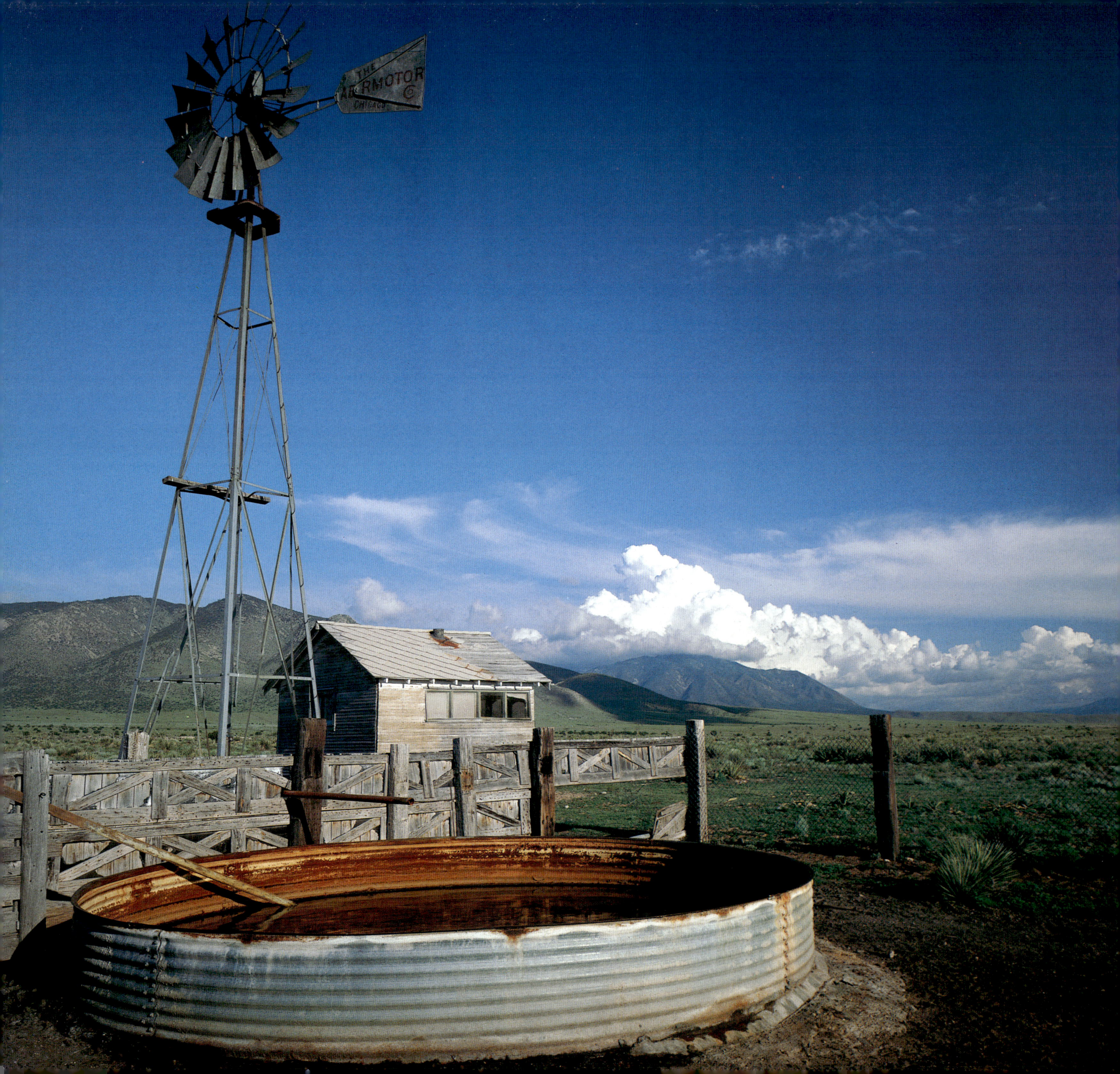
THE
RMOTOR

A cattle ranch near Carrizozo in southeastern New Mexico still exudes all the wide-open romance of the Old West, where many a legend were born and others laid to rest, sometimes violently.

Several major cattle routes crisscrossed this area, bringing fortune to cattle barons who sold their stock to railroad companies and army outposts that used the beef to feed their employees and soldiers.

As a consequence of this prosperous industry, range wars developed among rivalrous ranchers and merchants. One of the most famous in this area, of course, was the Lincoln County War, which spawned New Mexico's most famous outlaw legend — William McCarty, a.k.a. Billy the Kid.

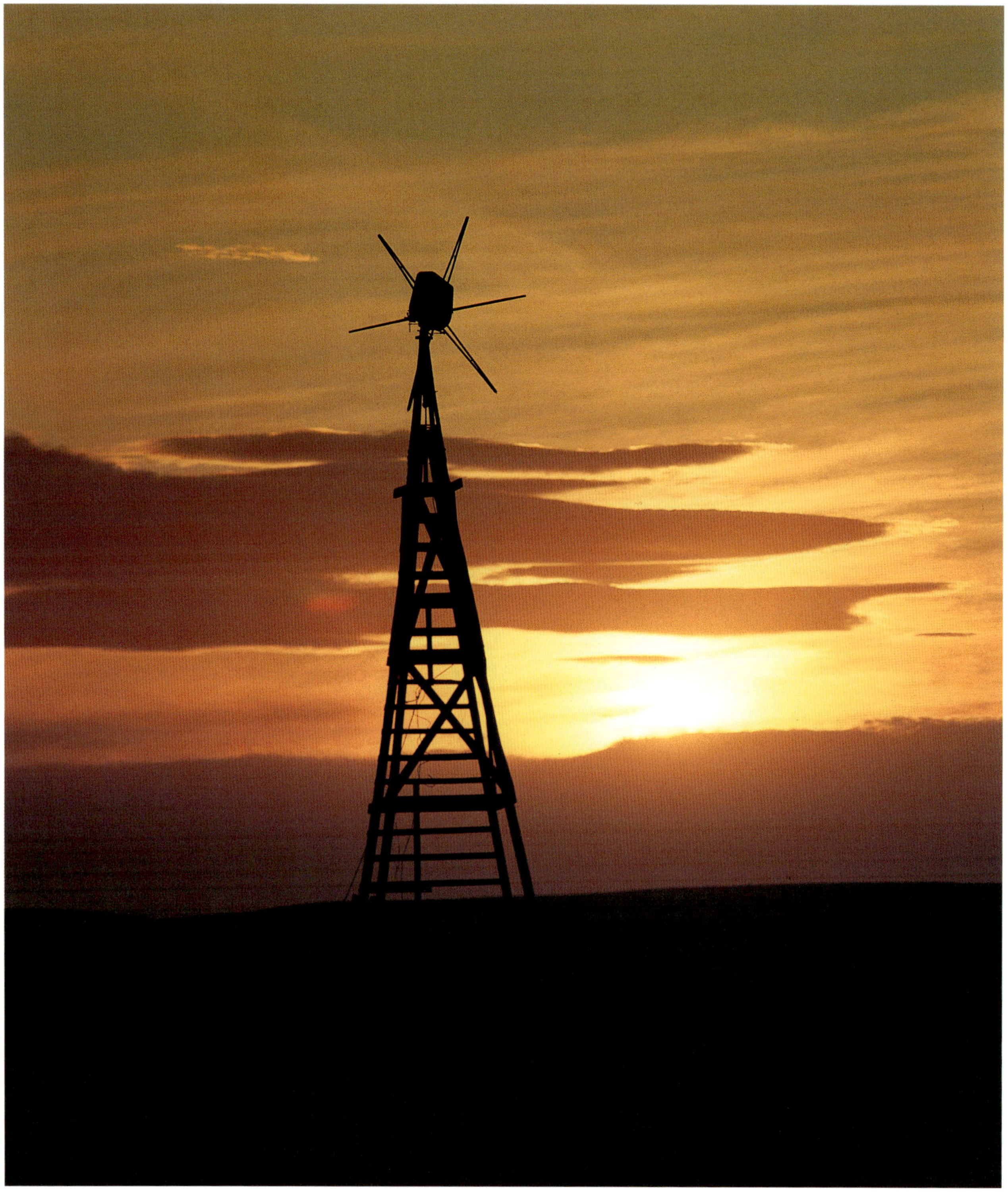

Sky Spinner

A lone windmill silhouettes before a golden evening sky near Carlsbad.

No longer the quintessential water-pumping tool, the windmill

remains a common sight in rural New Mexico.

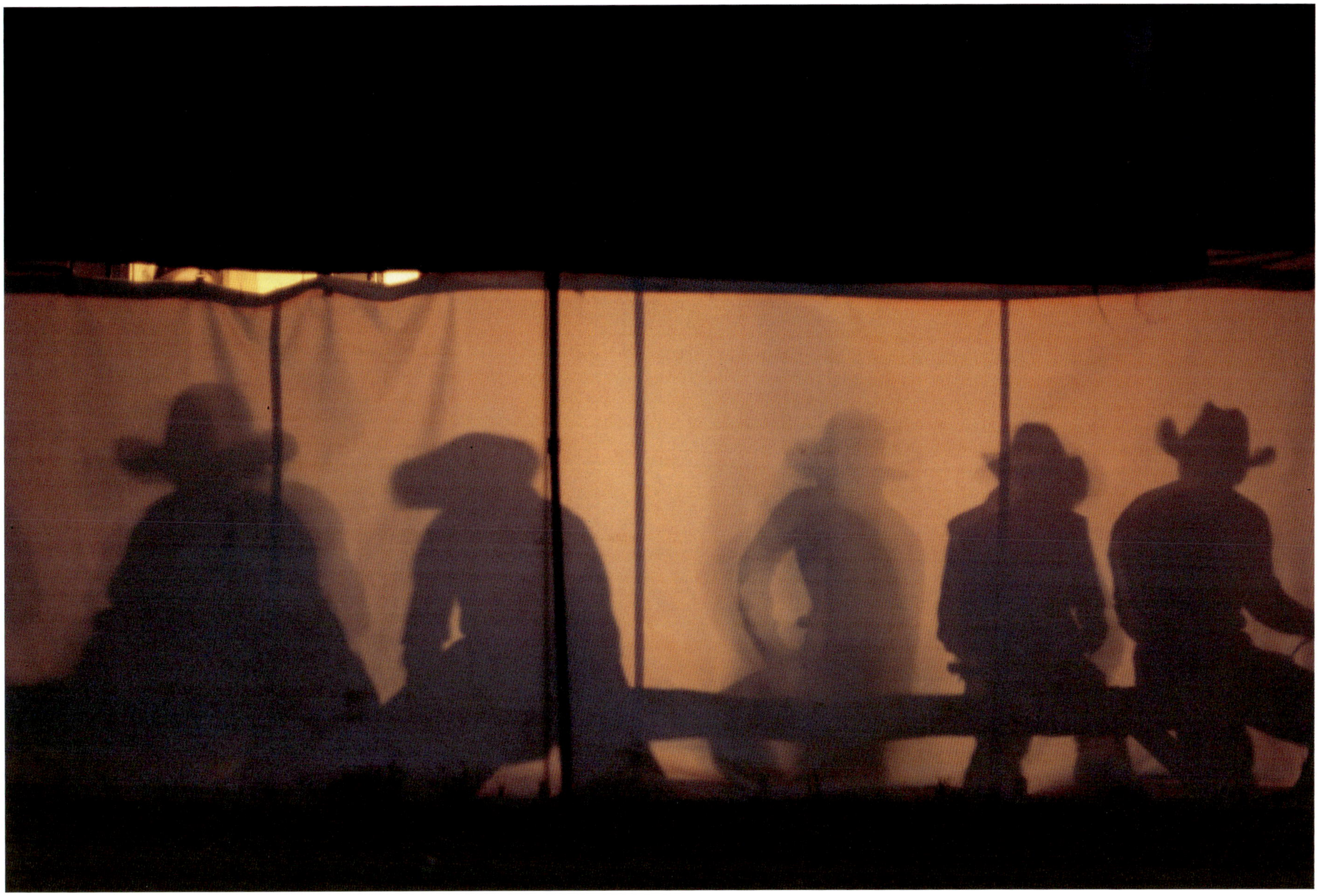

Round 'em up

Real working cowboys on the Bell Ranch in northeastern New Mexico gather at the chuck wagon for some hearty 3 a.m. grub before a hard day's work on the range.

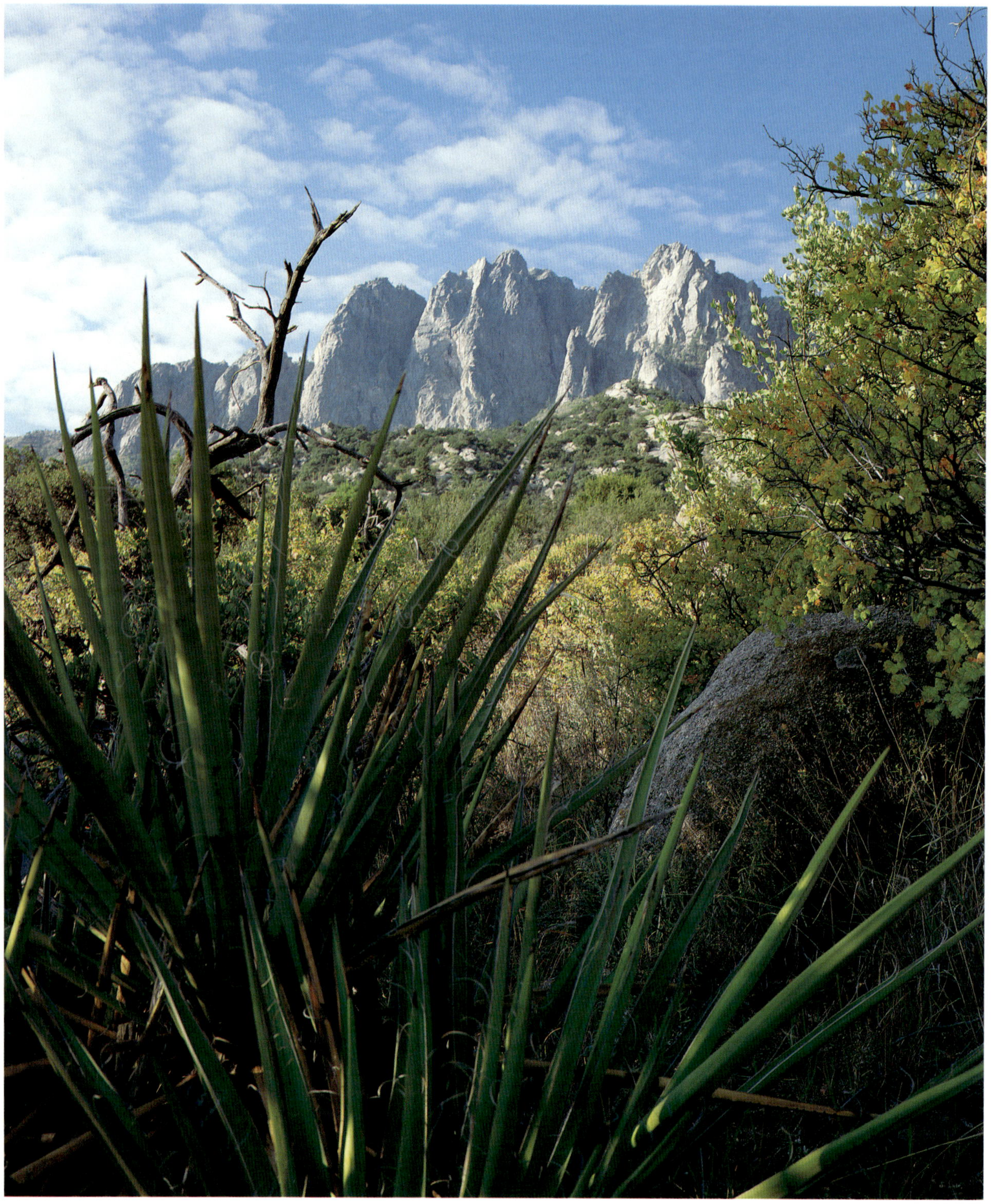

Bushwhacking Bonanza

Yucca plants dominate this view of the Organ Mountains from Aguirre Springs campground near Las Cruces. Native Americans once utilized the desert plant to make shampoo.

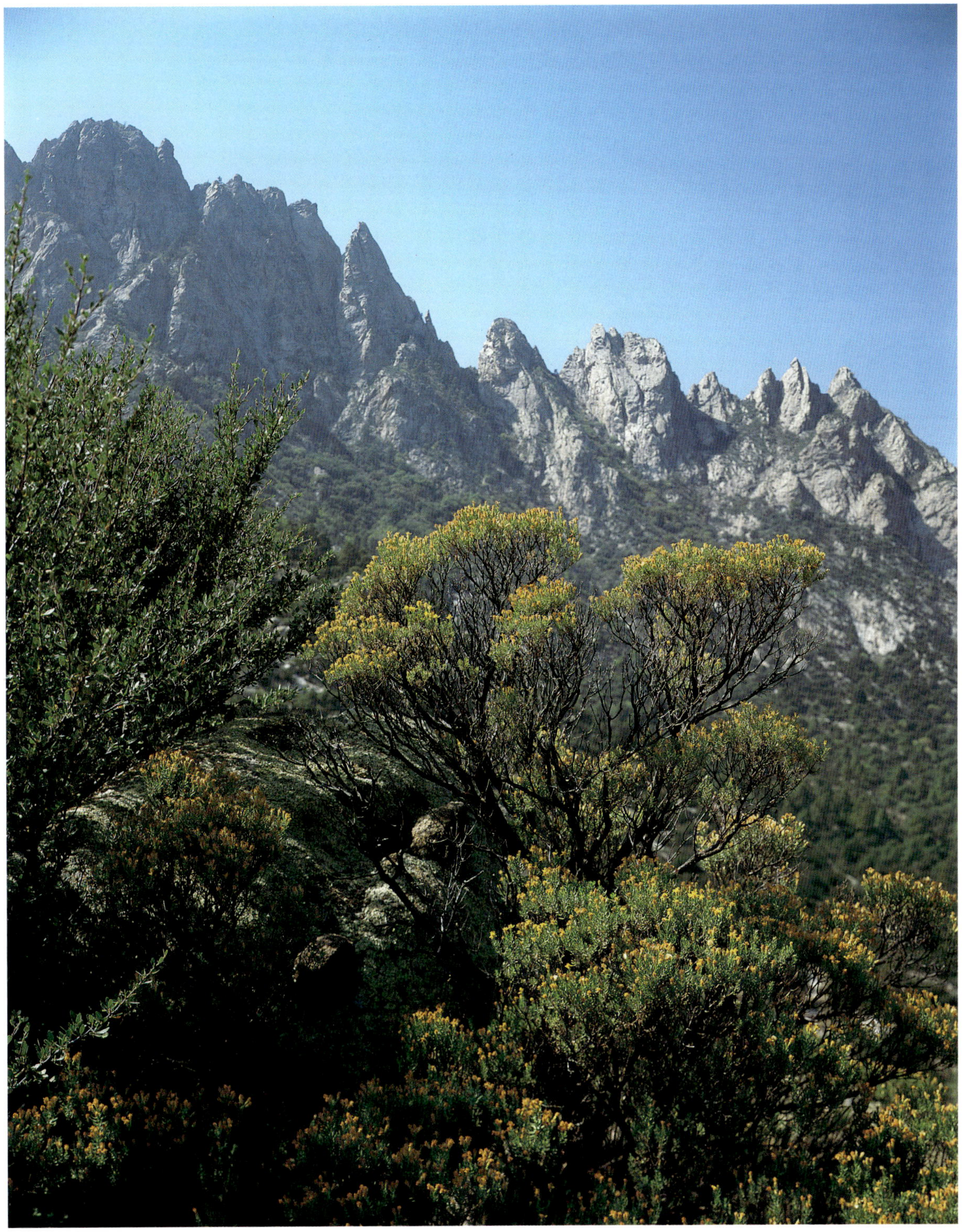

Touch the Sky

It's impossible to miss the distinct peaks of the Organ Mountains at Aguirre Springs. Although Spanish explorers called the range many names, the current name stuck because so many believed the spires resembled organ pipes.

The moon rises over a partially illuminated Sombrero Peak near Abiquiú. According to Robert Julyan, author of *The Place Names of New Mexico*, Arthur Newton Pack founded the Ghost Ranch conference center in 1933. A guide told Pack that the property previously was called Rancho de los Brujos (ranch of the witches) because it was supposedly haunted by evil spirits.

Pack said that people eventually began to refer to the property as Ghost Ranch and the name stuck. Legend has it that cottonwood trees on the property were used to hang cattle thieves, Julyan wrote. The area was settled in the late 19th century by the Archuleta family and a stockade they built out of cedar poles came to be known as the Ghost House.

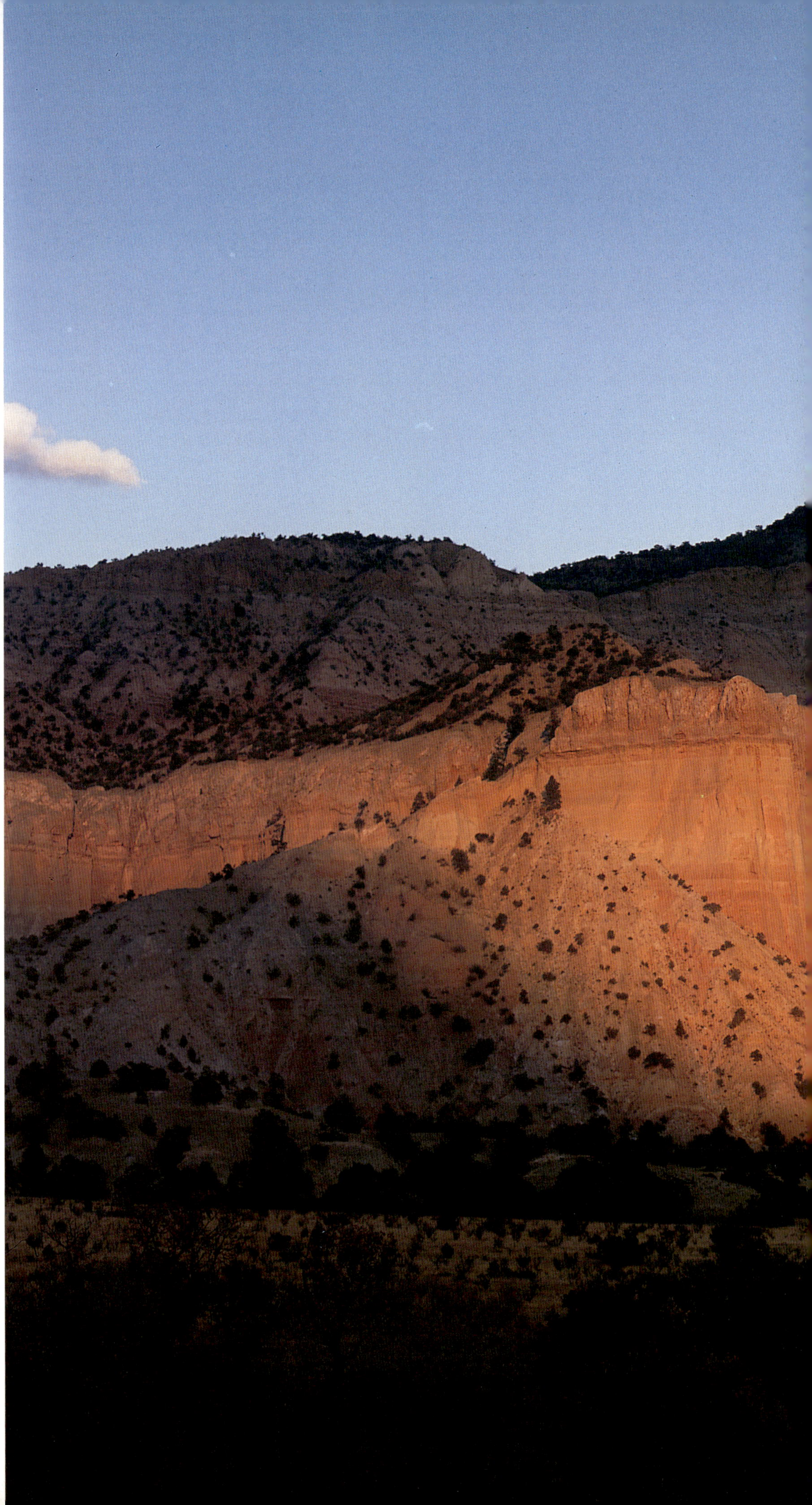

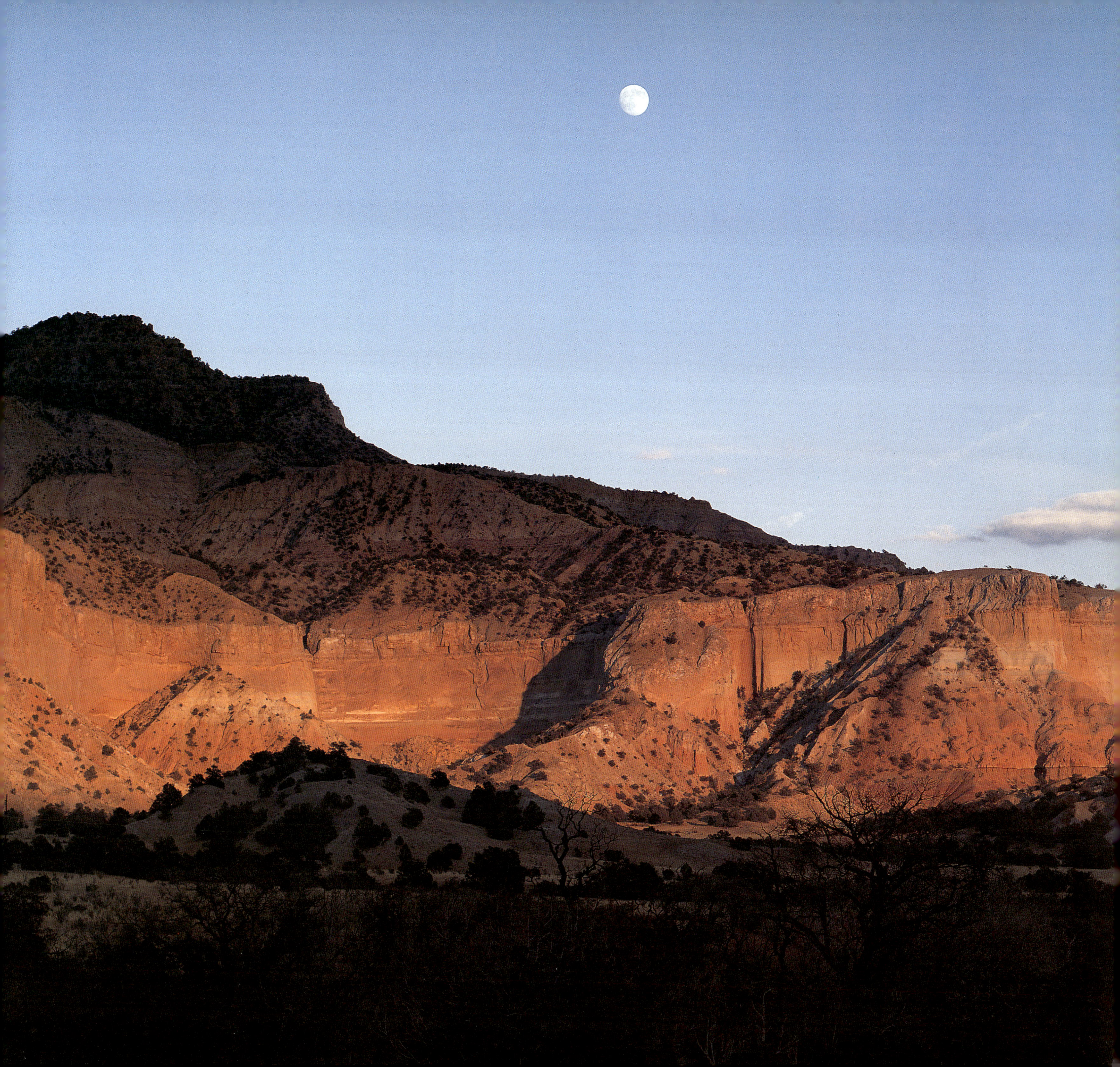

Every year members of La Iglesia de Santa Cruz de la Cañada, or the Church of the Holy Cross of the Brook in Santa Cruz, participate in services and processions to celebrate the Holy Triduum, the days between the crucifixion and resurrection of Jesus of Nazareth (Good Thursday through Easter Sunday).

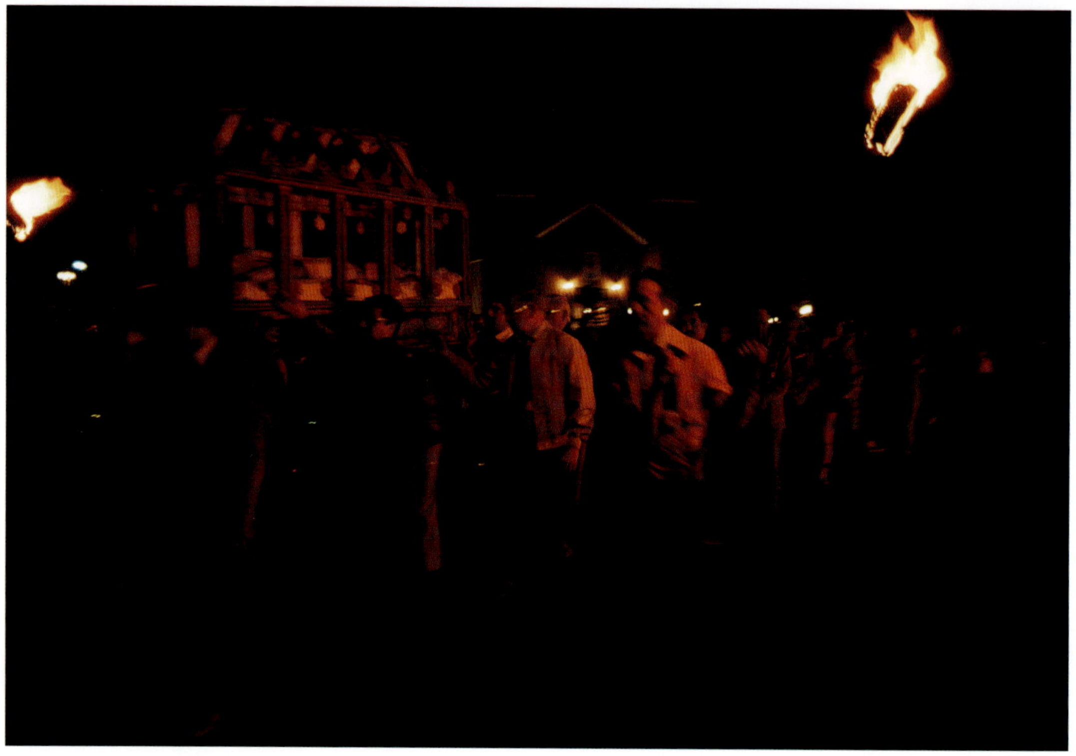

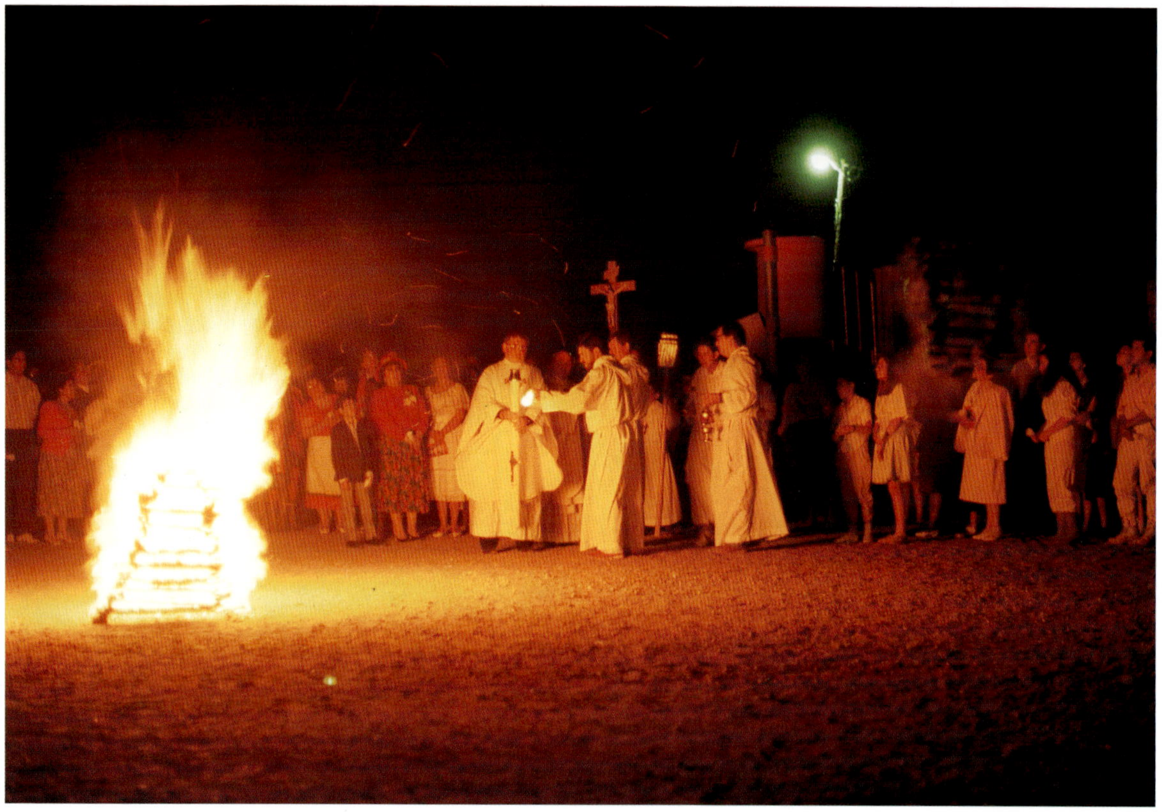

Above — Members of the Hermanos de Nuestro Padre Jesus (*Penitentes*) and Los Hermanos de la Santisima (*Trinitarios*) alternate each year in singing *alabados* (hymns) and carrying a casket with the wooden Santo Entierro, after Veneration of the Cross services on Good Friday. The Santo Entierro is believed to have been carved in the 1760s by Fray Andres García.

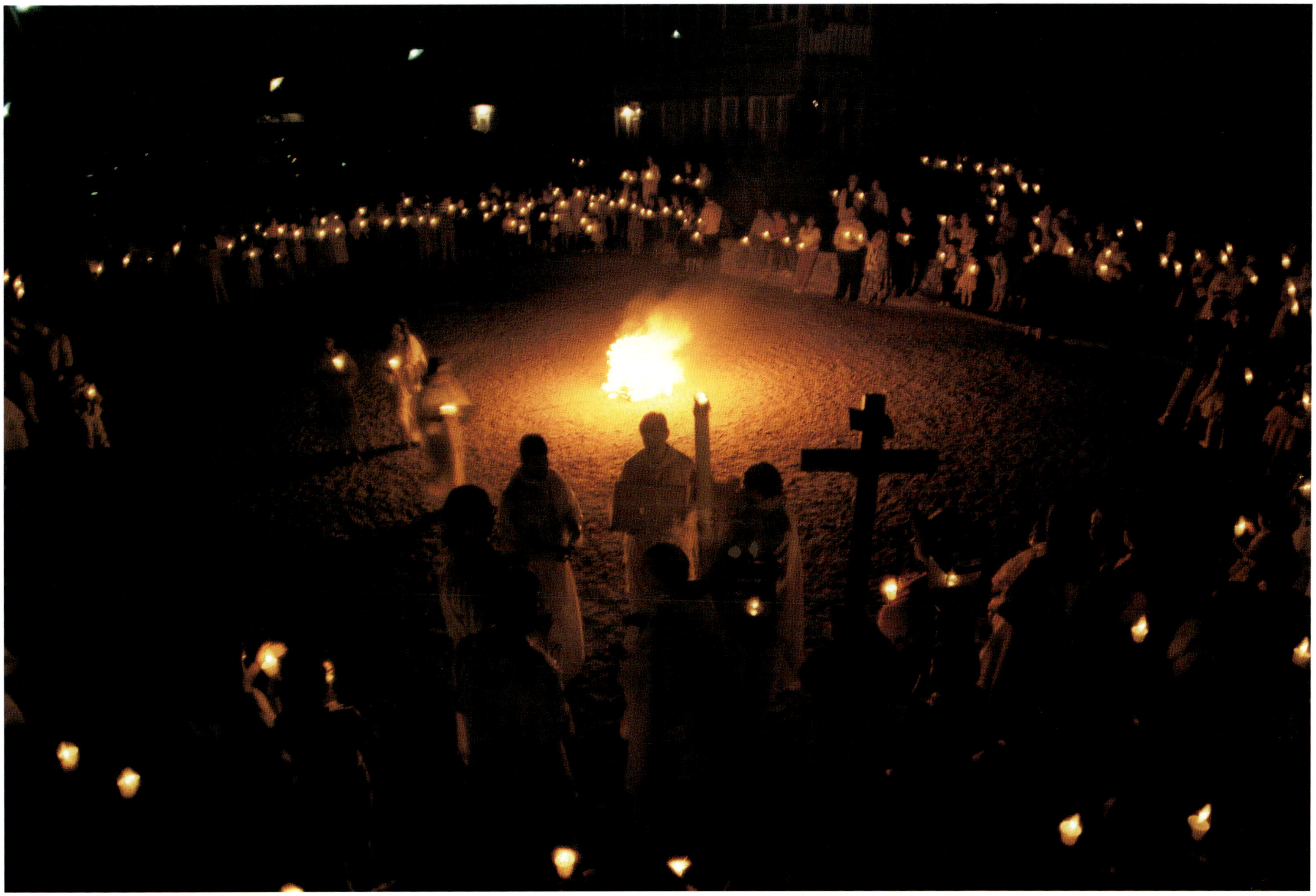

Above – The Paschal Candle, which represents the resurrected Christ, is used to light individual candles held by parishioners who then surround the sacred fire. Each individual candle represents its holder's baptism, while the sacred fire is symbolic of the light, heat and warmth of God.

Opposite below – Holy Cross Church authorities light the Paschal (Easter) candle with flame from the sacred fire (also called the new fire) during the Holy Saturday Easter vigil.

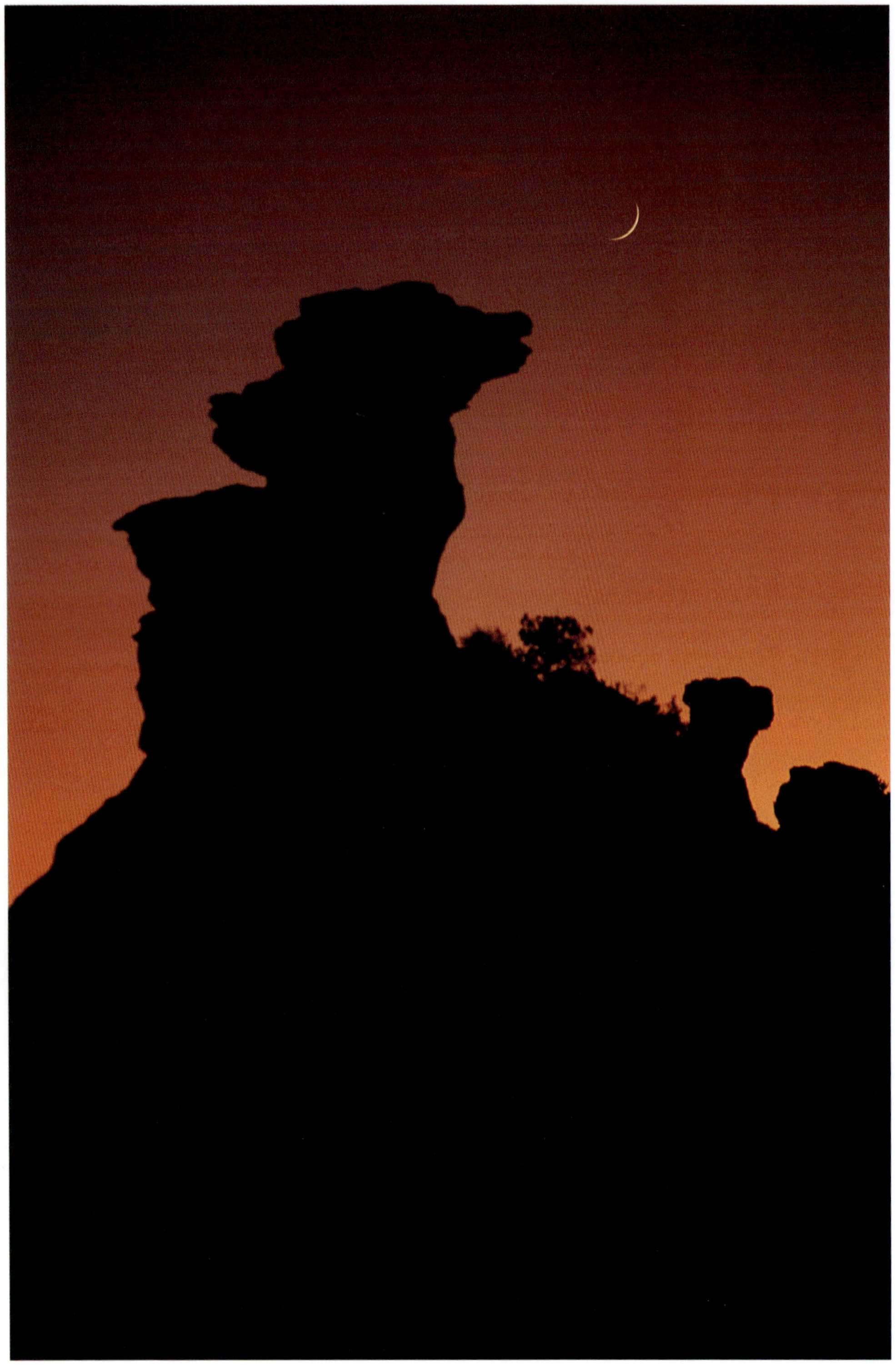

Magic Moods

While a slivered moon enchants from above, twilight's evening magic illuminates the sky and silhouettes an eroding sandstone formation south of Chimayó.

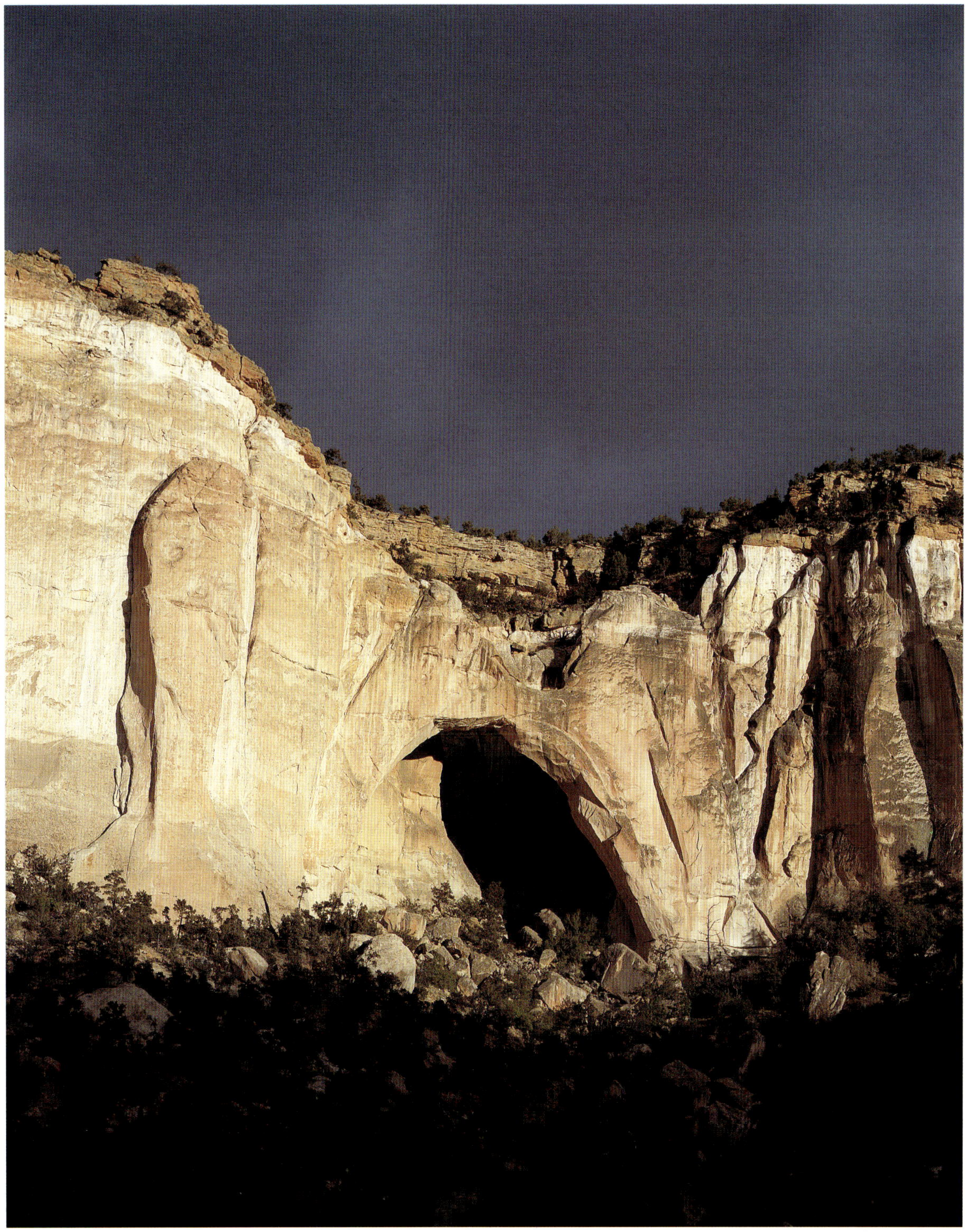

Chiseled in Stone

Mother nature always proves to be the ultimate architect, especially with this natural stone arch formed from a stunning cliff side at El Malpais National Monument.

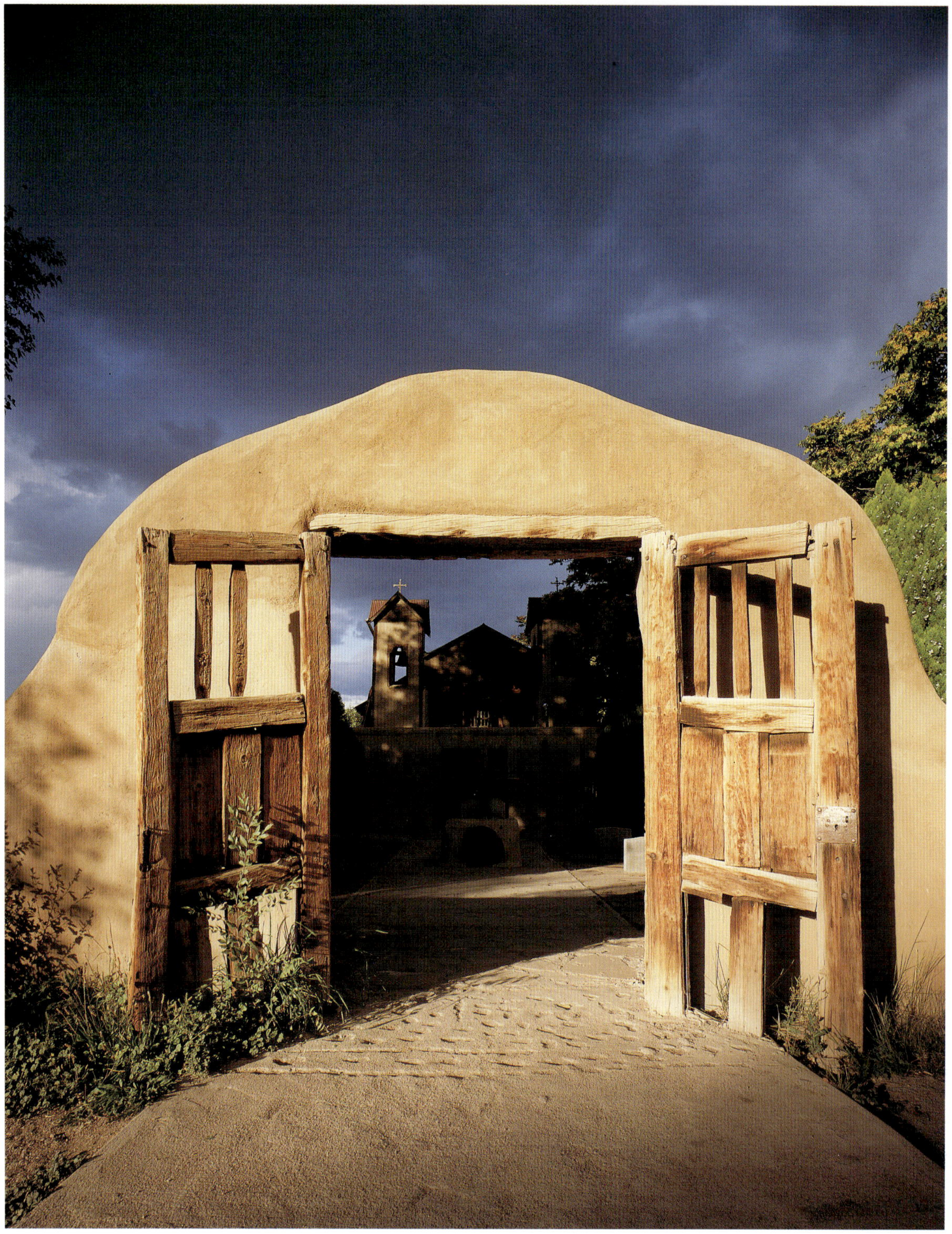

Gateway to Healing

Late-afternoon sunlight warms the adobe entrance to El Santuario de Nuestro Señor de Esquipulas in Chimayó. Construction began on this excellent example of Spanish colonial architecture in 1813.

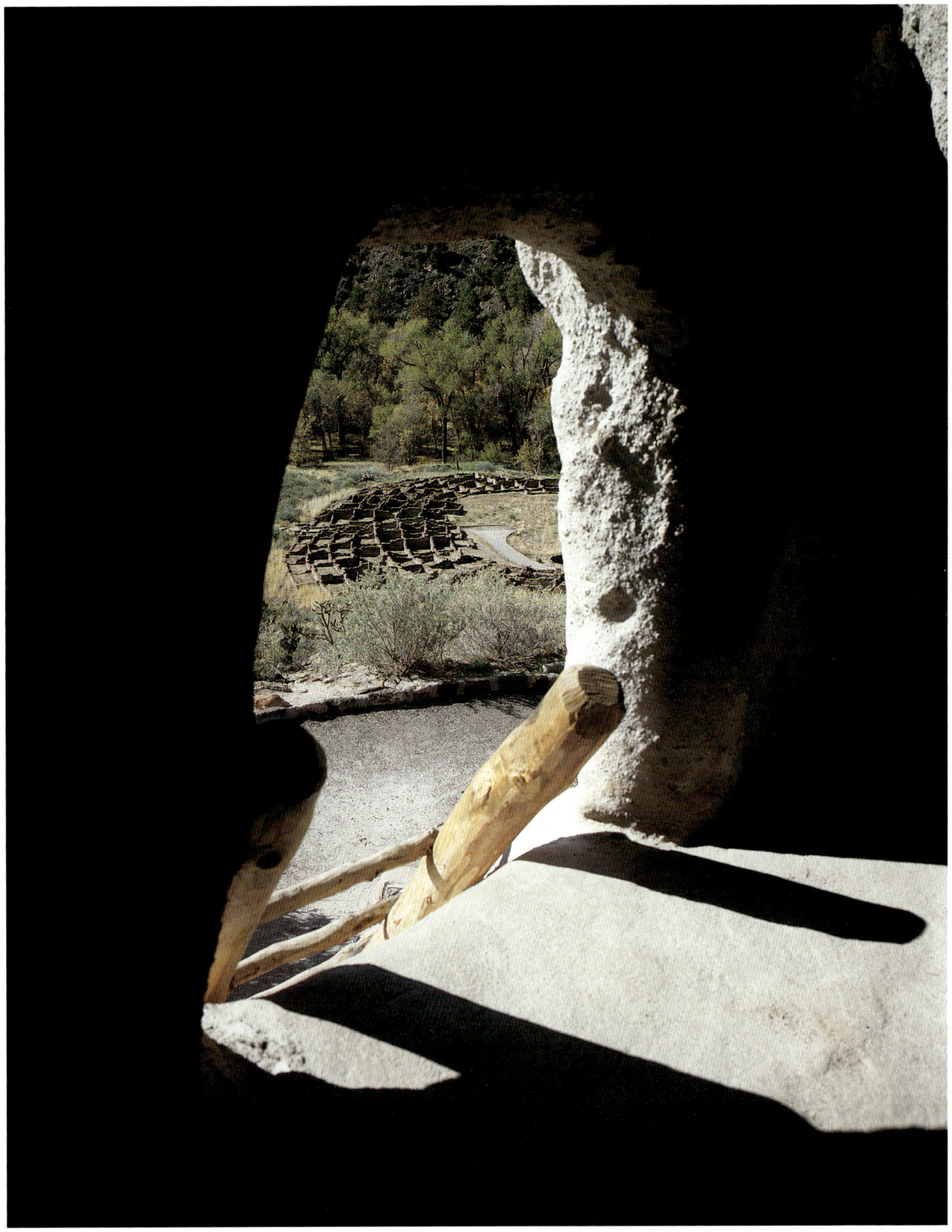

Come On In!

The soft volcanic tuff at Bandelier National Monument enabled ancient Indians to carve their homes into the walls of steep cliffs centuries ago.

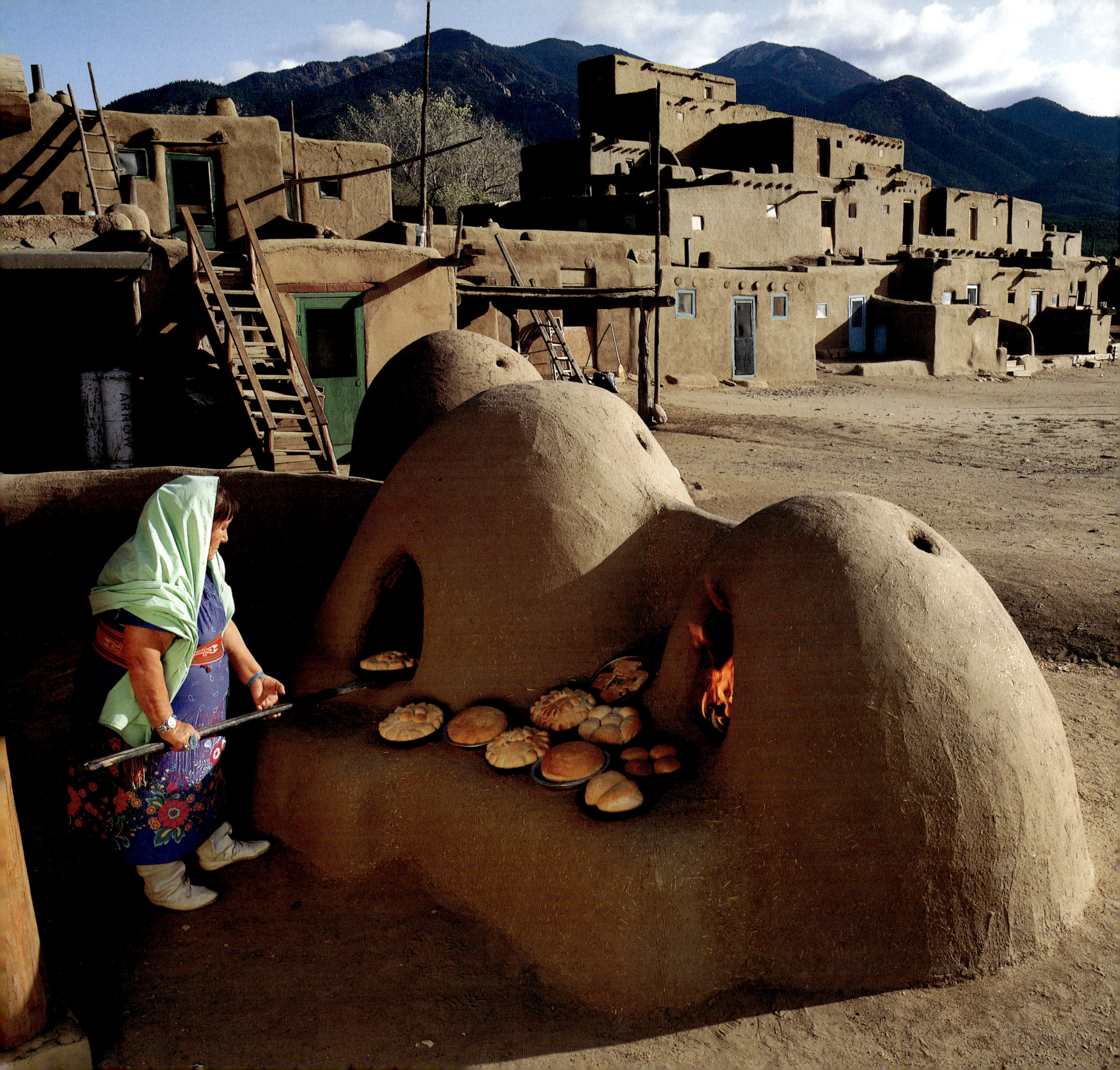

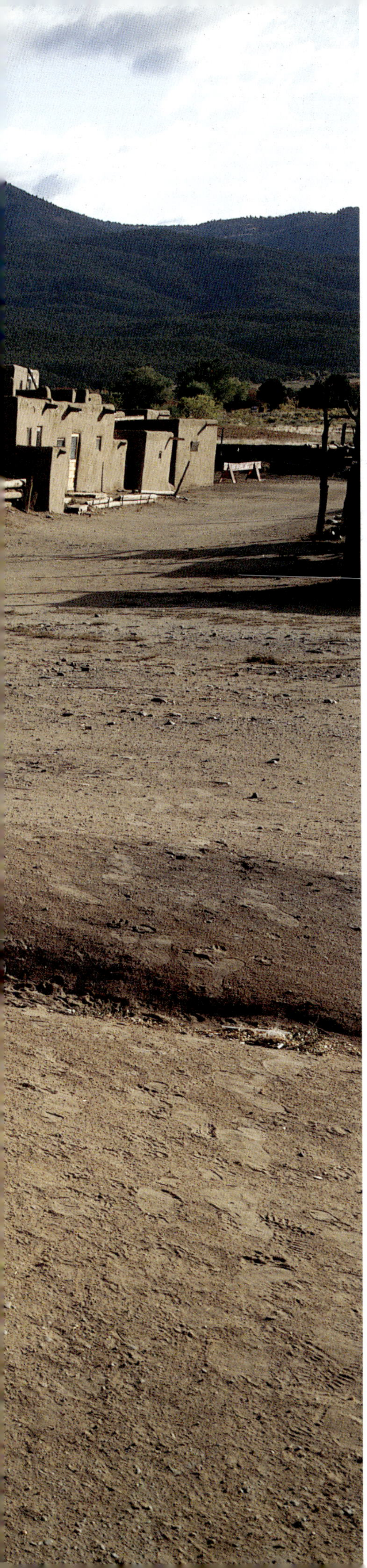

CRUCITA ROMERO

DISPLAYS THE FRUITS OF HER TRADITIONAL BREAD-BAKING EFFORTS ON A SET OF SIDE-BY-SIDE ADOBE *HORNOS* AT TAOS PUEBLO. THE LOCATION HAS LONG BEEN A TRADING CENTER BETWEEN DIFFERENT CULTURES EVEN BEFORE THE SPANISH ARRIVED IN THE SOUTHWEST IN THE 1500S.

PLAINS INDIANS USED TO TRADE HERE WITH THE PUEBLOS AND THEY LATER WERE JOINED BY SPANISH SETTLERS, FRENCH FUR TRADERS AND OTHER ROUGH MOUNTAIN MEN OF SORTS.

HISTORIANS BELIEVE ALL OF THESE DIFFERENT FACTIONS SET ASIDE THEIR CULTURAL DIFFERENCES ONCE A YEAR TO TRADE THEIR GOODS IN PEACE AT TAOS PUEBLO.

HOWEVER, THERE WERE SOME ACCOUNTS OF PLAINS INDIAN WARRIORS TRADING IN PEACE AT THE FAIR AND LATER AMBUSHING OTHER TRADERS ON THE TRAIL, RE-ACQUIRING THEIR ORIGINAL WARES AND, PERHAPS, A LITTLE MORE.

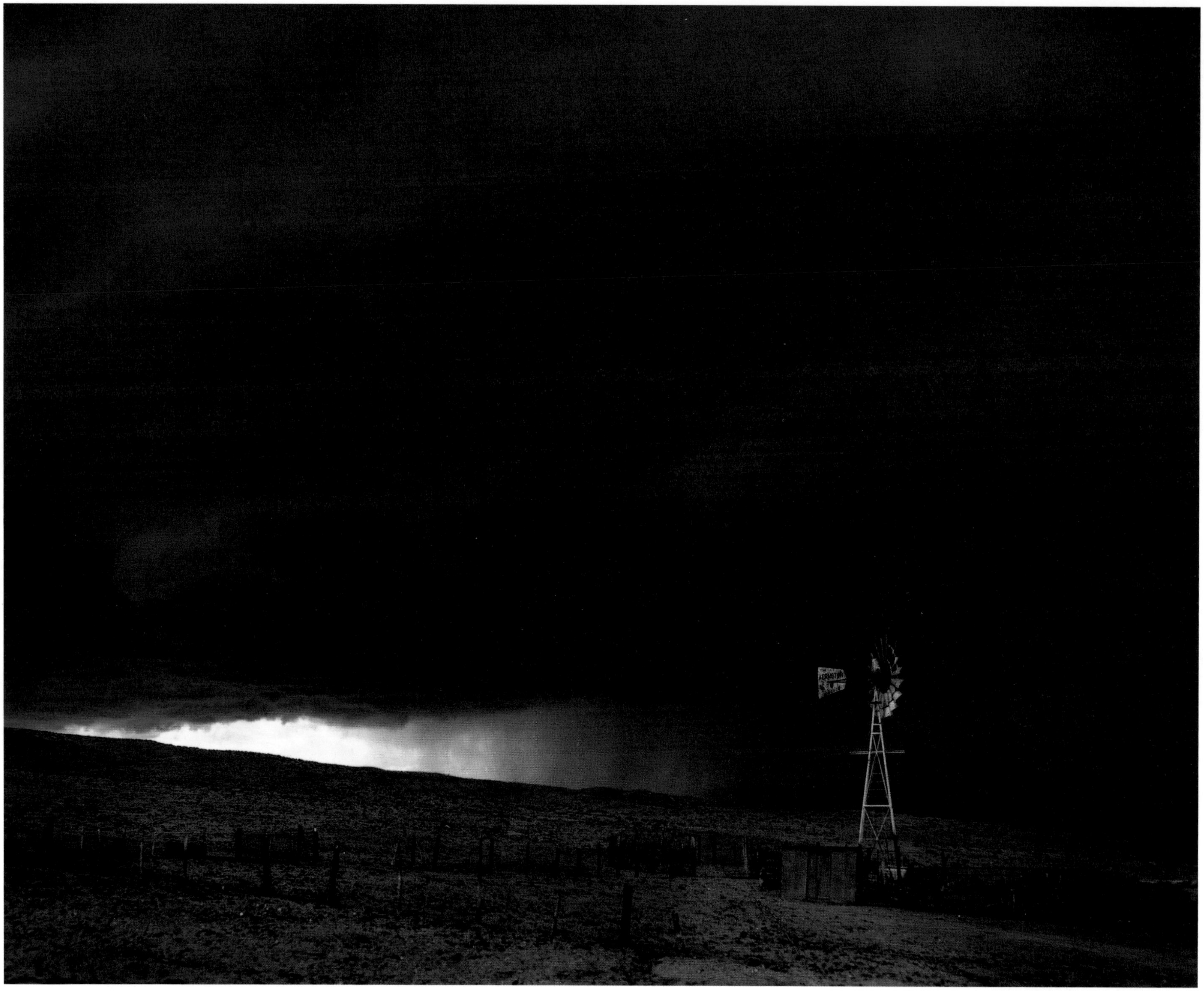

Power From Above

Mother Nature prepares to unleash her overwhelming force onto a small stock-yard and barren range on the West Mesa near Albuquerque.

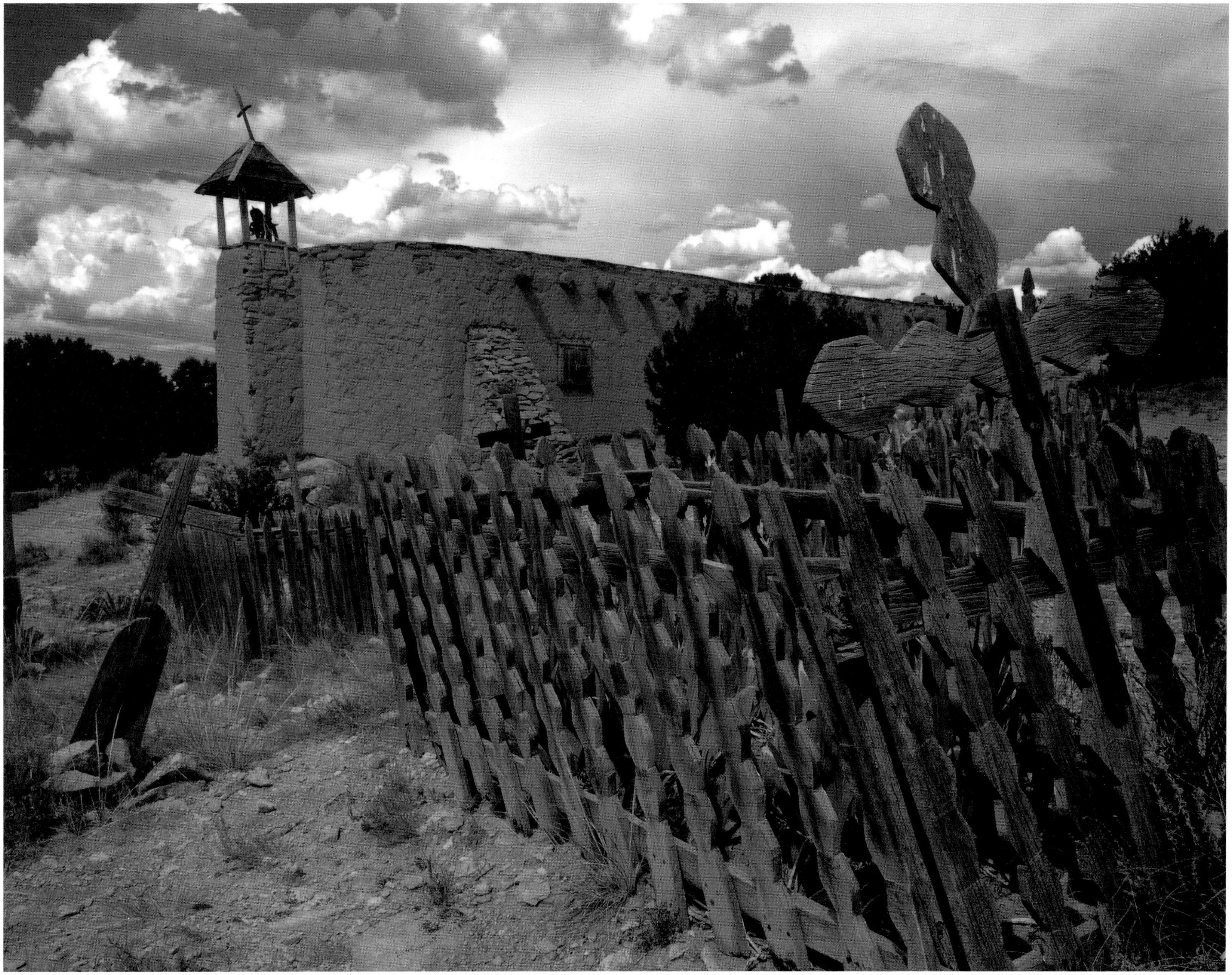

Valuable Vestiges

Showing the effects of time and weather, a *camposanto* (churchyard cemetery) outside a *morada* at El Rancho de las Golondrinas near Santa Fe exudes the flavor of the past.

A stock spring partially reflects an old wooden barn in a green valley in the Zuni Mountains of western New Mexico.

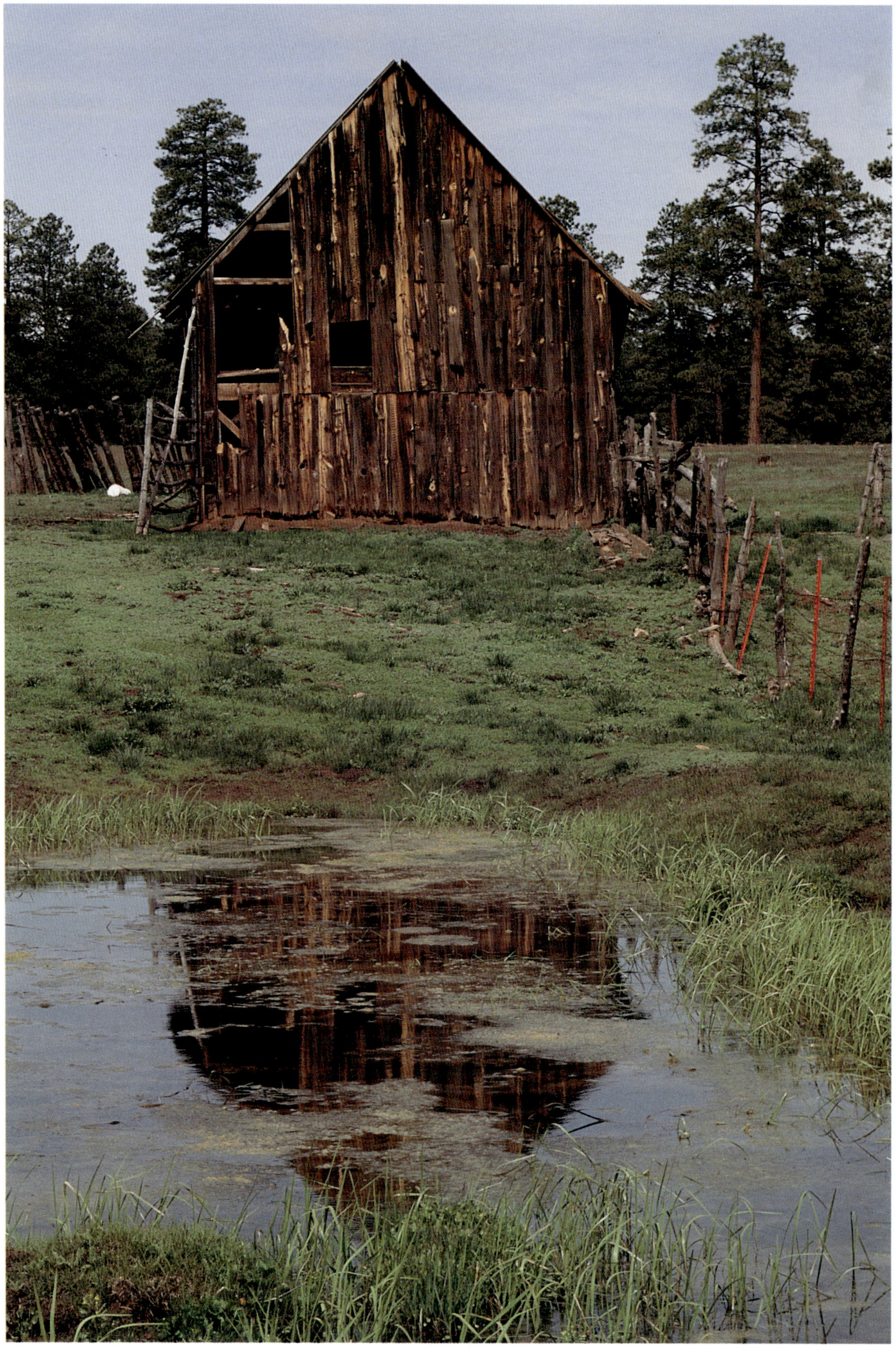

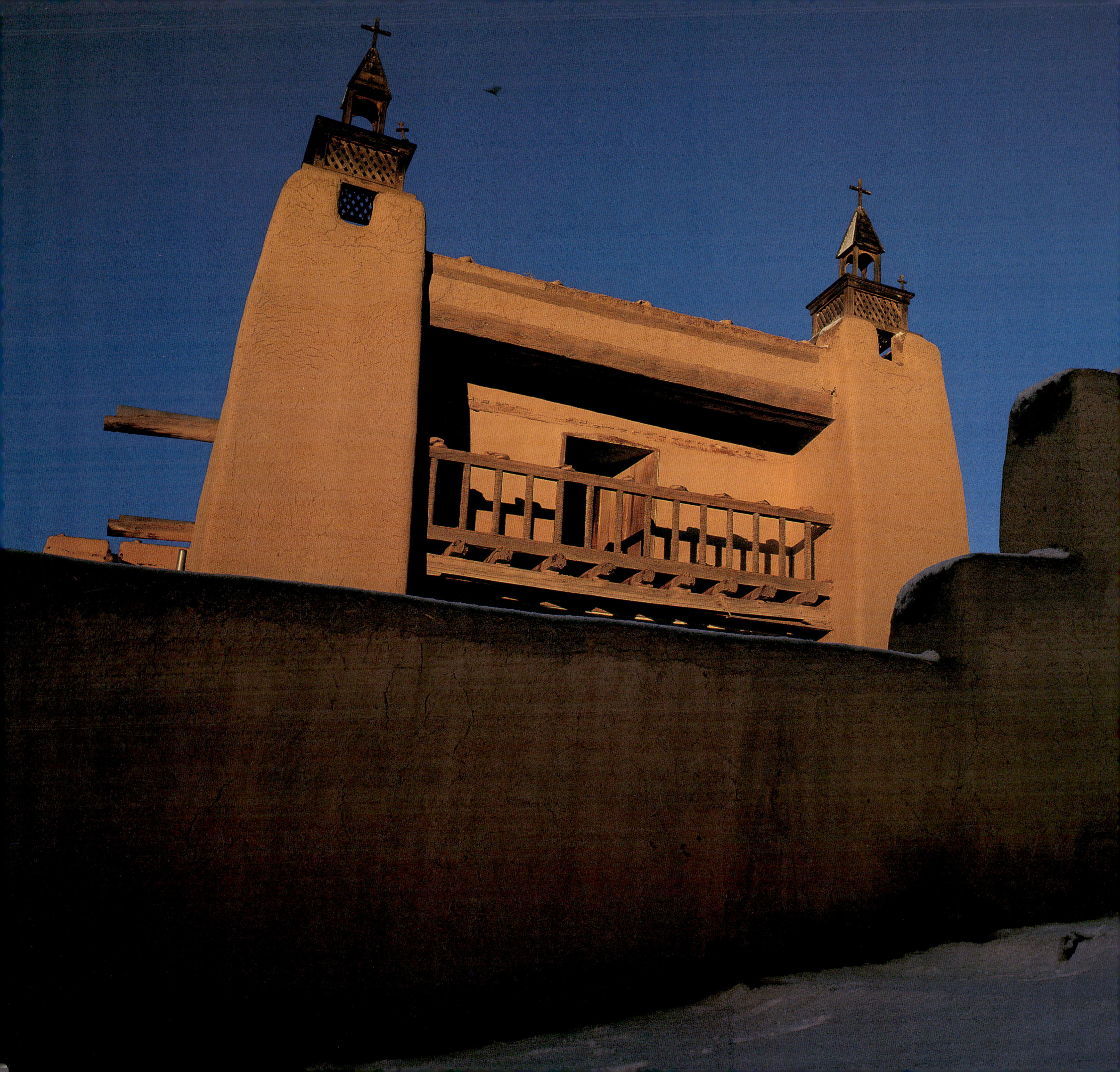

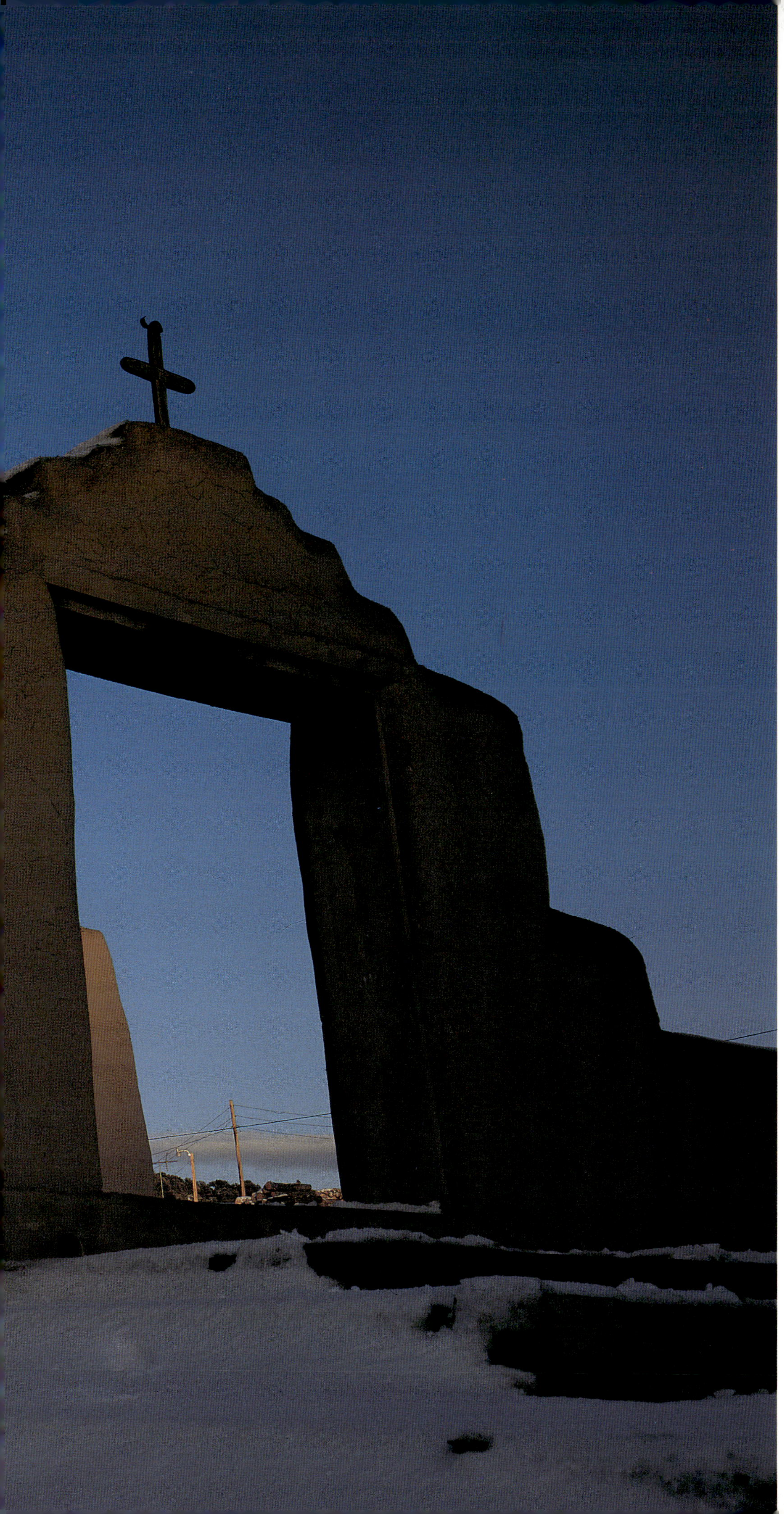

Historians believe the San José de Gracia Las Trampas Church was built around 1760. It's now called one of the "best preserved" colonial churches in New Mexico, although its first major renovation didn't occur until the early 1930s. This adobe building is one of the only historic churches with two belfries — the one on the right is called *Gracia* to symbolize the appreciation for gifts from the Lord; and the left one is named *Refugio*, meaning a place of refuge. Inside, the church is furnished with a wealth of colonial artifacts — *santos*, *bultos*, *reredos*, *retablos* and other items — that date back to the 18th and 19th centuries. For centuries the people of Las Trampas and other nearby villages have cared for the church, which is also a gathering place for a local *penitente* group.

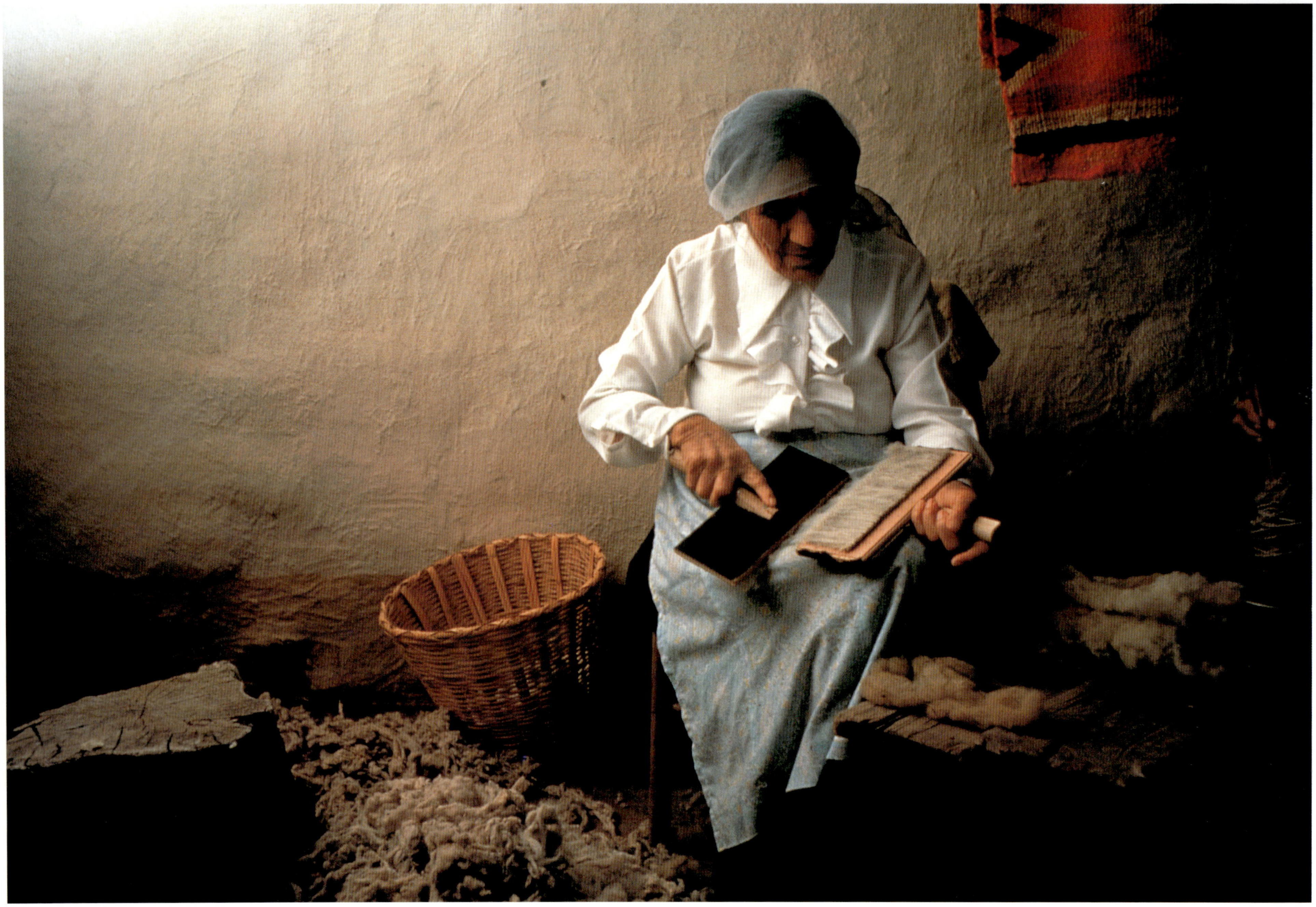

Enduring Tradition

Ferminia Leyba cards wool during a festival at El Rancho de las Golondrinas, a historic Spanish colonial village museum south of Santa Fe dedicated to preserving traditional Hispanic folkways.

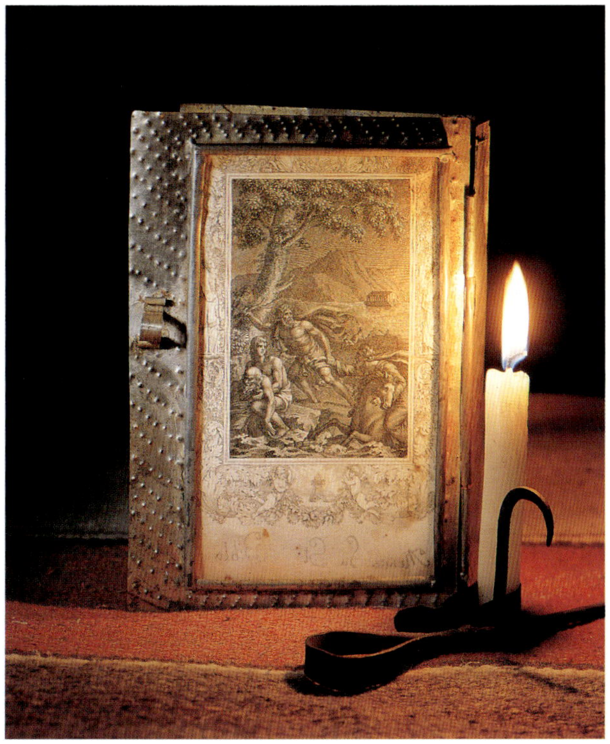

Scarcity of manufactured goods forced early Spanish settlers to be resourceful with tools, clothes, food, building materials and other common household items. In this spirit, *colonistas* fashioned *aforros* out of cloth, leather, tin and wood to protect their few precious books. Some believe this tin *aforro* was made in the late 1700s by Wilfredo C de Baca of Peña Blanca.

The Hispanic Legacy

by

Arnold Vigil

In a rare evolution that only time and virtual isolation can produce, New Mexico's Hispanic culture has developed into one of the most unique in the world. The culture has retained elements not only from its European and Moorish roots, but it also exudes traits influenced by the rugged landscape as well as Native Americans who flourished in this area for hundreds of years before the Spanish arrived.

Historically, save the last 60 or so years, life for New Mexico Hispanics remained relatively unchanged for more than three centuries. Most of the original 205 Spanish families who arrived with Juan de Oñate to colonize just north of Española in 1598 were lured north from prosperous Mexico with promises of land, noble status and, of course, gold.

But instead of magnificent golden cities and verdant valleys teeming with crops and wildlife, the *colonistas* found little food, constant threat of Indian attack, dry soil, harsh winters and hardship in nearly every aspect of their newly crestfallen lives.

The pioneering families and future generations of their offspring endured a mostly Spartan existence, facing daily hardships and shortages while constantly having to wrestle with an inhospitable land from the high mountains in the north to the hot, dry deserts of the south. Their remarkable tenaciousness for centuries to come played a major role in creating the charming New Mexico of today.

While faith already figured significantly in the *colonistas'* day-to-day lives, the religious conviction of the Hispanic settlers grew even stronger in the absence of any luxury or security they might have once enjoyed in their motherlands of Spain or Mexico.

Many wanted to abandon the effort to colonize New Mexico shortly after the Oñate expedition arrived because it was quickly realized there was no prosperity to be exploited from what some considered a barren and forsaken land. But papal authorities convinced governmental leaders that colonization was essential because too many Indians had already been Christianized and it would be unholy to abandon the cause.

The Pueblo Revolt of 1680, however, taught the Spanish a violent lesson that they couldn't force Native Americans to totally reject their ancient beliefs to accept Christianity. The mission churches were the first monuments of the Spanish to be destroyed, signifying a deep, native resentment against being strong-armed to worship a foreign god and pay tribute in the form of labor and food to unwanted and repressive neighbors.

A dozen years after being rousted from New Mexico in the Revolt, the Spanish, a group of *genízaros* (Christianized Indians of mixed blood) and other native allies returned with Diego de Vargas with a newfound tolerance toward the beliefs of the Pueblo Indians.

While some pueblos resisted their return, others quickly allied with the Europeans against hostile Plains, Navajo and Apache Indians who pillaged many of the peaceful northern pueblos during the hiatus. The revitalized alliance naturally provided for a more mutual exchange of culture between the Spanish and the Pueblos. This set the stage for what the Hispanic culture has evolved into today in terms of religion, cuisine, architecture, folklore and other elements that make Hispanic New Mexico unique from other Latino populations in the world.

During the Spanish period (1598-1821), the provincial government strictly enforced a xenophobic policy of forbidding contact with any other Europeans encroaching from the East. This isolated Hispanic New Mexicans not only from foreign ideas and wares, but also from their own status-minded leaders who did little to ease their hardships let alone protect them from hostile Indians.

Many rural Hispanic villages in New Mexico were established in the 1700s as buffer communities between the more populated areas and the known haunts of unfriendly natives. Settlers of these communities, mostly *genízaros* who were granted lands by the crown to homestead, quickly developed hardy, independent and self-sufficient traits that are still characteristic of their descendants today.

When Mexico achieved independence from Spain in the spring of 1821, New Mexicans didn't learn they were under new jurisdiction until the following September. The well-established chasm between New Mexicans and their leaders changed little under the new cash-strapped Mexican government, which like its predecessor, taxed disproportionately to what was returned in service.

The new government, however, did tolerate visitors and trade from the East, and profit-motivated Americans wasted no time in developing the Santa Fe Trail, providing some Hispanics with the opportunity to prosper.

Most Hispanics, essentially for the first time, were exposed to other cultures, including the aggressive Americans, French and English explorers, and decades later, Orientals and emancipated black slaves working on the railroad. But overall, the sheer vastness of New Mexico along with a lack of monetary means relegated most of them to a continued existence of isolation with the usual shortages of manufactured goods.

Despite the absence of money, Hispanics never really considered themselves poor until the newcomers pointed it out to them. They lived a hearty life. They grew their own crops, raised livestock, hunted game in

DECADES OF TRIAL AND ERROR AT THE LOOM ENABLED THE SKILLED HANDS OF THE LATE NOBERTO VIGIL OF CUNDIYO TO CREATE BEAUTIFUL RÍO GRANDE-STYLE BLANKETS AND TAPESTRIES.

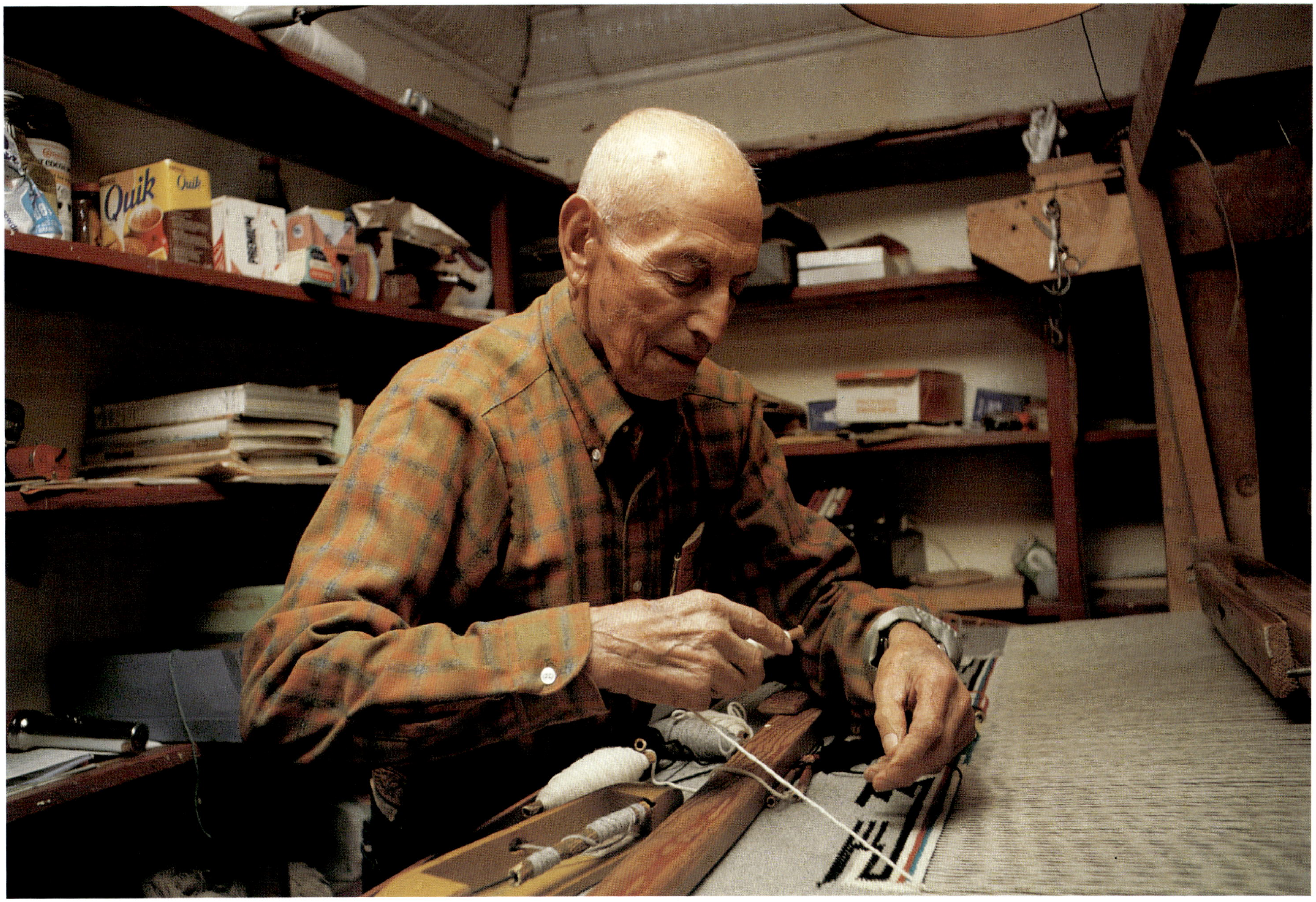
Quik
Quik

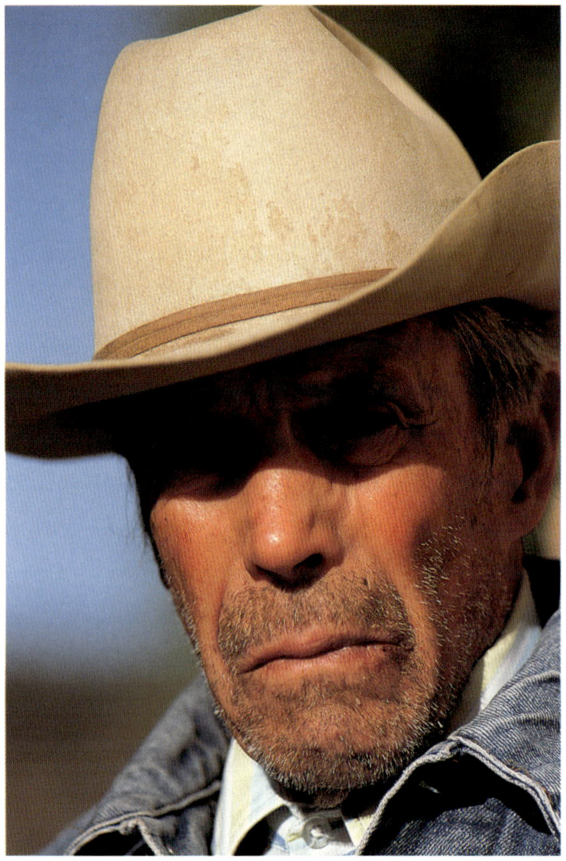

THE HARD AND HUMBLE LIFE OF RURAL NEW MEXICO HISPANICS THROUGHOUT THE CENTURIES IS SOMEHOW SYMBOLIZED IN THE DISTINCT FACE OF FLORENCIO QUINTANA OF EL CERRITO, A SMALL VILLAGE BETWEEN SANTA FE AND LAS VEGAS.

the vast wilderness. They listened to colorful stories handed down through the generations and developed a close, wondrous relationship with nature and God.

In areas where they experienced want or extreme need, their faith carried them through. In general, humility became second nature for these poor people. Generation after generation were taught to share with others and that God, hard work and family were the most important things. Their good nature, naiveté and inability to speak English made it easier for some unscrupulous Americans to take advantage of them after the U.S. takeover in 1846.

But Hispanics remained entrenched in their culture and many struggled to learn English and the new ways of the conquerors from the East. Most succeeded in becoming model Americans before and after statehood in 1912, actively participating in their new government and economic system, and fighting honorably when required to serve in times of war.

An unfortunate consequence, however, resulted from the personal sacrifices some Hispanics made to assimilate into the American mainstream. Many Hispanic parents who moved to cities after World War II vowed to themselves that their children would learn only English. They didn't want their youth to also experience the humiliation, confusion and penalization of not knowing English in school and being at an automatic disadvantage by not understanding the American system.

Their children grew up speaking only English and assimilated just fine into western culture, but they never learned Spanish and an important cultural link to their ancestry came dangerously close to being lost. The pendulum inadvertently swung the other direction.

This didn't occur in all Hispanic families, however, especially those still living in the traditional isolation of the rural areas. But economics are taking their toll on the centuries-old culture there, also. Many young Spanish-speaking Hispanics realize they cannot live off the land like their ancestors and they have no alternative but to leave their roots to make a living in the cities.

Realizing that much of the culture in New Mexico was handed down only orally, many contemporary Hispanic scholars are actively recording customs and interviewing their elders. As more and more of the old ones pass away, the number of stories and traditions they might relate also dwindles. The race is on, so to speak, to preserve as much culture as possible before it is too late.

Fortunately, many traditions have been documented, some for the first time, and a growing number of young Hispanics who don't speak Spanish are making concerted efforts to learn the language so that they can pass what customs they absorb along to their children.

But contemporary Hispanics are living in somewhat of a paradox as they seek to regain their Spanish-speaking roots. They essentially must defy a nationwide fervor to make English the official language of the United States and deal with a growing resentment against Mexican citizens illegally entering this country that also undeservedly targets themselves – even as U.S. citizens. But more English-speaking Hispanics are realizing the importance of learning and passing along their culture despite any ignorant opposition.

This current transitional period is crucial, perhaps more important than any other in the four previous centuries of Hispanic culture in New Mexico. As western civilization continues to influence the world, for better or worse, Hispanics here certainly aren't alone in their struggle to keep their traditions alive. As is *always* the case, only time will dictate what perseveres.

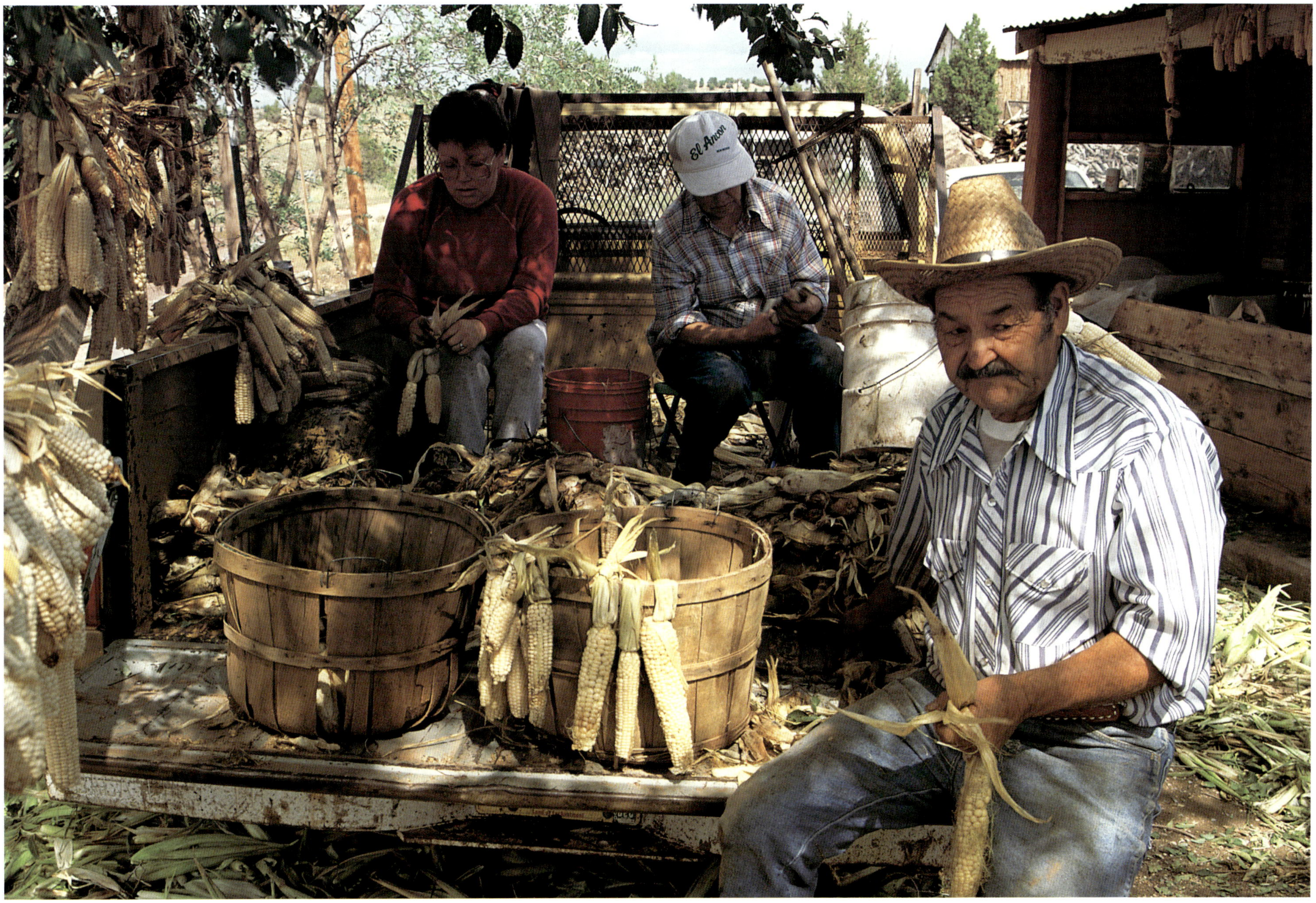

Food for Thought

Bonafacio Montoya and his family shuck ears of corn to make chicos on their farm in Ribera. The centuries-old technique of preservation today is being practiced by a rapidly dwindling number of traditional families.

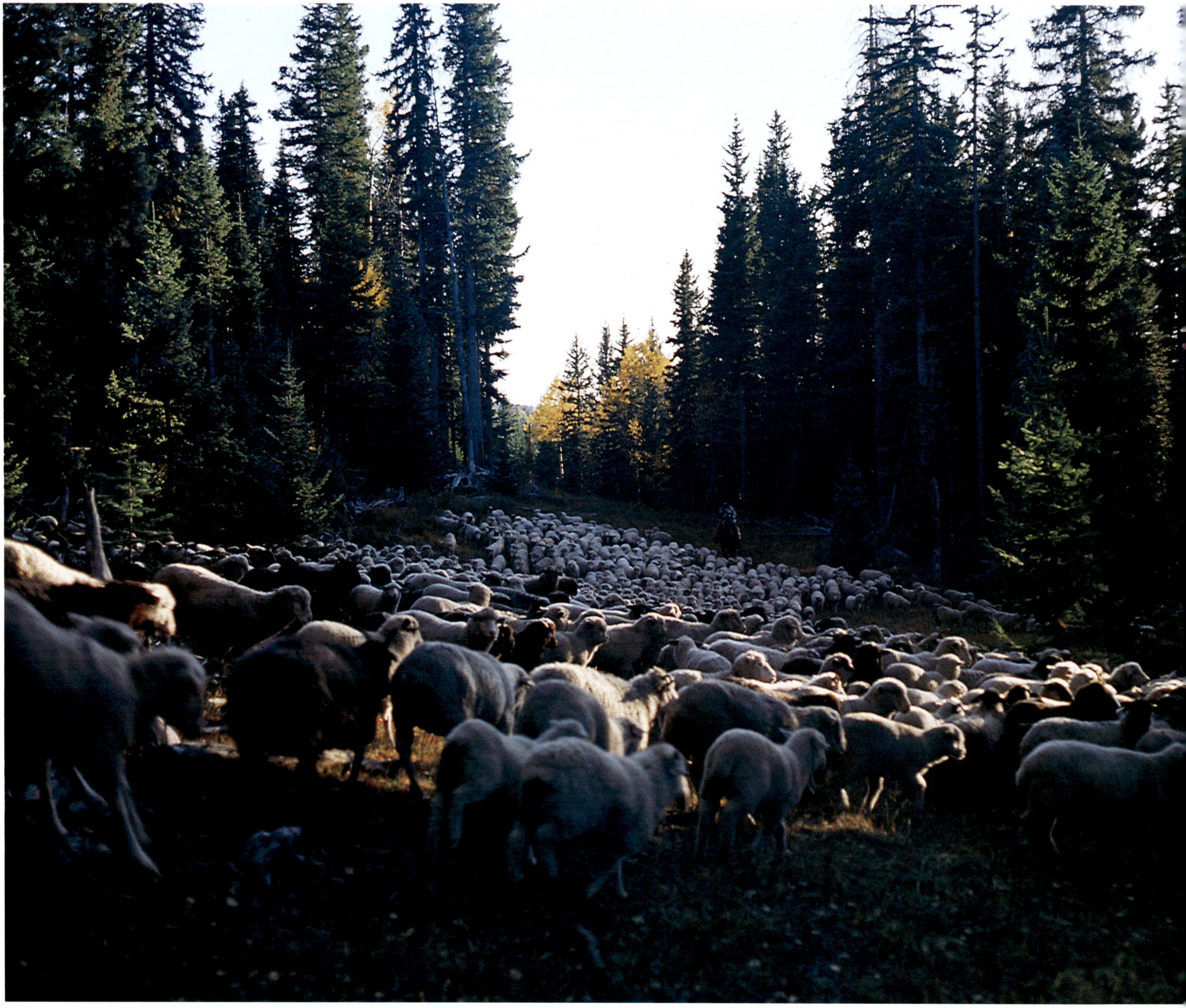

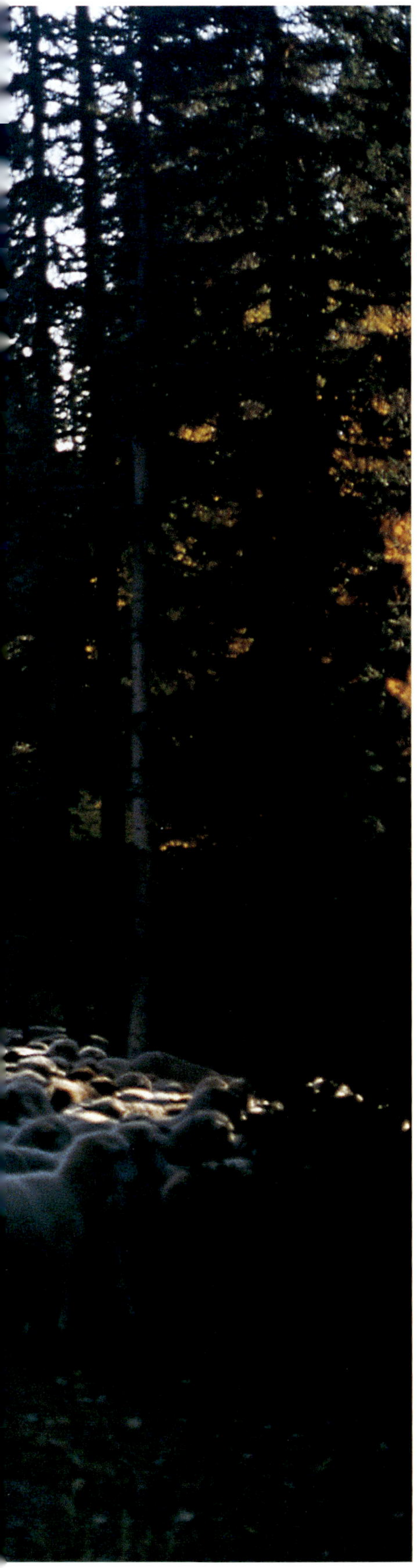

A HORSEBACK SHEEPHERDER DRIVES HIS GRAZING FLOCK THROUGH A GREEN MOUNTAIN VALLEY NEAR THE NORTHERN VILLAGES OF CHAMA AND BRAZOS.

THIS AREA'S RECENT PAST HAS BEEN A HOT BED OF ACTIVITY FOR HISPANIC CAUSES. IN 1967, REIES LÓPEZ TIJERINA AND A GROUP OF ARMED LAND GRANT ACTIVISTS SEIZED THE RÍO ARRIBA COUNTY COURTHOUSE. THEY TOOK HOSTAGES IN PROTEST OF THE U.S. GOVERNMENT'S NON-COMPLIANCE WITH TERMS OUTLINED IN THE TREATY OF GUADALUPE HIDALGO REGARDING THE RECOGNITION OF SPANISH AND MEXICAN LAND GRANTS ISSUED PRIOR TO THE AMERICAN TAKEOVER.

IN THE LATE 1980S, THE COURTS RULED THAT A POOR TIERRA AMARILLA MAN, INDEED, HAD ANCESTRAL RIGHTS TO HUNDREDS OF ACRES THAT WERE THEN OWNED BY AN OUT-OF-STATE CORPORATION.

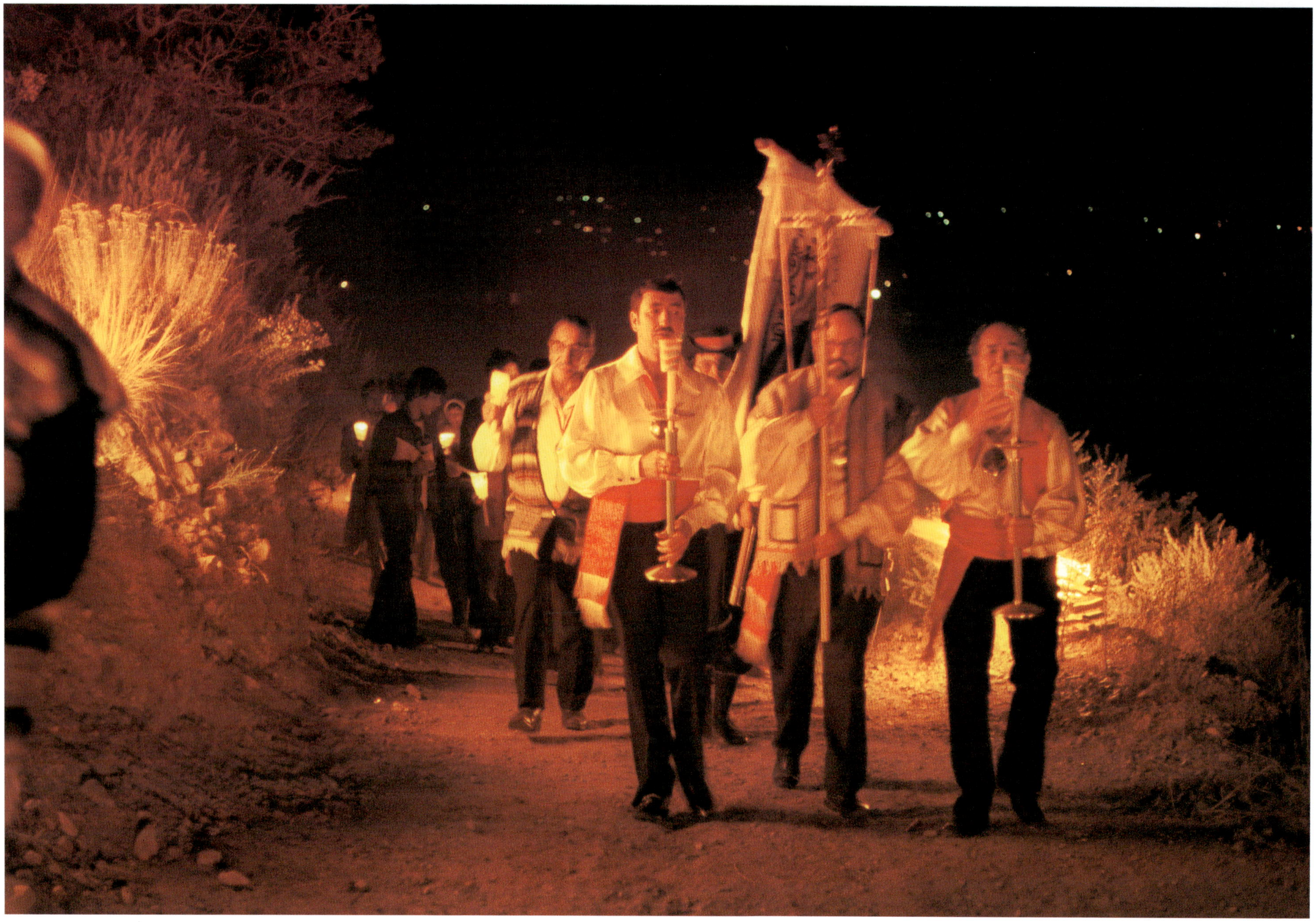

March of Faith

As part of the official closing ceremonies of the annual La Fiesta de Santa Fe, faithful members of the Roman Catholic Church hold candles and march through downtown streets to the crest of the hilltop Cross of the Martyrs.

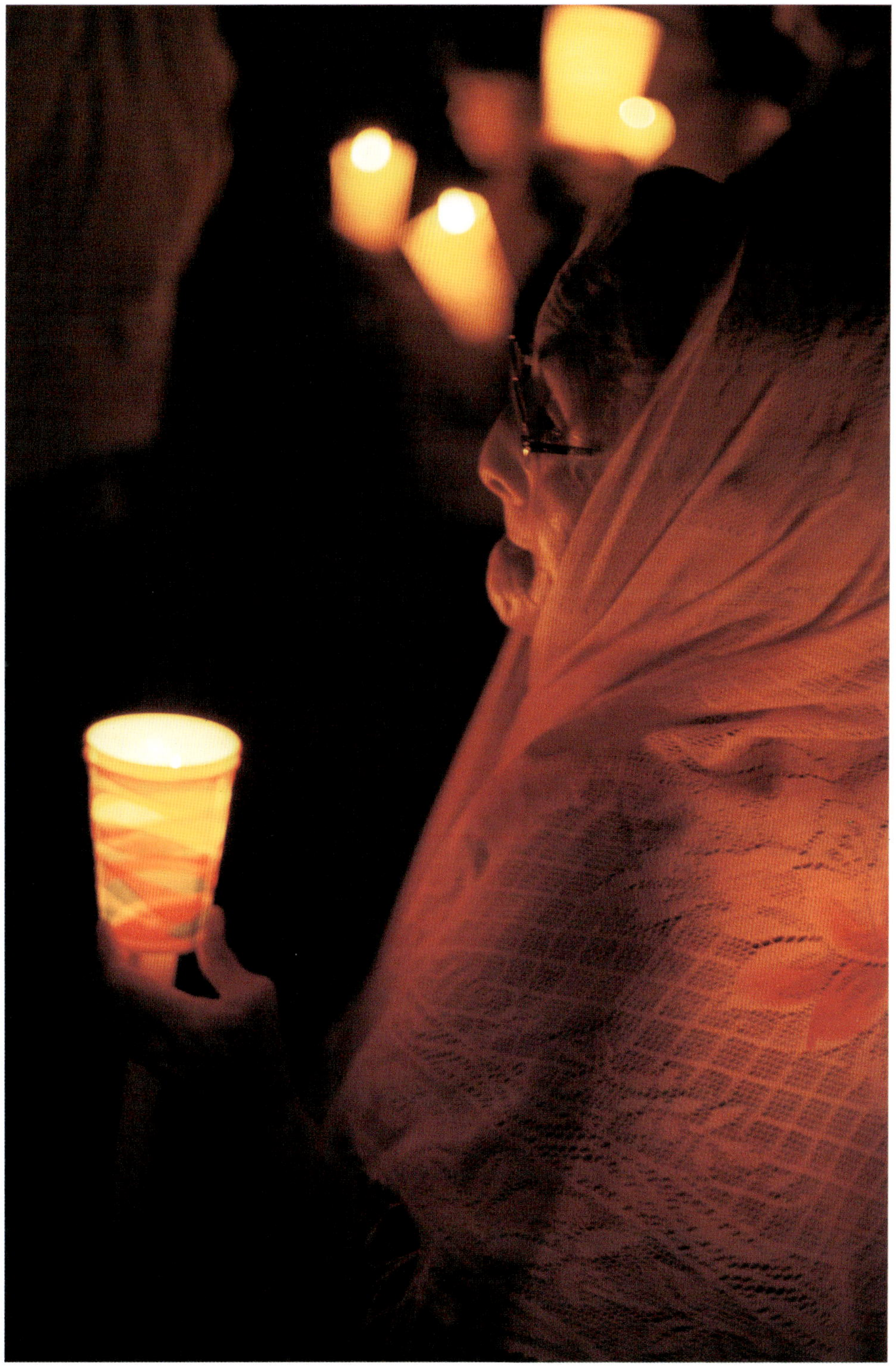

TRUE CONVICTION

AN ELDERLY SANTA FE WOMAN PRAYS DURING THE CANDLELIGHT PROCESSION OF LA FIESTA DE SANTA FE. THE ANNUAL CELEBRATION BEGAN IN 1712 TO HONOR THE RECONQUEST OF NEW MEXICO BY DON DIEGO DE VARGAS.

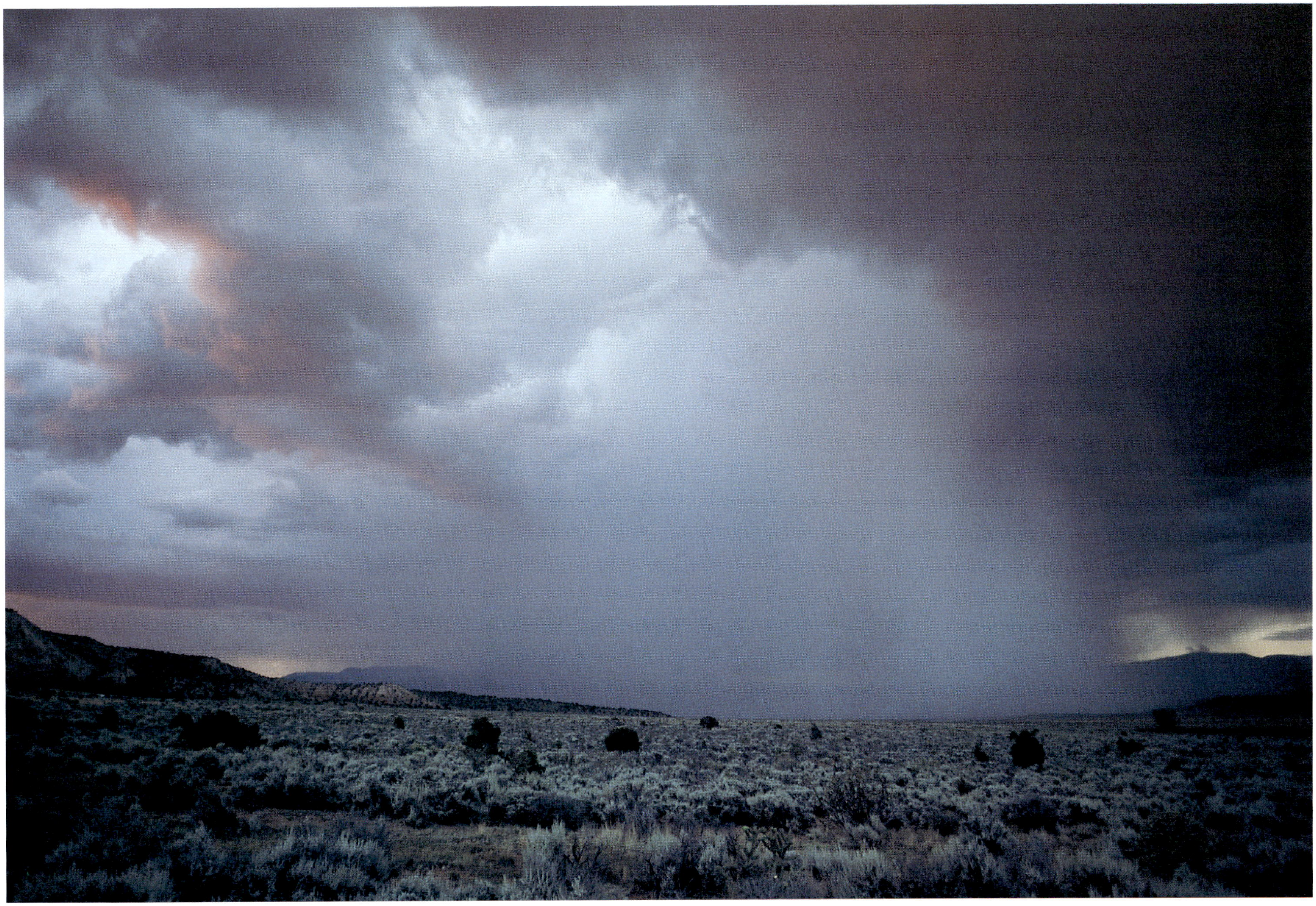

Cloudburst

A thunderstorm explodes onto the Mesa de las Viejas near Abiquiú. Any moisture from the sky is sacred to all people and animals of semi-arid New Mexico.

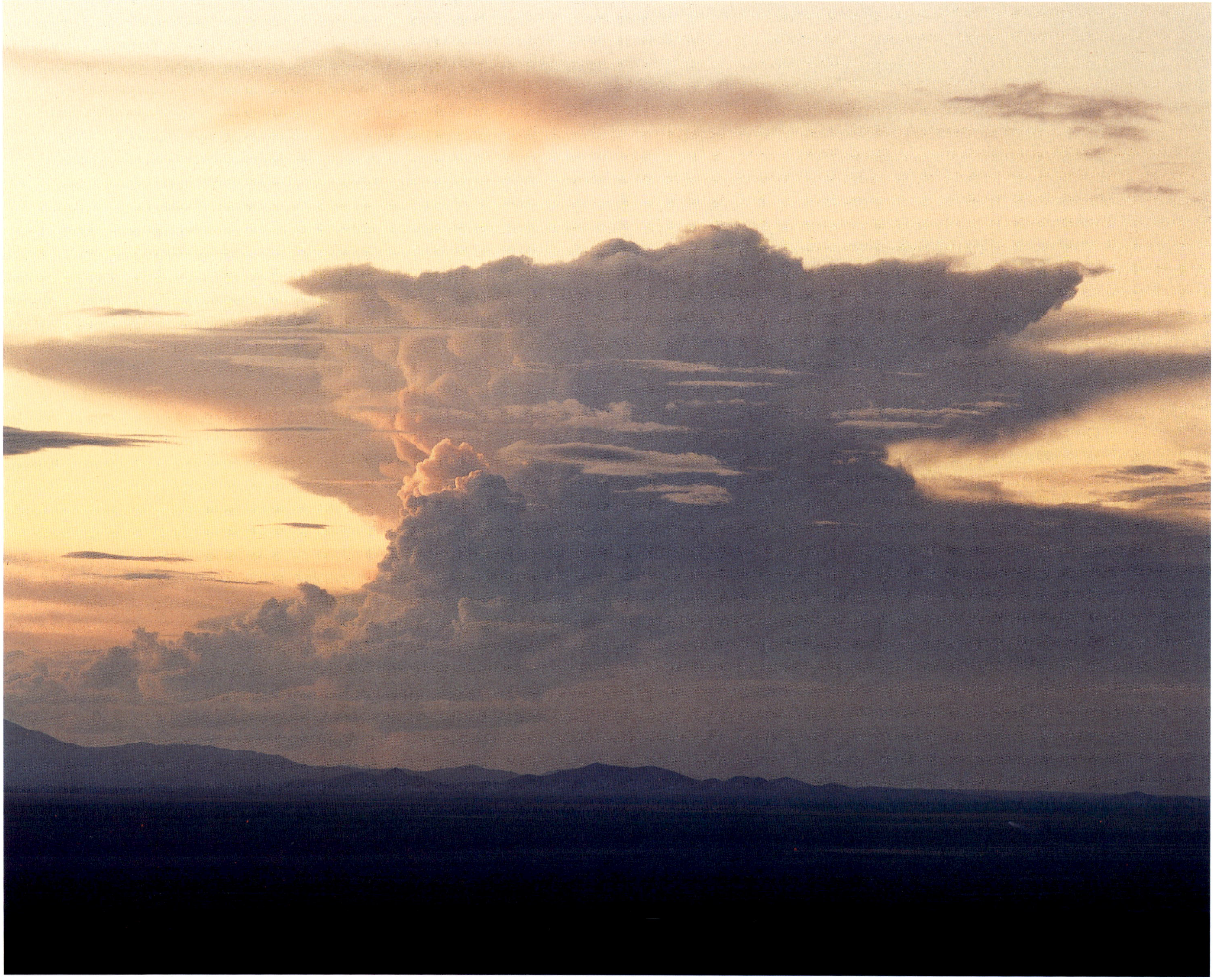

Sky Almighty

A towering anvil cloud develops over the Tularosa Valley, a huge basin separating the Sacramento Mountains from the San Andres Mountains to the west.

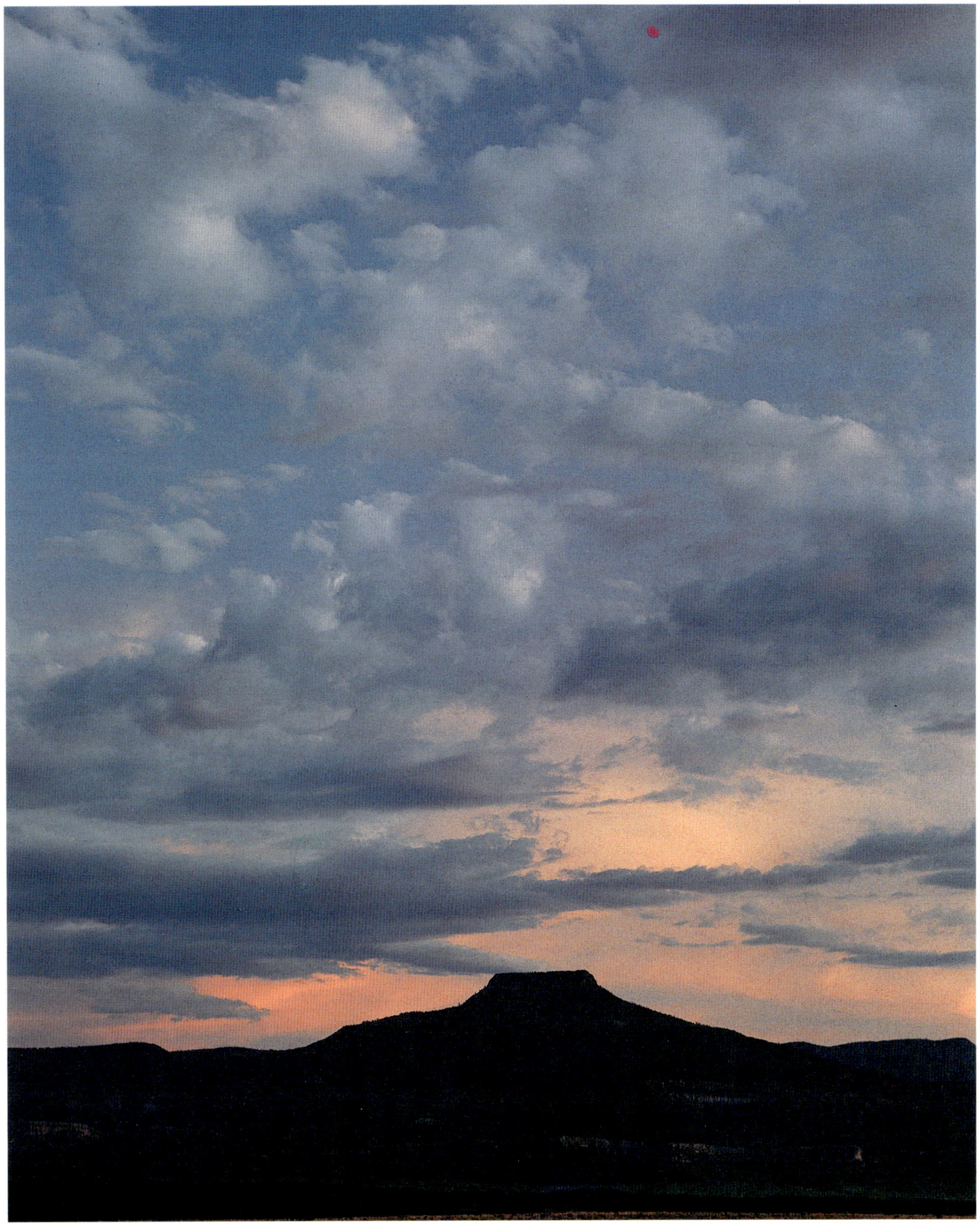

Landmark Legend

Cerro Pedernal near Abiquiú silhouettes in the early morning light. The name of the 9,862-foot peak in the north Jémez Mountains means "flint mountain" in Spanish. other names in Tewa and Navajo hold similar meanings.

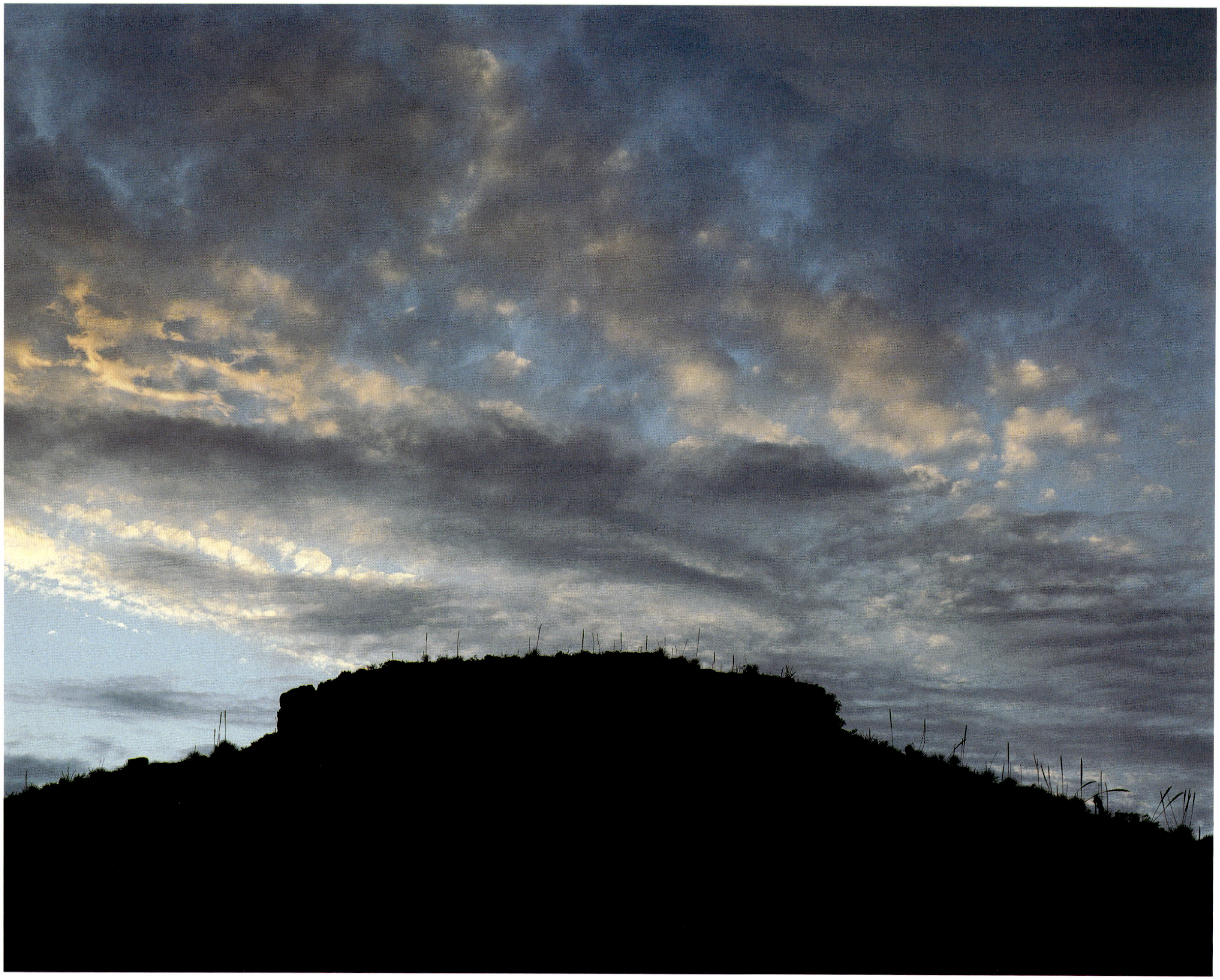

Morning Herald

Stalks from a lineup of yucca plants atop a mesa in Carlsbad Caverns National Park pierce the brightening morning sky in southeast New Mexico.

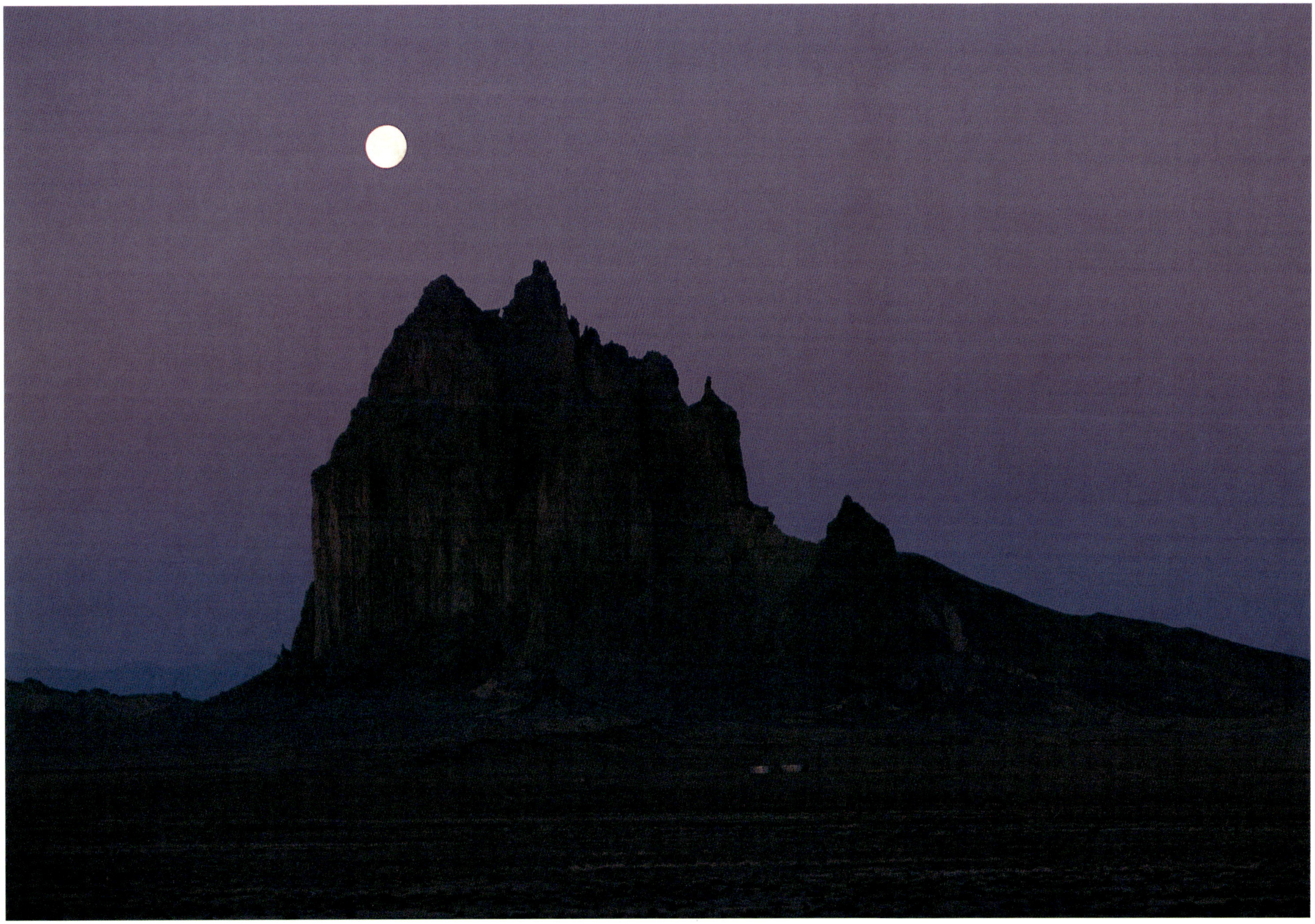

SACRED MOUNTAIN

A RADIANT FULL MOON SETS OVER SHIP ROCK IN NORTHWESTERN NEW MEXICO.
THE 7,178-FOOT PEAK IS SACRED TO THE NAVAJO PEOPLE AND THEY FORBID ANYONE TO CLIMB TO ITS SUMMIT.

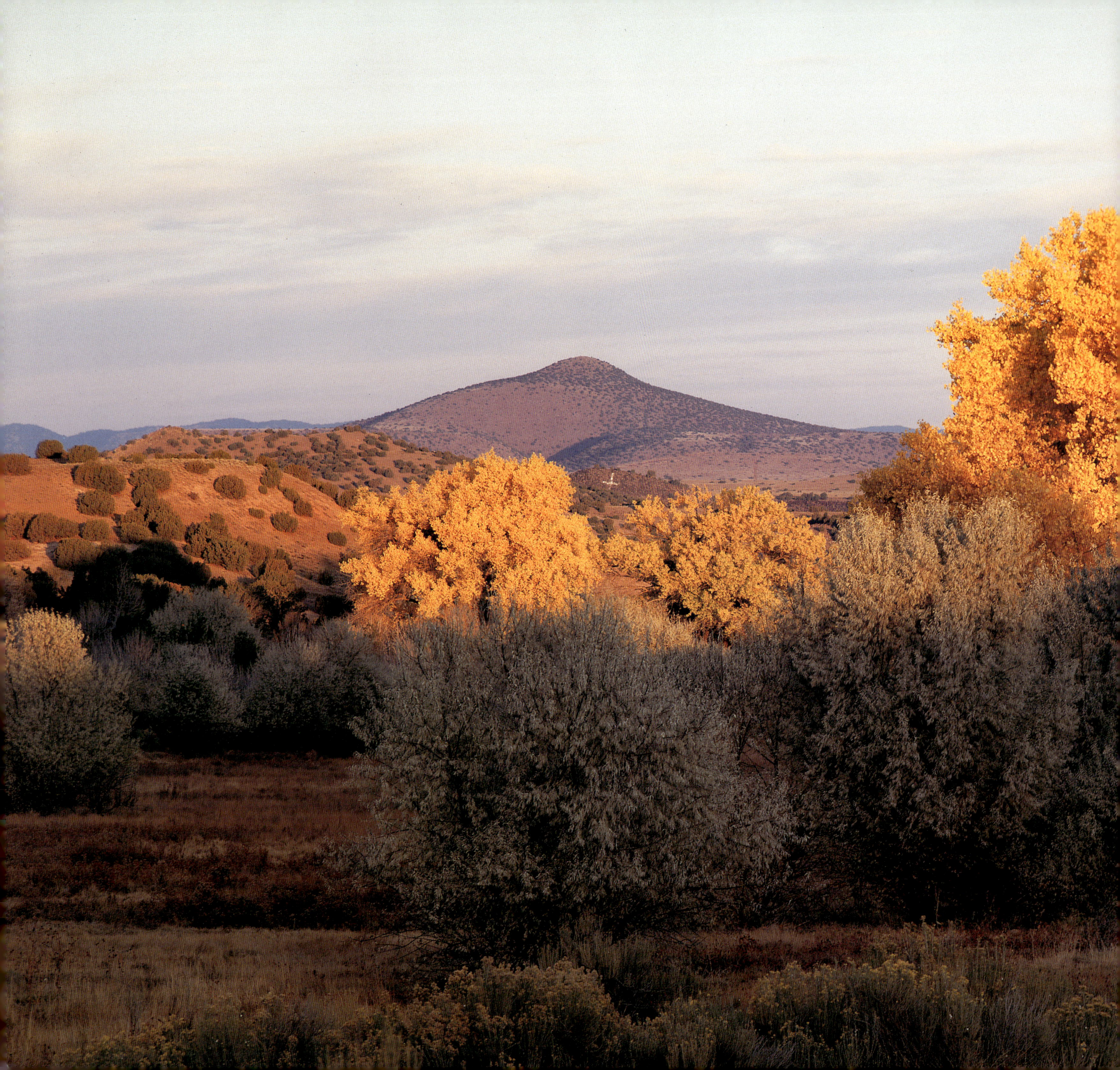

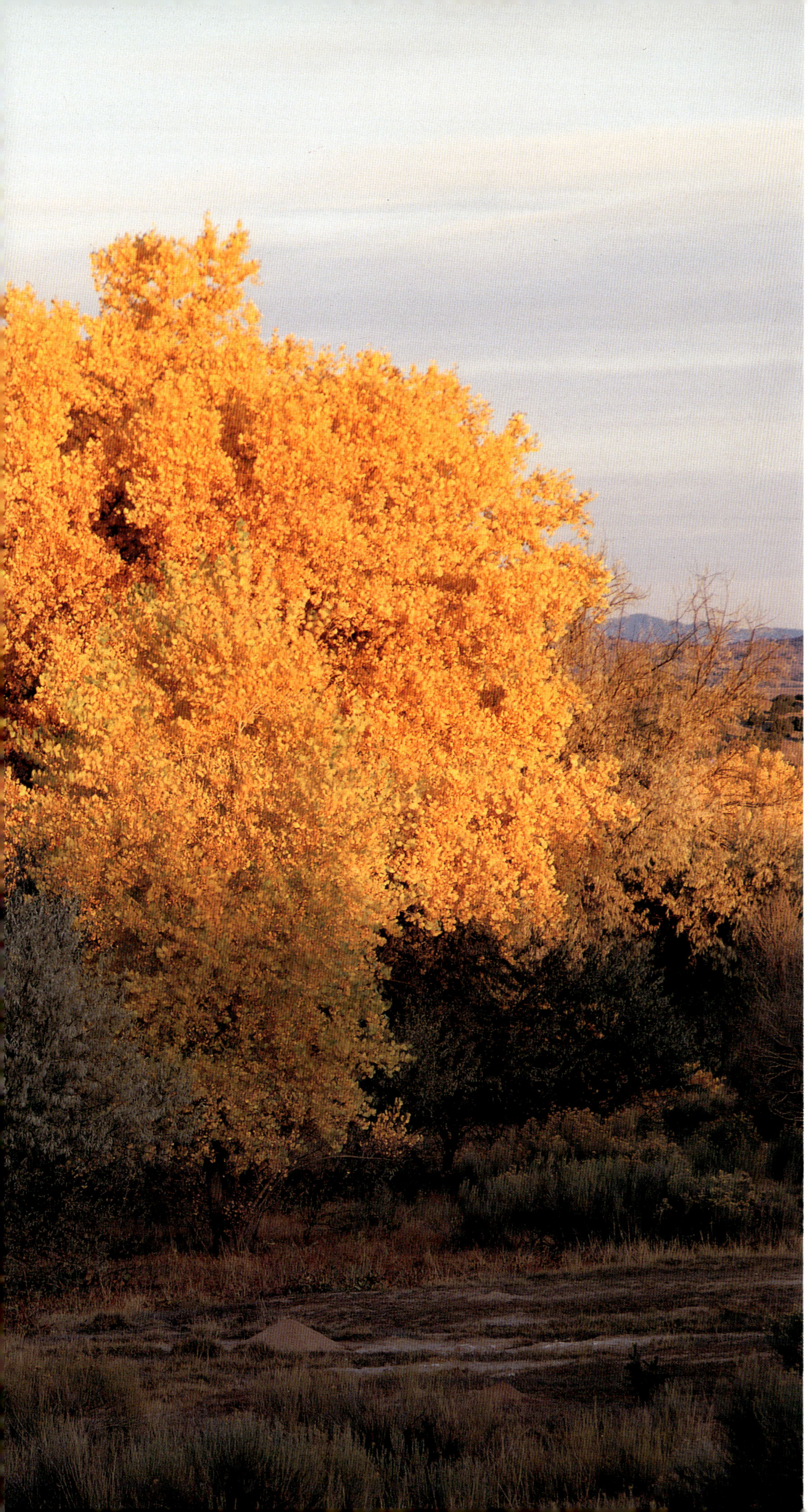

Yellow-turned cottonwood trees in La Cienega trumpet autumn's official arrival in the late-afternoon sun as 7,206-foot Tetilla Peak basks in the background. This scene lies adjacent to El Rancho de las Golondrinas, a restored Spanish colonial era village dedicated to the preservation of Hispanic tradition and culture. In colonial times, this village was the last overnight stop before reaching Santa Fe for wagon trains coming north from Mexico on the rugged Chihuahua Trail and El Camino Real. Travelers usually celebrated in gusto after reaching this location, having just endured a grueling trip that included the Jornada del Muerto (Journey of Death), a long, dry stretch of desert between Las Cruces and Socorro that spelled doom for many souls who ventured across it.

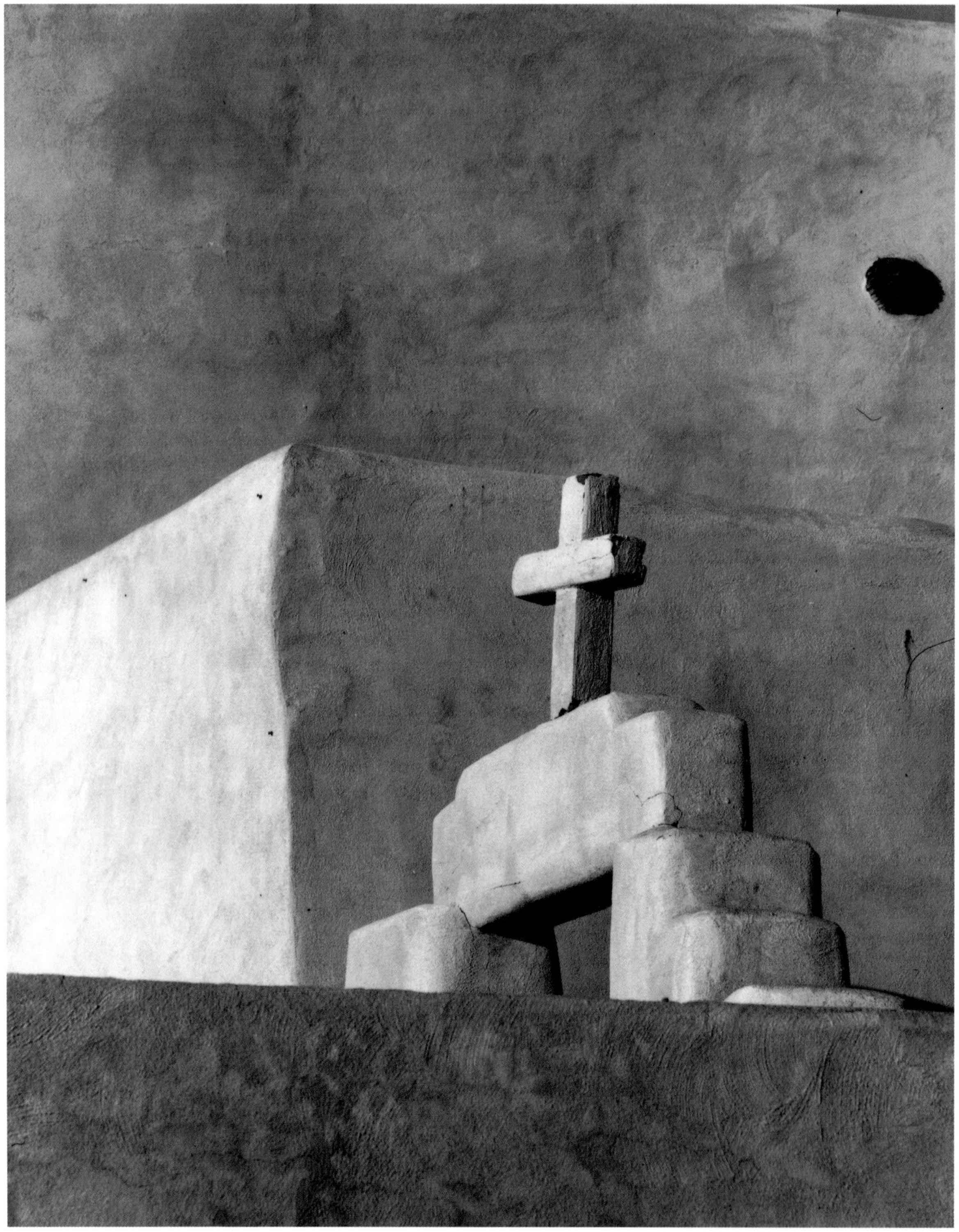

FAITH STANDS TALL

THE TEXTURED WALLS OF THE HISTORIC CHURCH AT LAGUNA PUEBLO NEAR GRANTS PROVIDE AN ARTISTIC BACKDROP TO A CROSS BASKING IN THE AFTERNOON SUN.

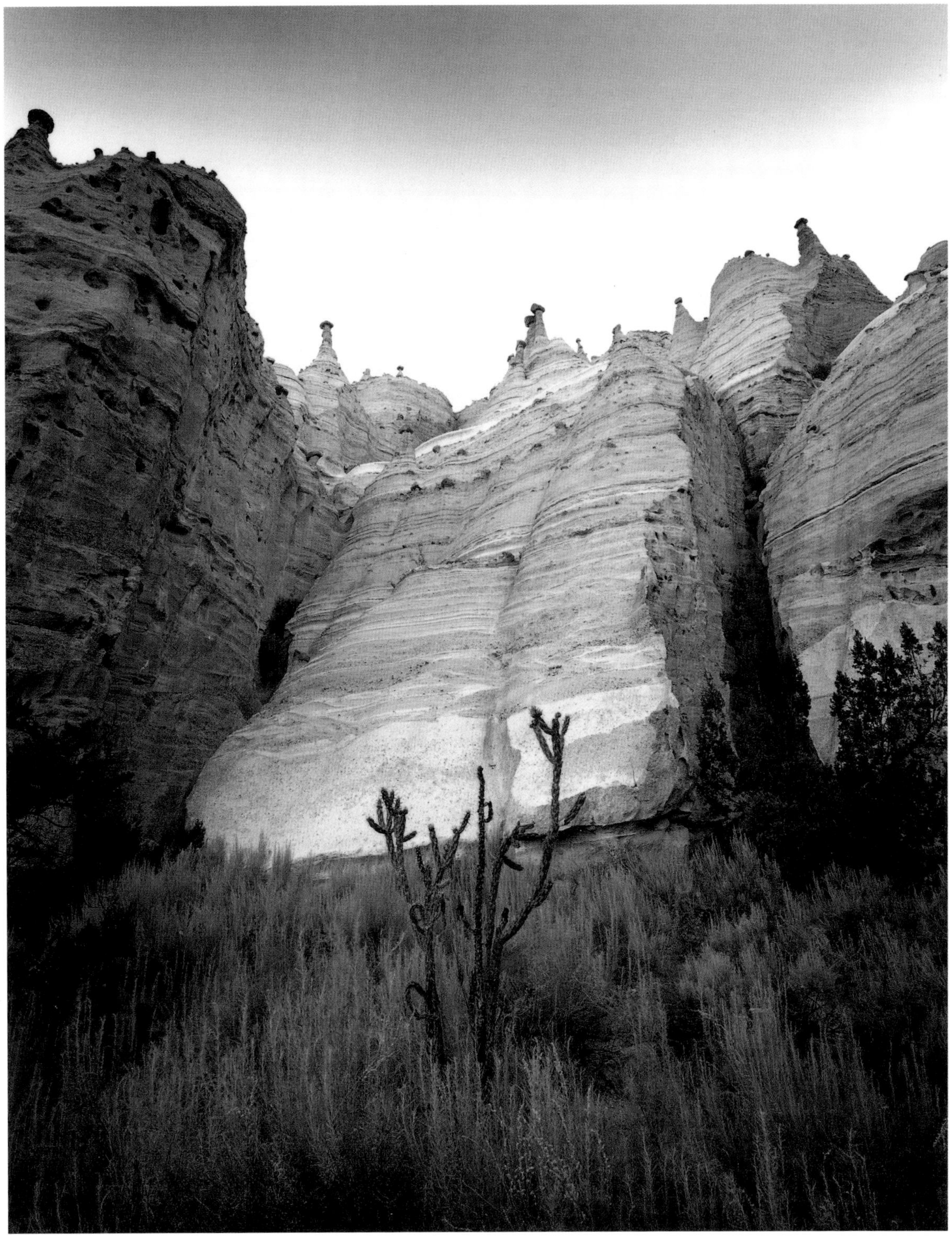

Pillars of Time

The fantastical columnar formations of Tent Rocks near Cochití Pueblo keep watch over cholla cactus growing on the valley floor.

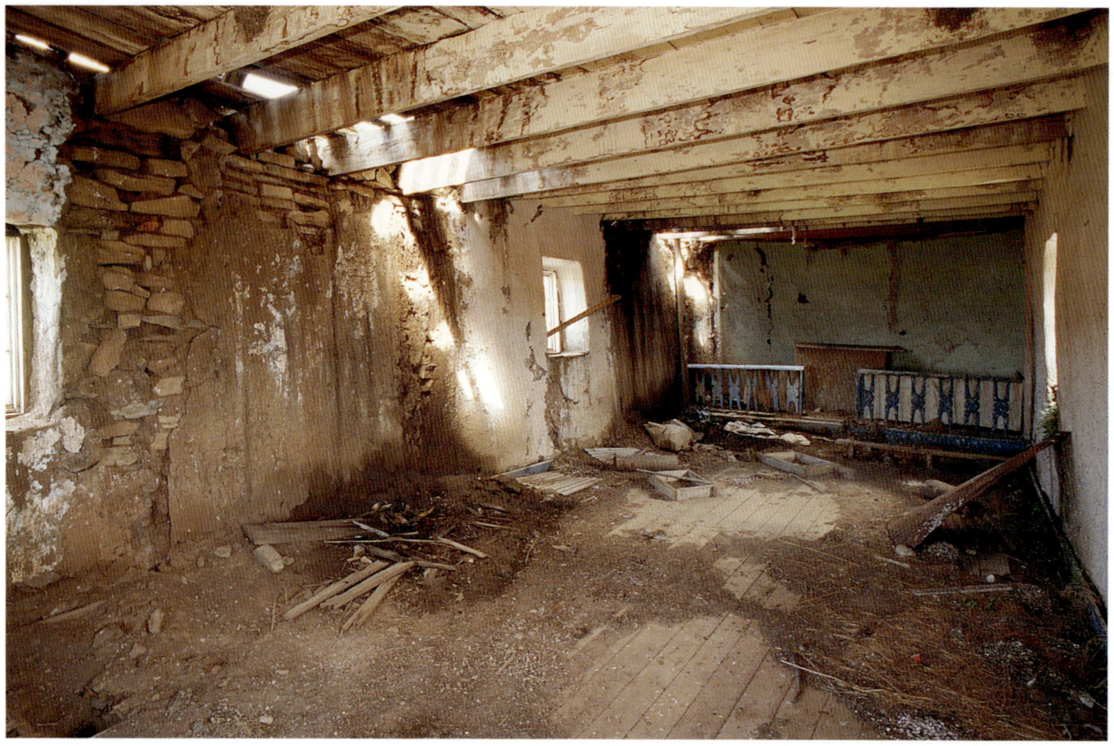

Two excellent examples of this are the restored San Jóse Mission in Upper Rociada, whose interior is shown below, and the inside of the rapidly dilapidating San Isidro Mission in Manuelitas Norte, left.

Both of the these northwestern San Miguel County missions were built around the late 1860s while under the jurisdiction of Bishop Jean Baptiste Lamy, who began revamping the whole Roman Catholic Church system in New Mexico upon his arrival in 1859.

Throughout the centuries the people living in isolated communities across the state built their own small chapels and missions to practice their faith. Today, many of these historically significant buildings are slowly returning to the earth from which they came. Only a handful remain intact, mostly through the restoration efforts of concerned residents and volunteers.

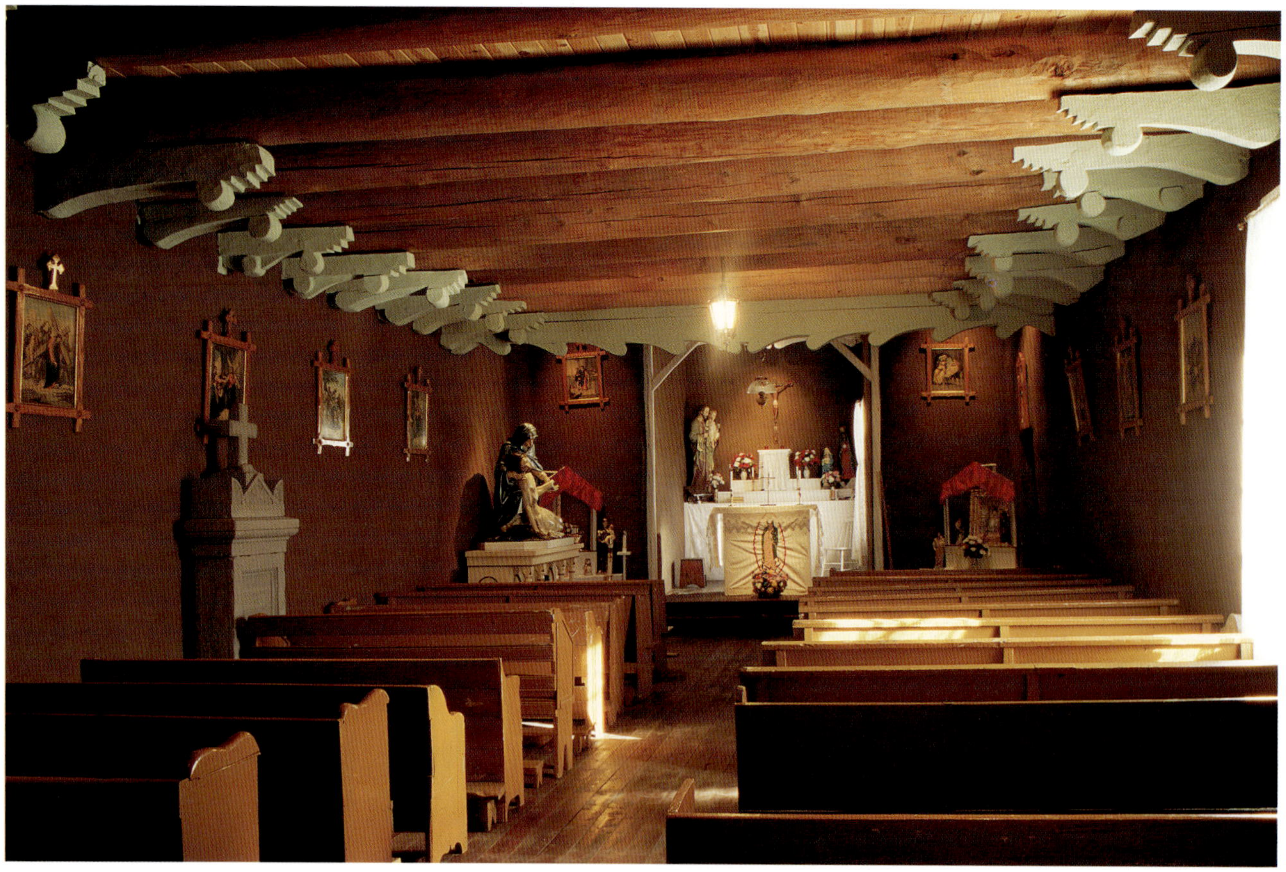

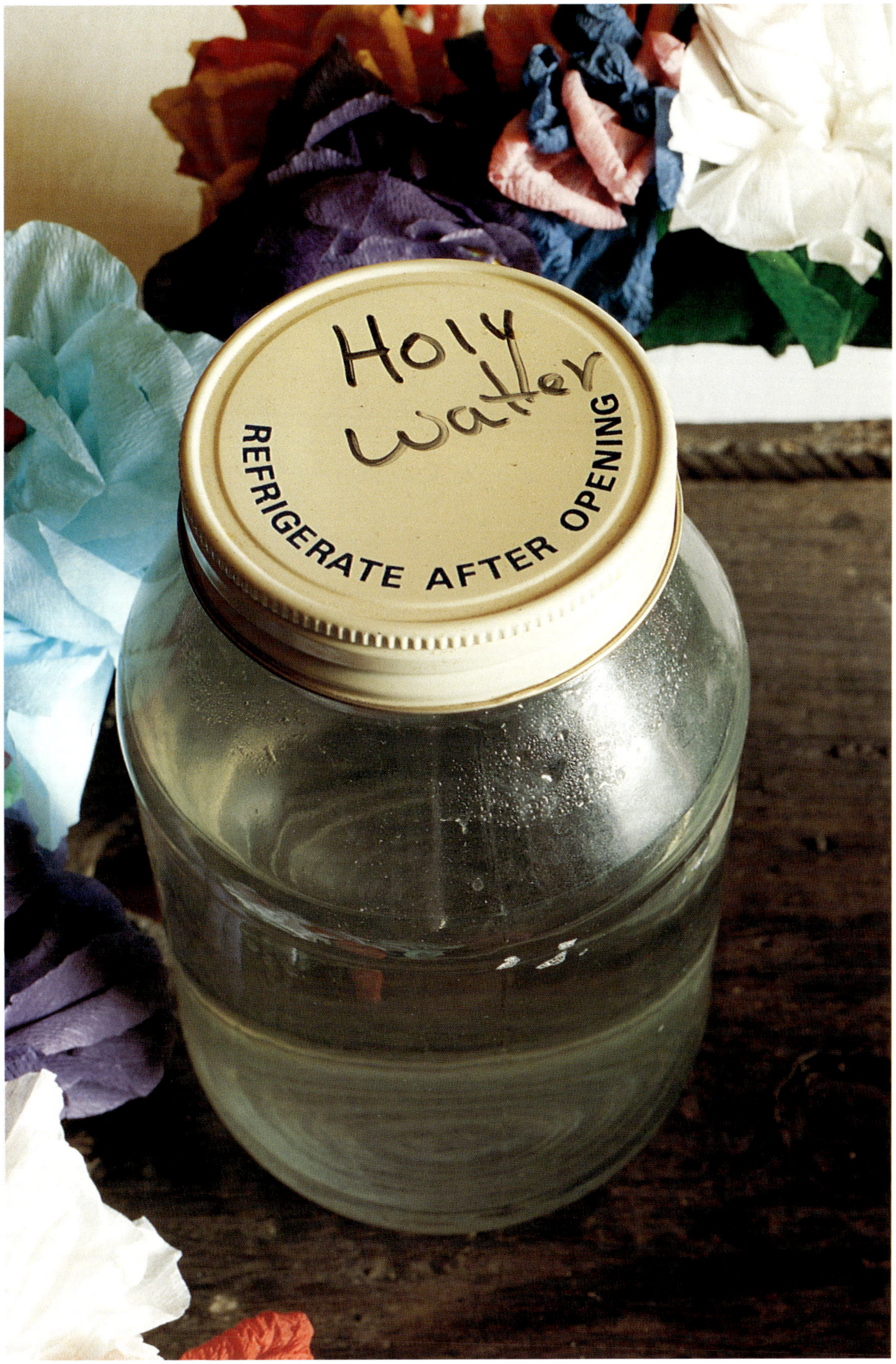

The San Jóse Mission was condemned by the state in 1985, but it was renovated by August 1994, when the Rociada community used Holy Water, left, to once again celebrate Mass. The community received help from Cornerstones Community Partnerships, a non-profit organization that gives technical assistance to communities that seek to restore old churches.

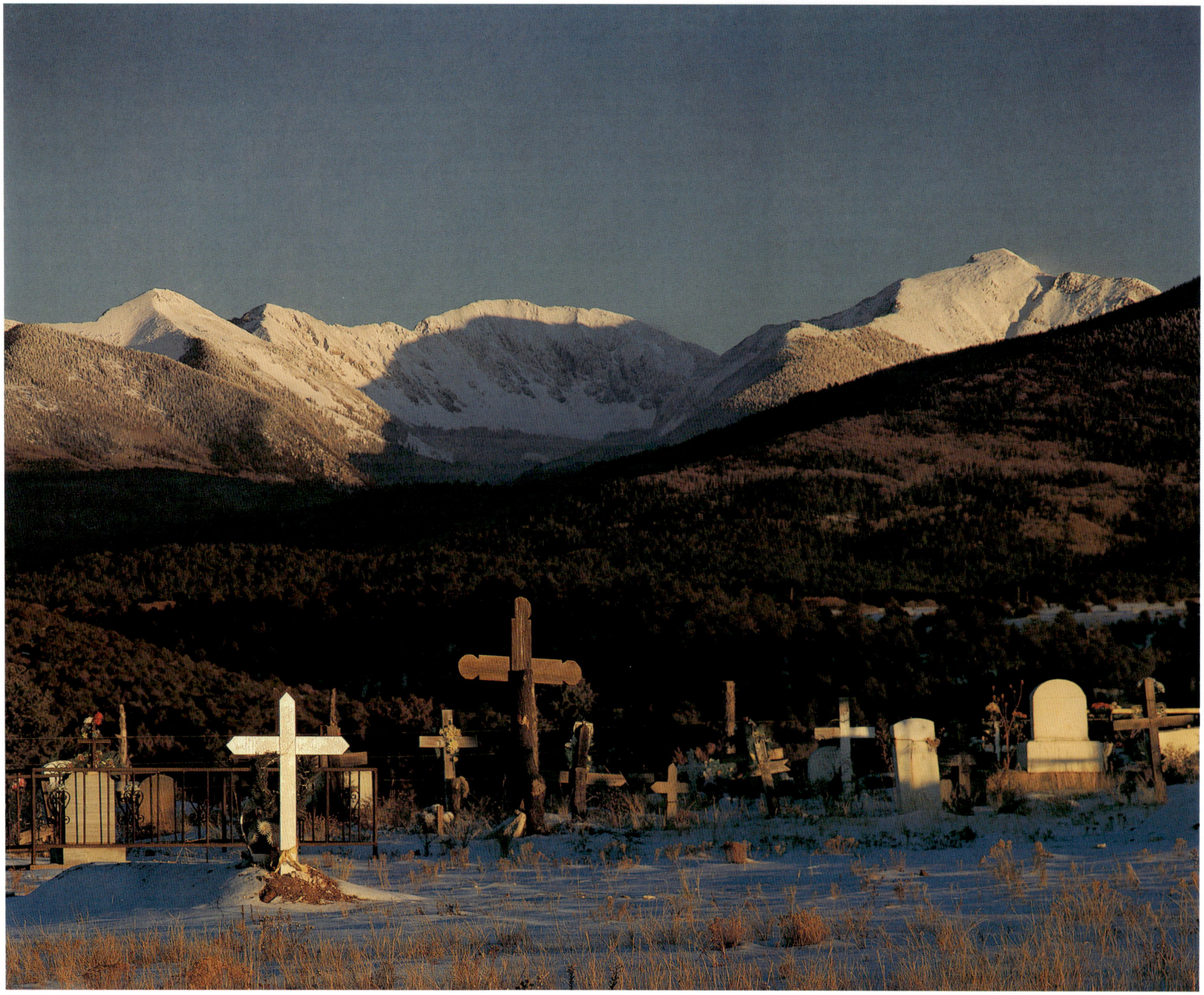

TRUCHAS GLORY

COLORED BY THE SETTING SUN AND RISING MORE THAN 13,000 FEET, THE SNOWCAPPED TRUCHAS PEAKS TOWER OVER THE CEMETERY OF TRUCHAS, A SMALL MOUNTAINSIDE VILLAGE MENTIONED AS EARLY AS 1752 IN SPANISH ARCHIVAL RECORDS.

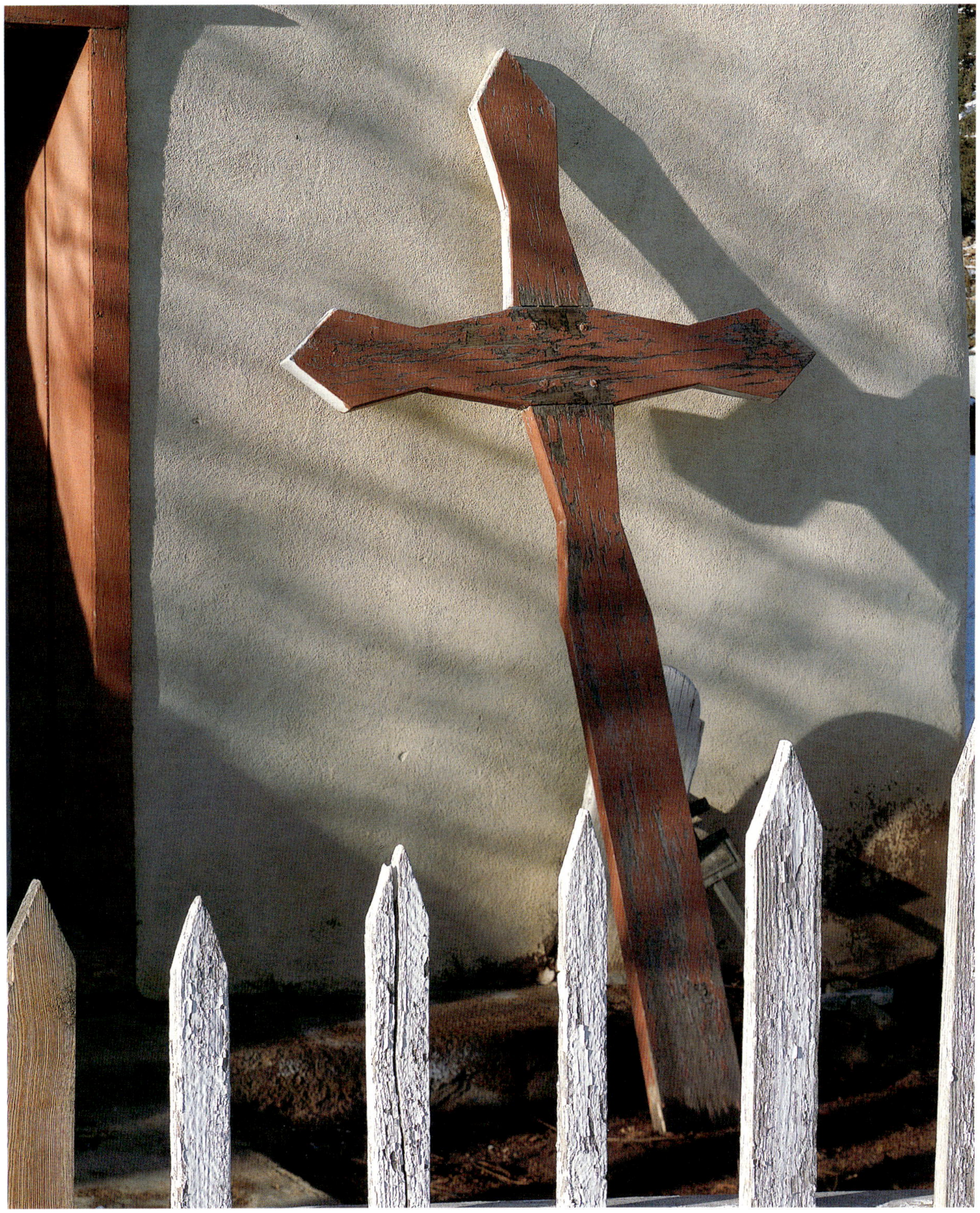

Resting Point

A hand-fashioned cross rests against the small roadside chapel in Cañoncito, which for many decades in the 1800s was the last stop before Santa Fe for travelers on the old Santa Fe Trail.

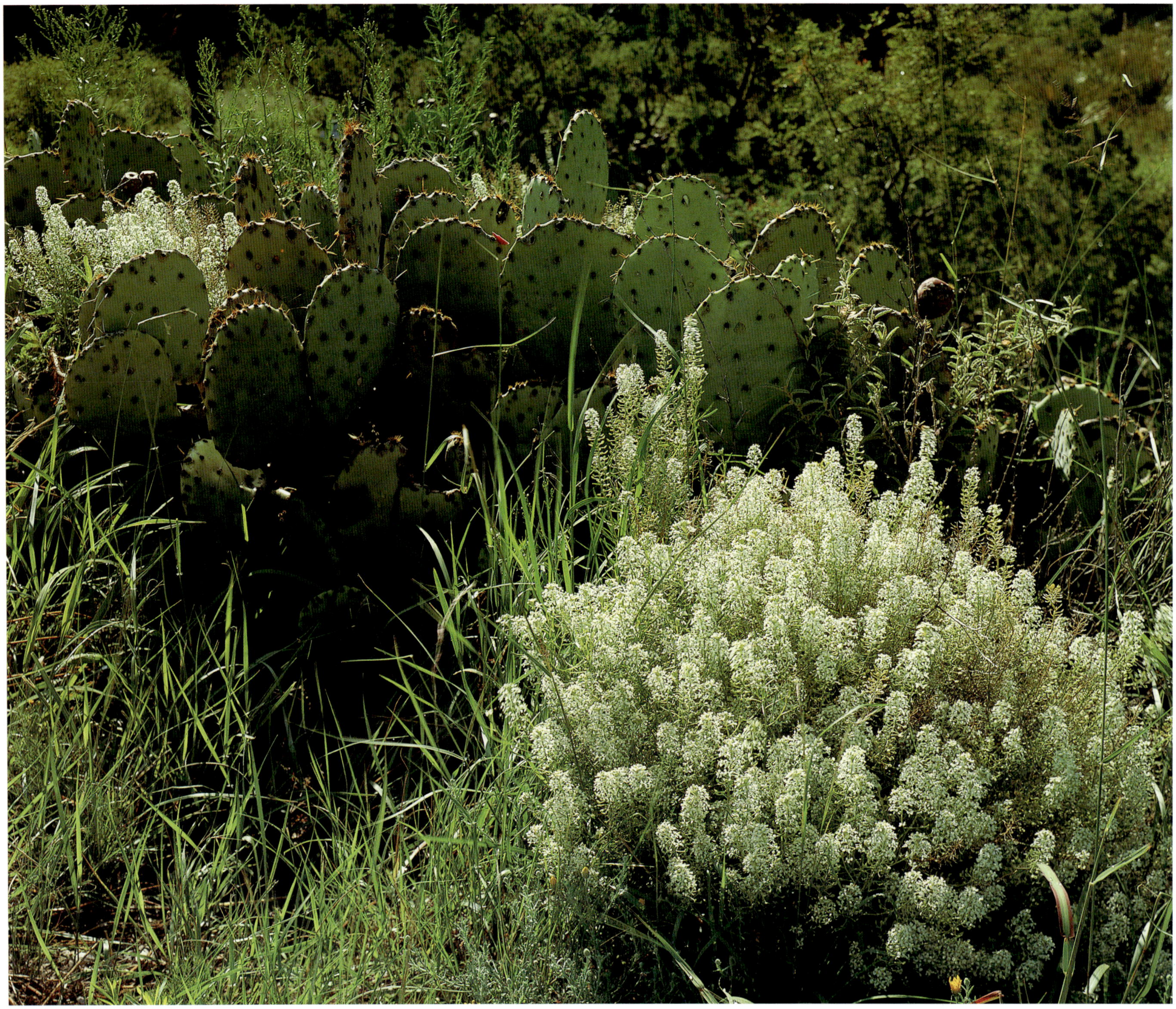

Desert Bloom

Prickly pear cactus grows alongside other indigenous plants in what might otherwise seem like an unusual patch of verdancy in the Chihuahuan Desert near Carlsbad.

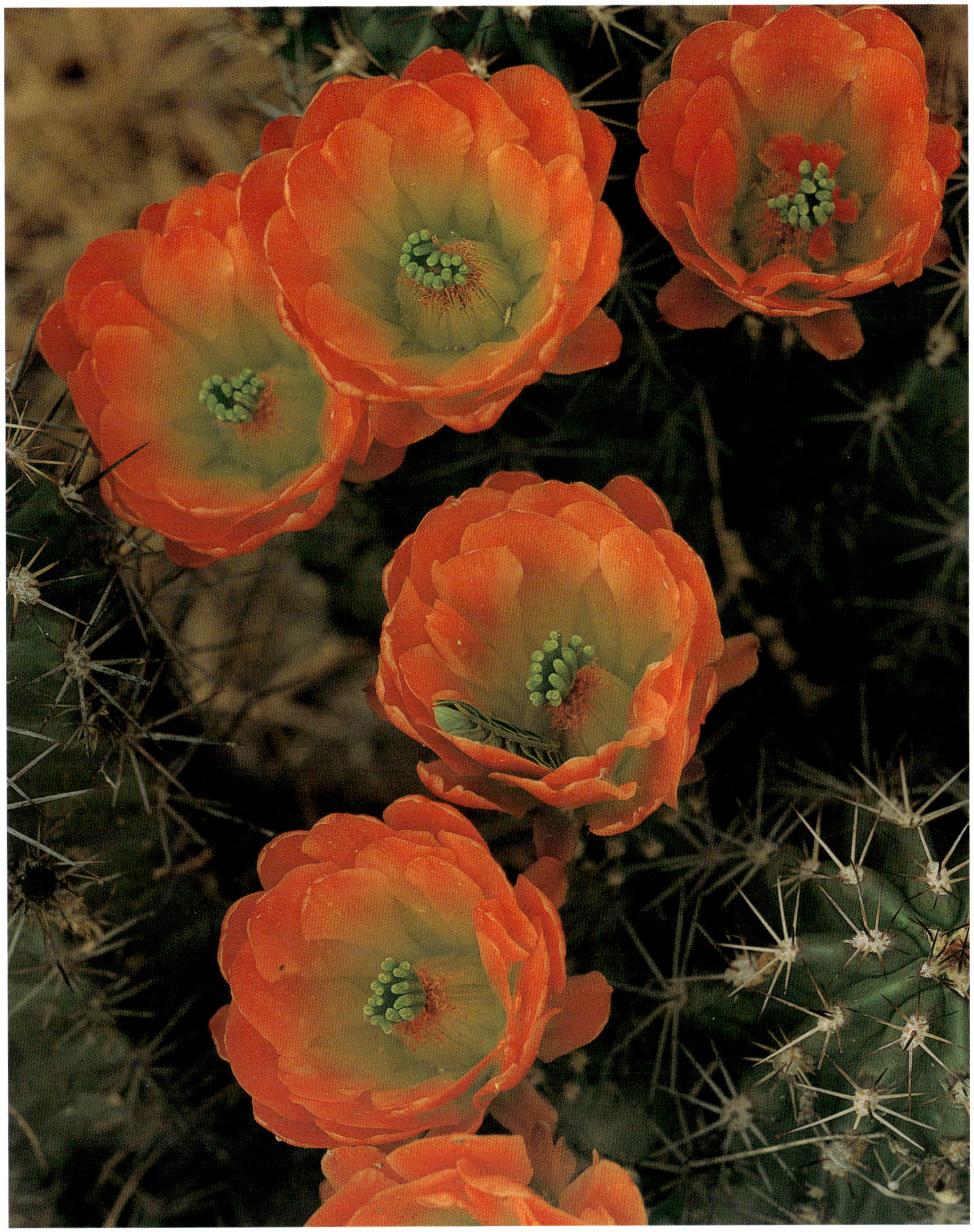

Fiery blossoms sprout from a cactus growing in the desert near Carlsbad. This area is one of the most geologically interesting on the planet, boasting among other things Carlsbad Caverns National Park, the largest known underground cave system in the world. The area is also rich in potash, a potassium compound used in agriculture and industry that was mined here for decades before the demand lessened.

More recently, the U.S.government chose the deep salt beds underneath this region to construct the Waste Isolation Pilot Plant (WIPP), a massive facility designed to store low-level radioactive waste from the nation's nuclear weapons research projects. The official opening of WIPP has been delayed many years, however, because of safety concerns raised by environmental groups.

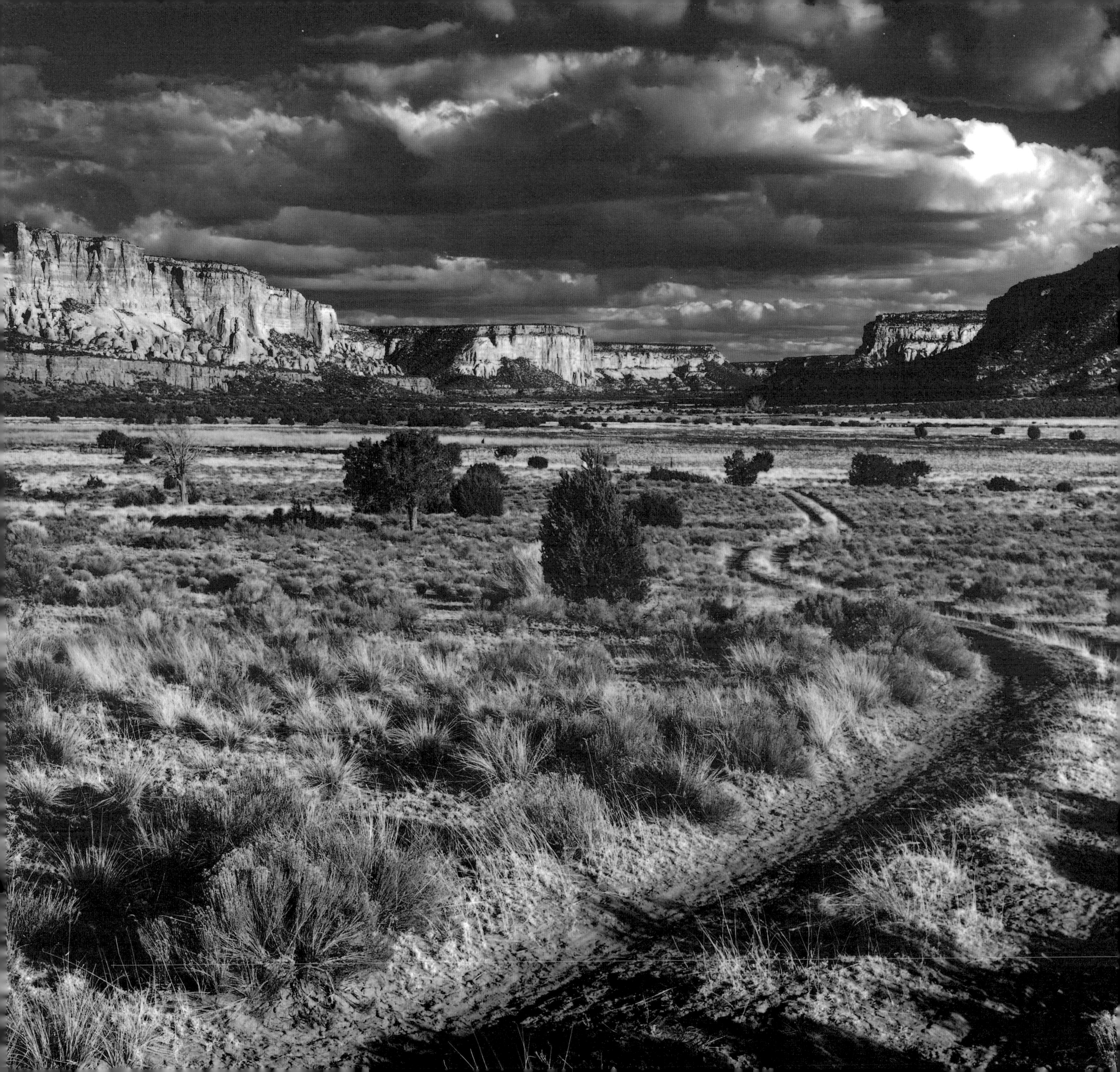

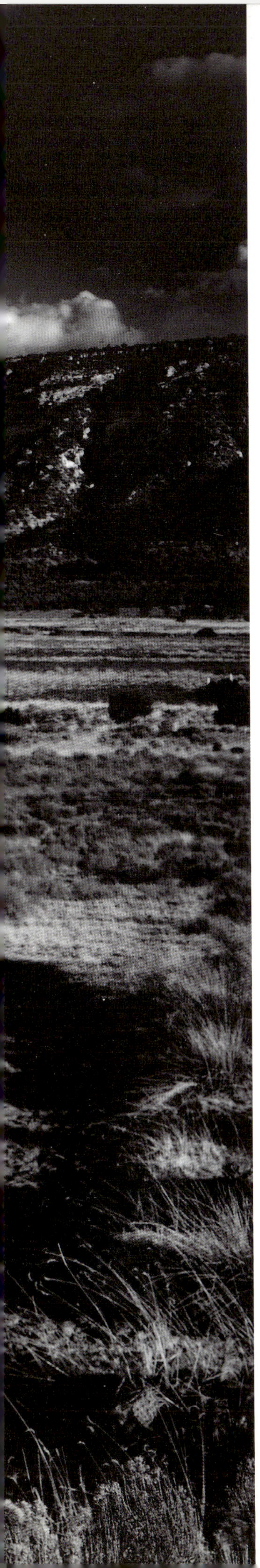

It's highly likely that Spanish conquistadors looking for the "Seven Golden Cities of Cíbola" saw these magnificent mesas near Zuni Pueblo in 1540. Disappointed at not finding gold or wealth in this area of western New Mexico, expedition parties of Francisco Vázquez de Coronado continued their fruitless search.

One outfit explored Arizona and discovered the Grand Canyon, while others reached the Río Grande, where they journeyed as far north as Taos and south to Socorro. Others in Coronado's party eventually made their way east across New Mexico, witnessing new lands in areas now known as north Texas, the Oklahoma Panhandle and central Kansas.

Although Coronado's epic journey across the Southwest yielded tremendous discoveries and maps for future expeditions, it was considered a failure at the time because they never discovered riches. It essentially left the ambitious Coronado a broken man.

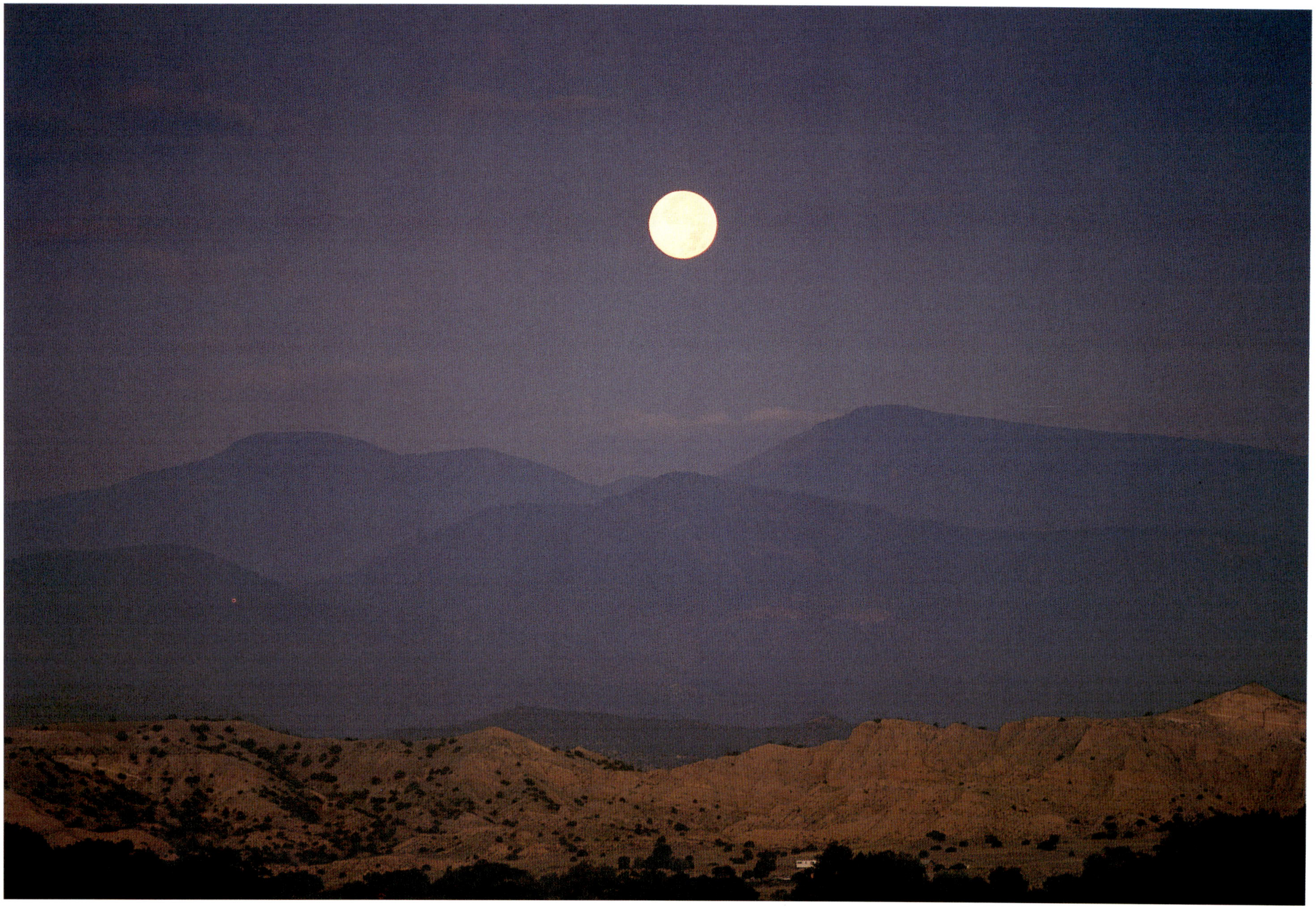

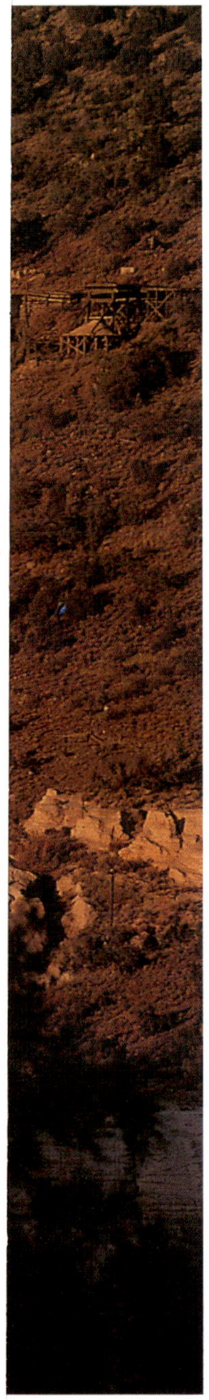

Moonset Above Valle Grande

A full moon begins its descent behind the Jémez Mountains, which were once a series of active volcanoes millions of years ago. Scientists have found debris from an ancient Jémez eruption as far away as Kansas.

e Fannie Mine in
town prospered
n it inevitably

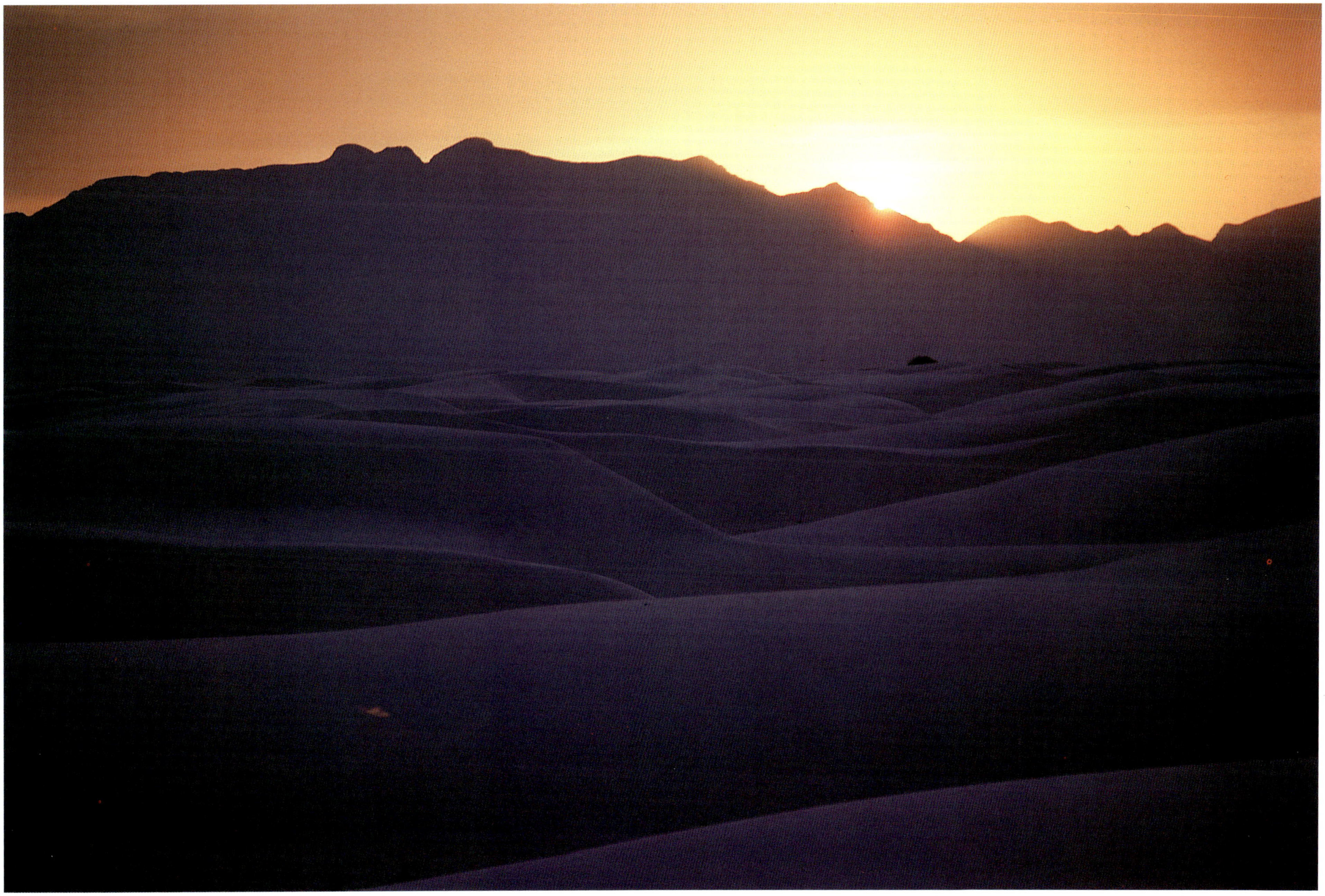

Desert Cooler

The smooth, free-flowing lines of White Sands National Monument in the morning light offer an inviting painterly version of the harsh desert climate of southern New Mexico.

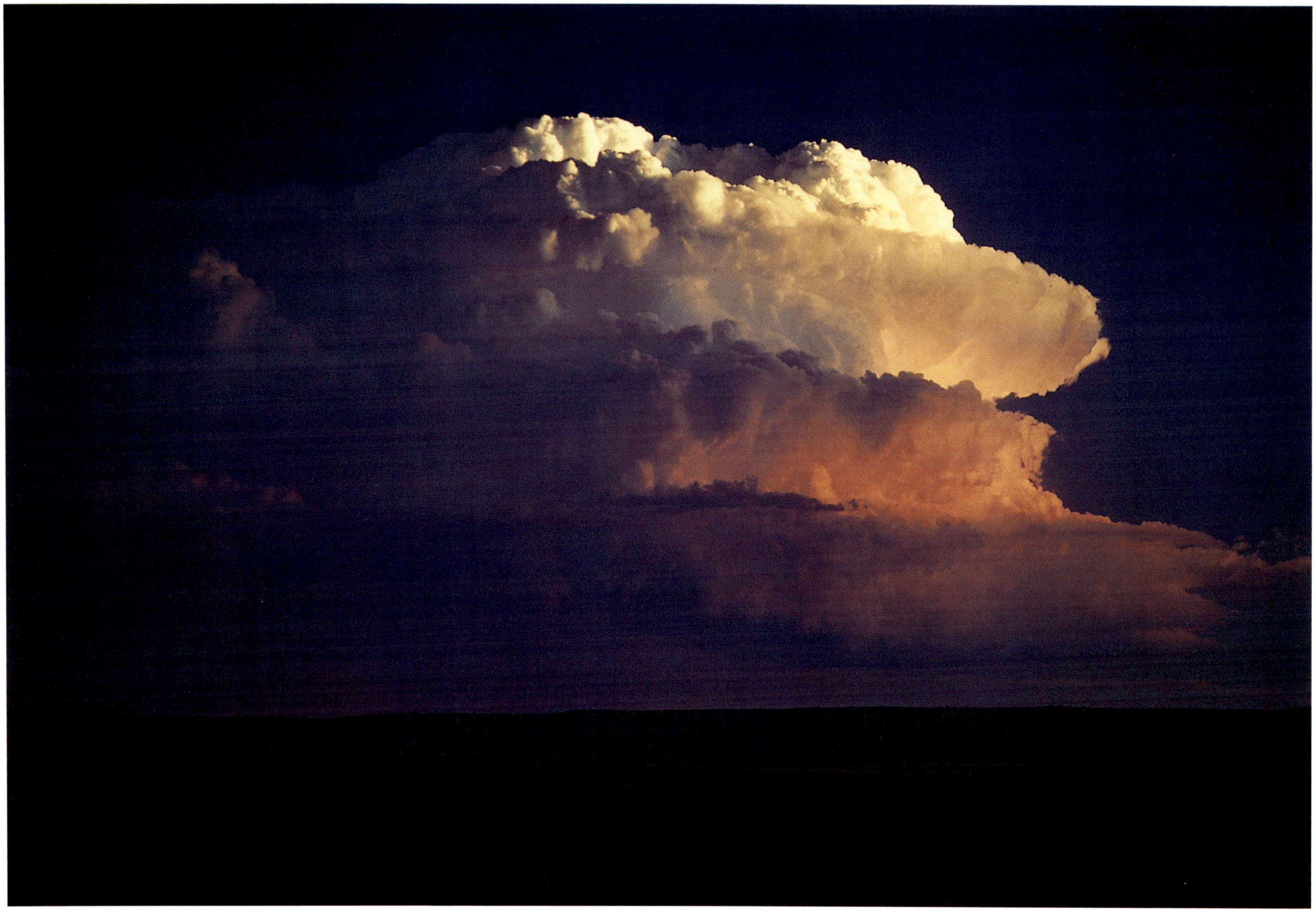

Sky Palette

The stacked layers of a spectacular anvil cloud rising over Tucumcari display a variety of hues on the color spectrum caused by the setting sun.

A winter snowfall dusts the chamisa bushes, cholla cactus, juniper trees and native grasses on the grounds of Bandelier National Monument. Drought and the depletion of topsoil are the most widely believed reasons that the Anasazi Indians abandoned this array of dwellings and caves centuries ago. Although the original inhabitants are long gone, the notion of a bustling native village thrives in the imaginations of the thousands who visit this area daily.

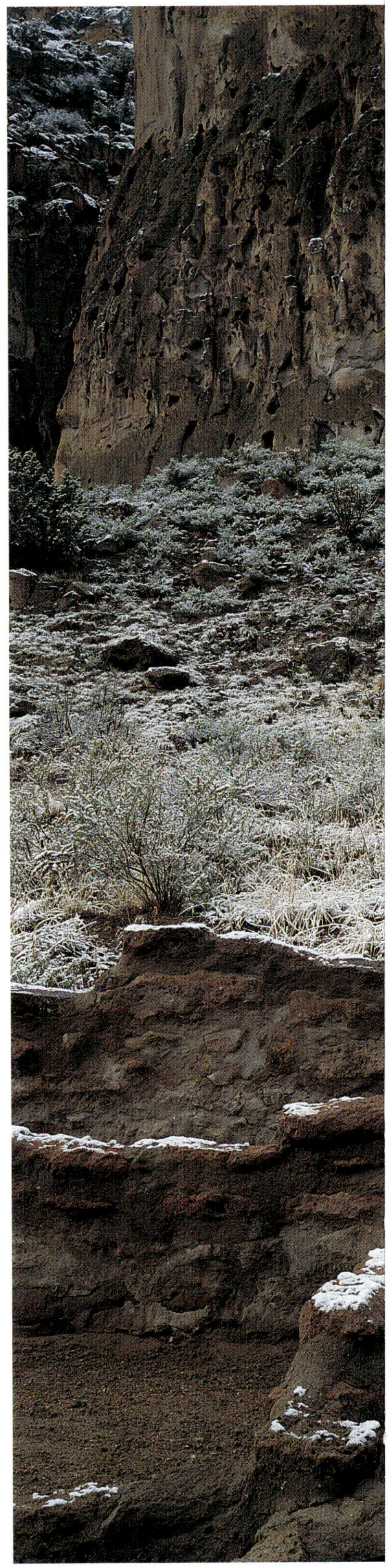

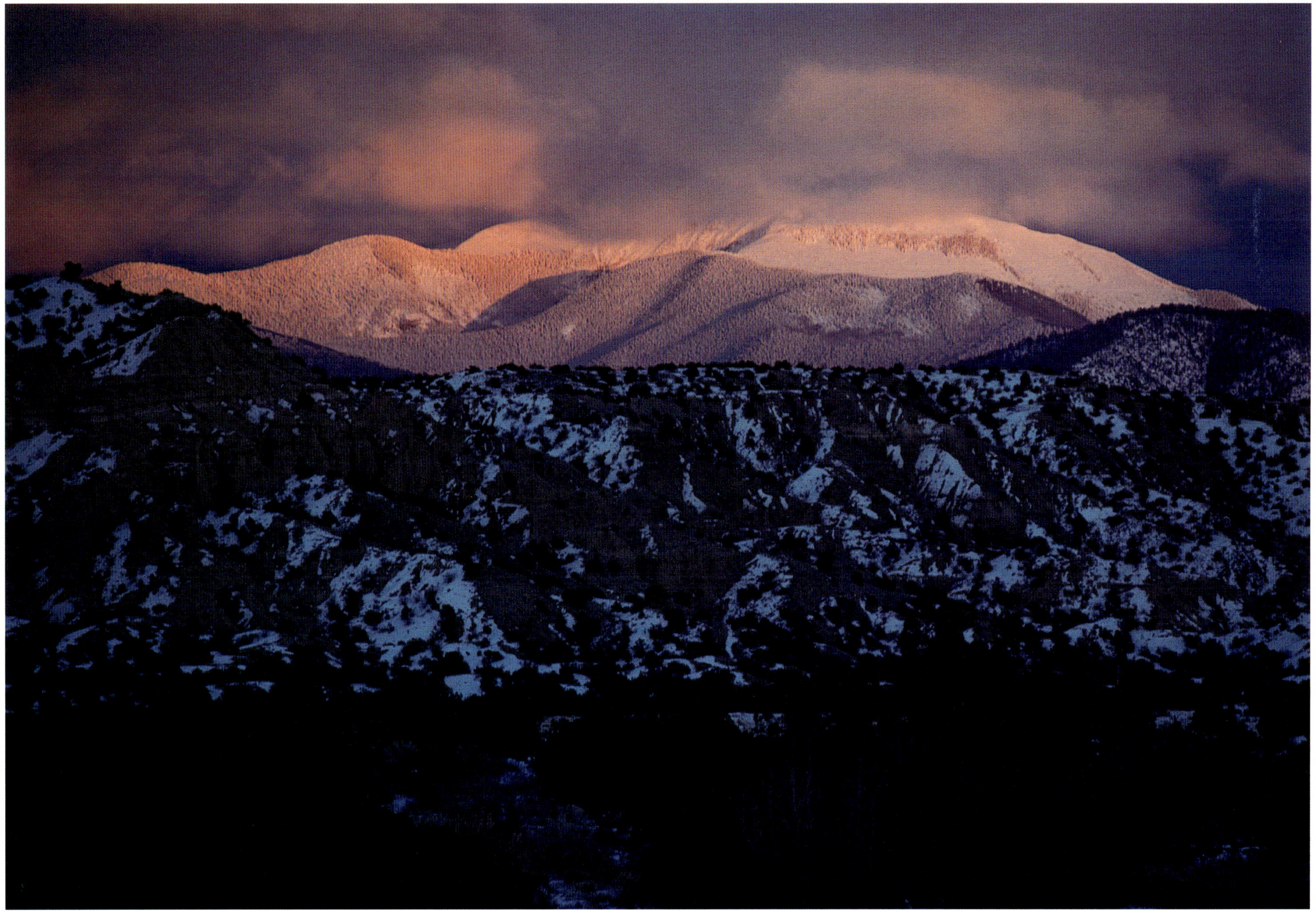

Mountain Freeze

Winter clouds at sundown hover over the snowcapped, 12,622-foot Santa Fe Baldy, ensuring an icy, stormy night in the Sangre de Cristo Mountains.

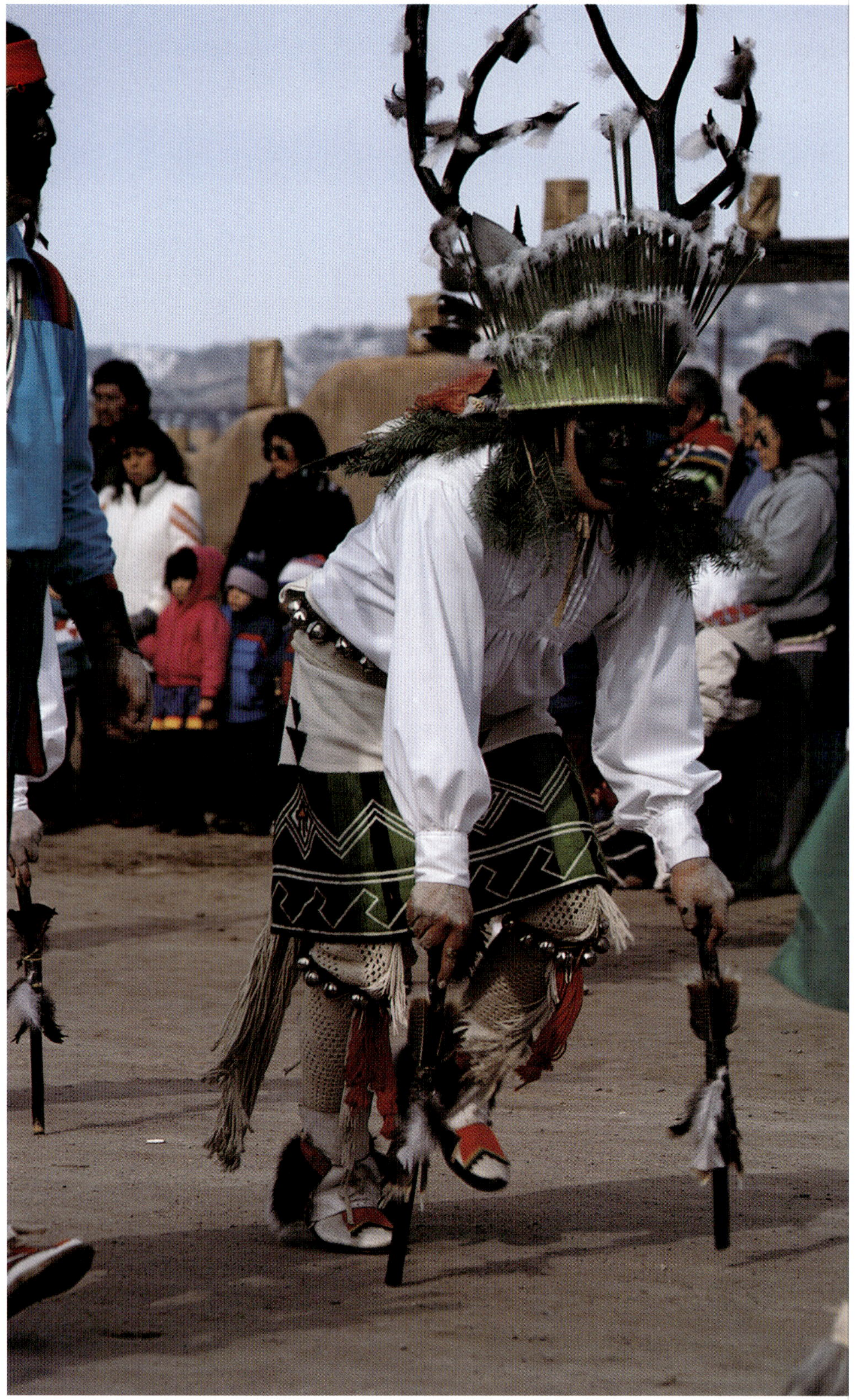

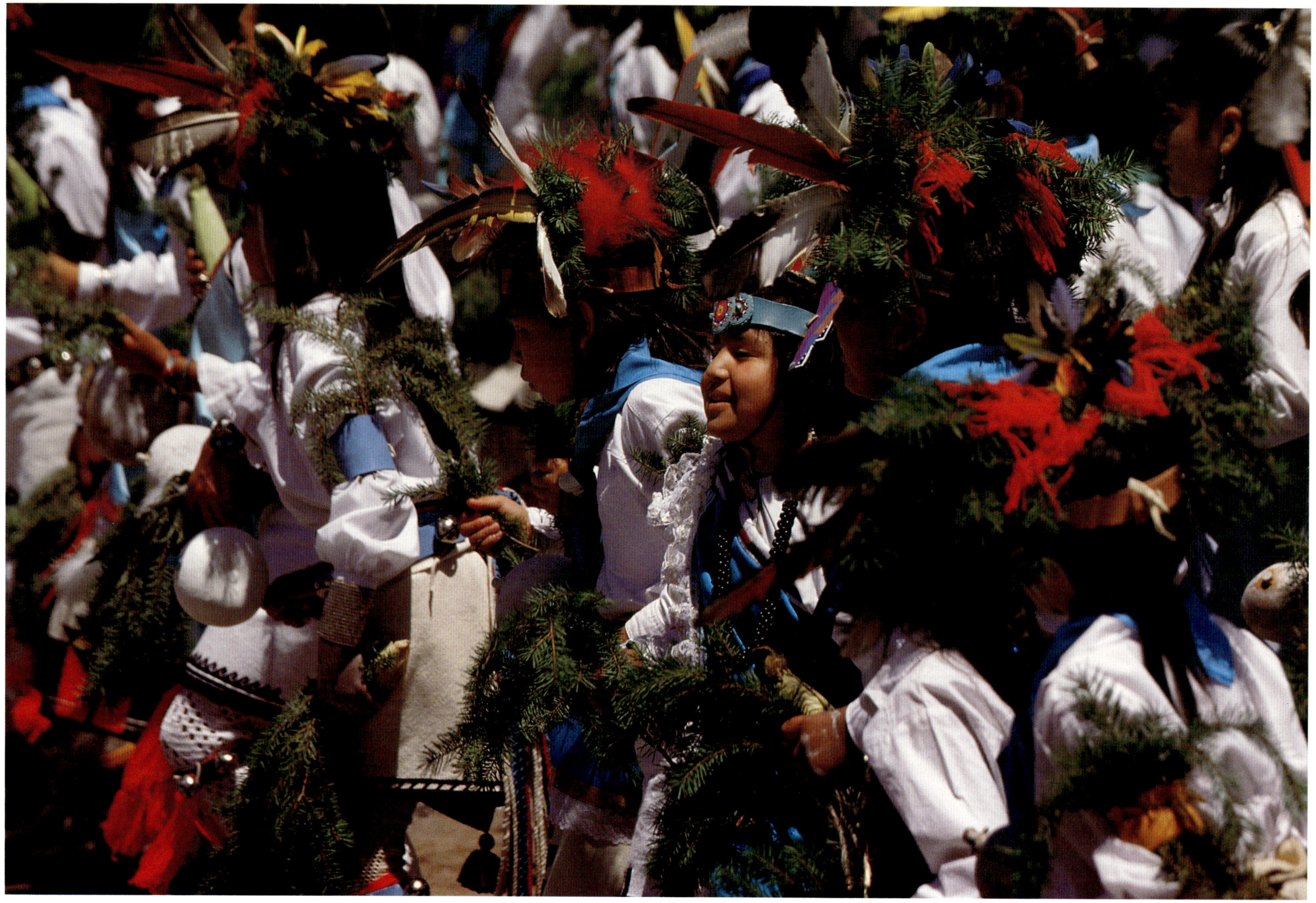

MEANINGFUL MOTION

YOUNG DANCERS KEEP TRADITION ALIVE WHILE PERFORMING ON FEAST DAY AT THE TEWA-SPEAKING SANTA CLARA PUEBLO ON THE WESTERN BANK OF THE RÍO GRANDE, SOUTH OF ESPAÑOLA.

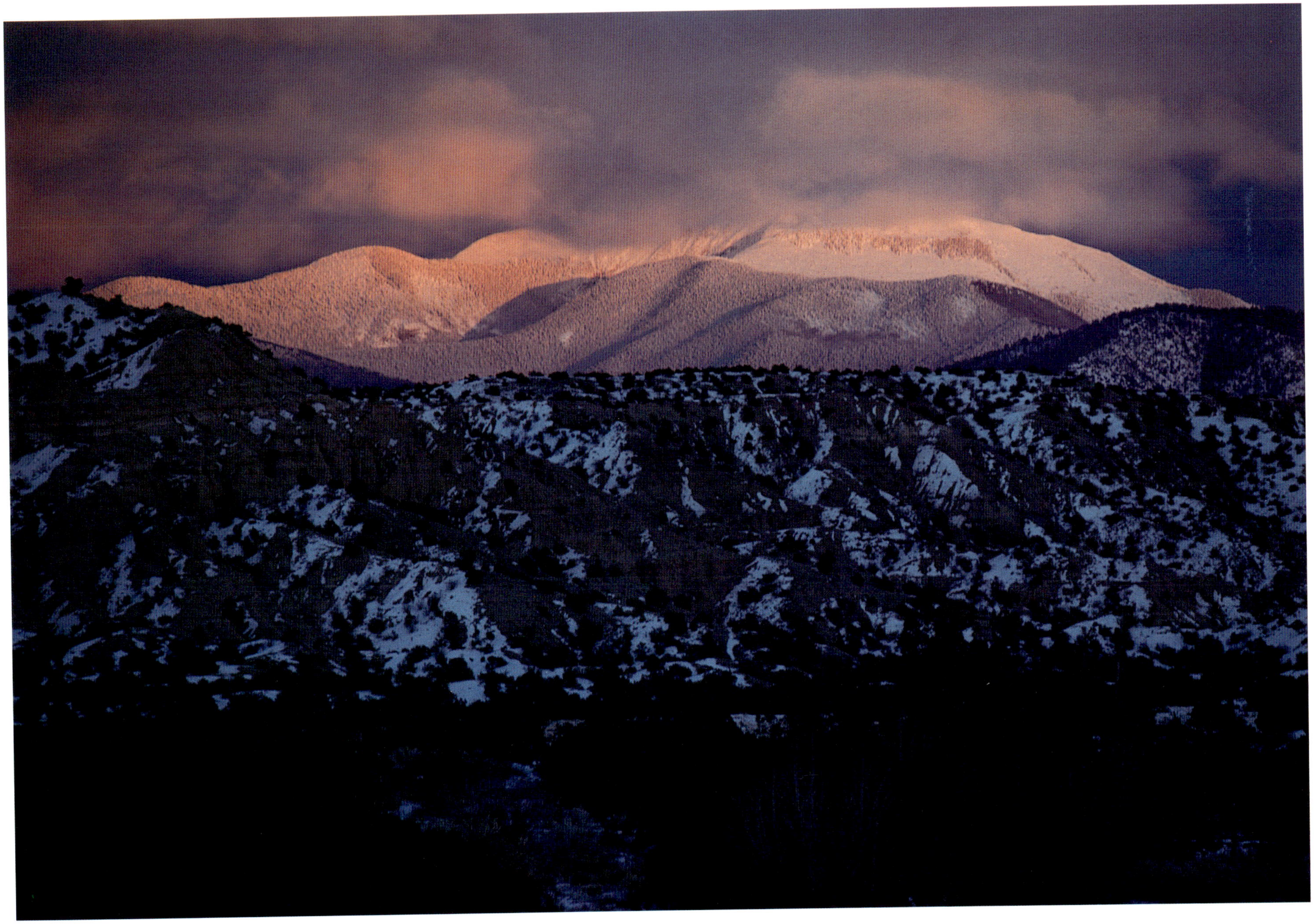

Mountain Freeze

Winter clouds at sundown hover over the snowcapped, 12,622-foot Santa Fe Baldy, ensuring an icy, stormy night in the Sangre de Cristo Mountains.

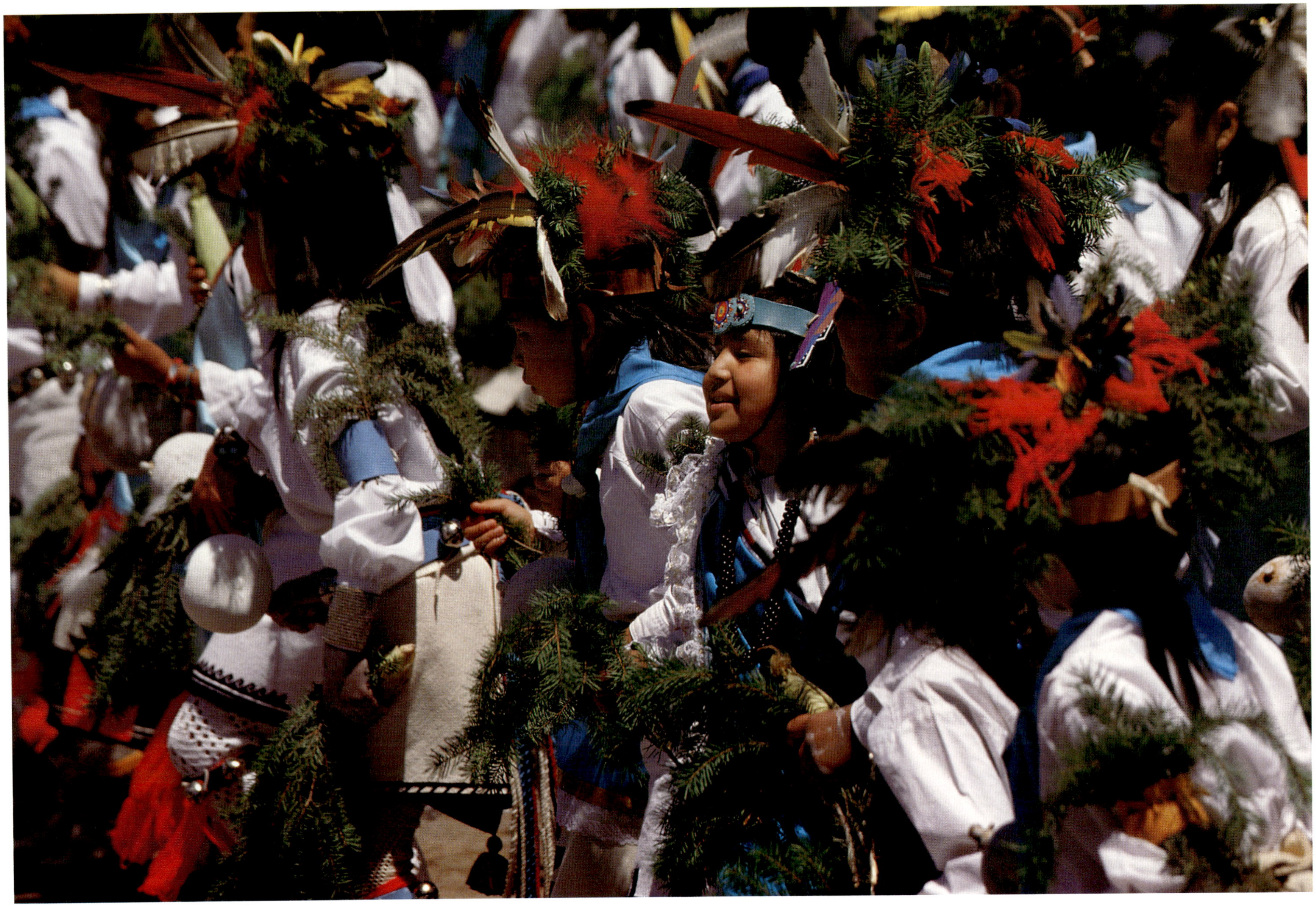

Meaningful Motion

Young dancers keep tradition alive while performing on feast day at the Tewa-speaking Santa Clara Pueblo on the western bank of the Río Grande, south of Española.

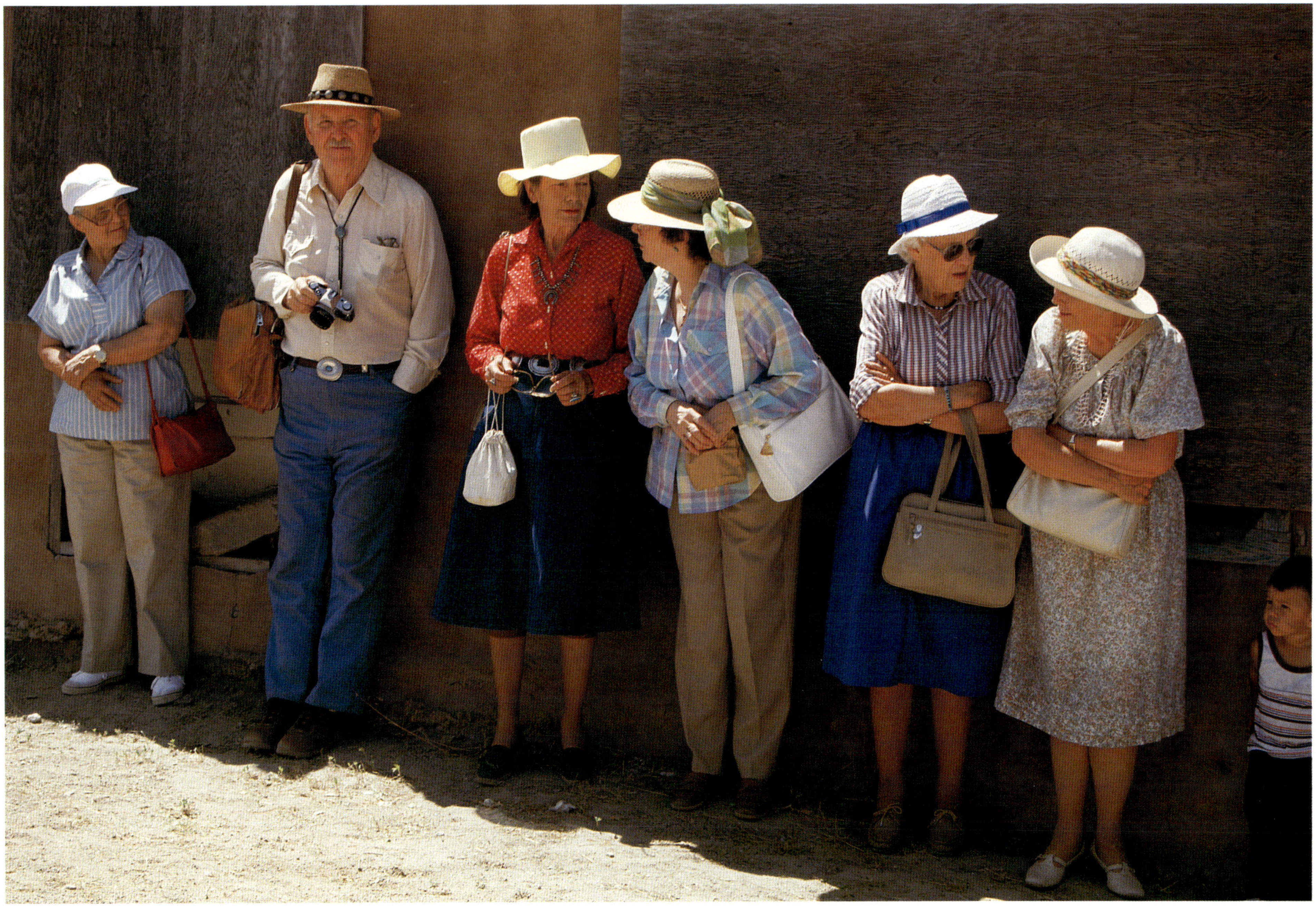

Pass the Sunscreen!

A group of hatted tourists takes refuge from the hot summer sun in a small patch of shade while watching traditional dances at San Juan Pueblo, just north of Española.

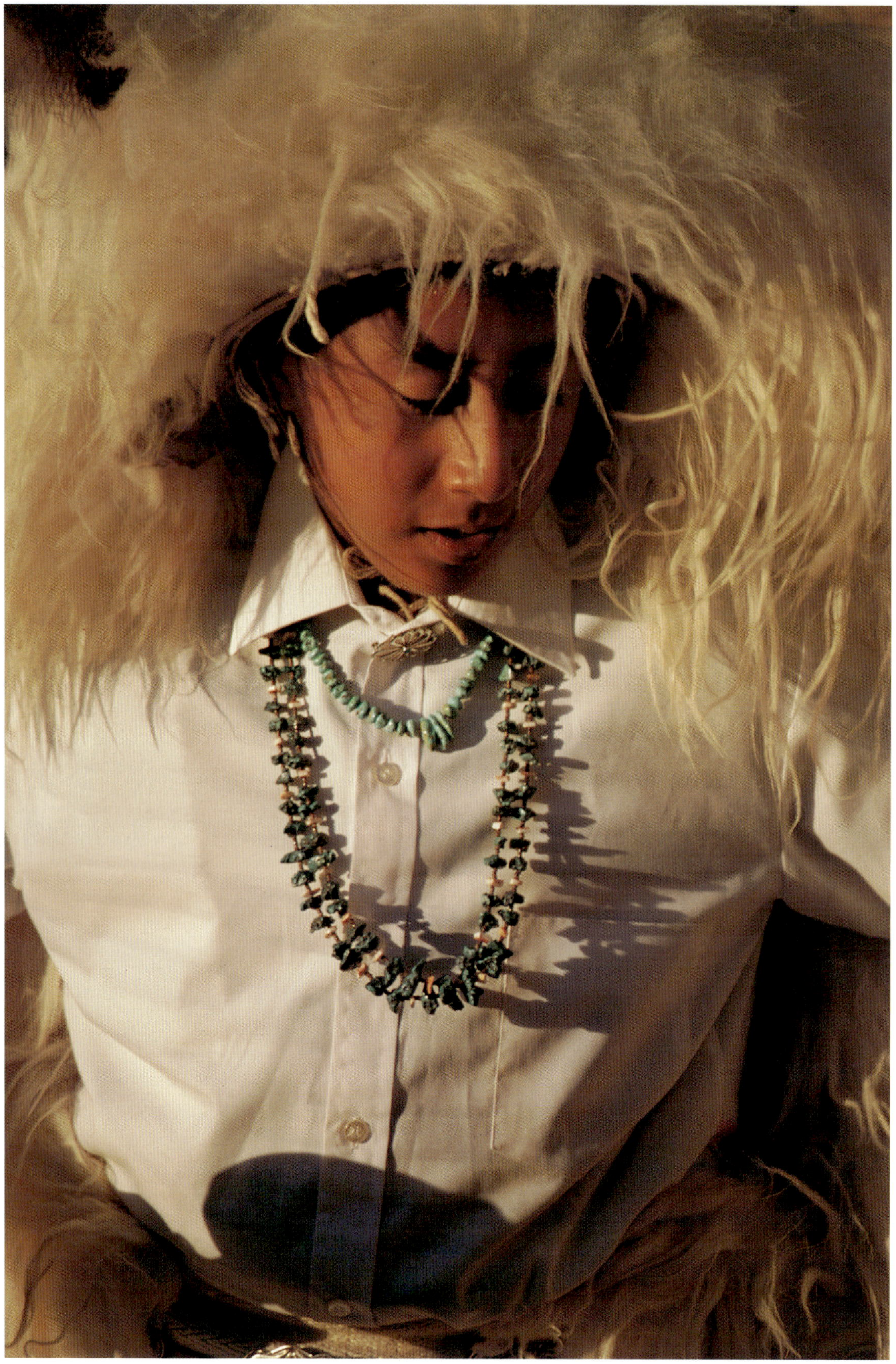

Soft light from the sun creates dramatic tones upon the body of Stuart Valdo, while he performs in the buffalo dance at Acoma Pueblo.

The feathered headdress and darkened face of a dancer at San Ildefonso Pueblo creates a stunning outline against the magnificent blue New Mexico sky.

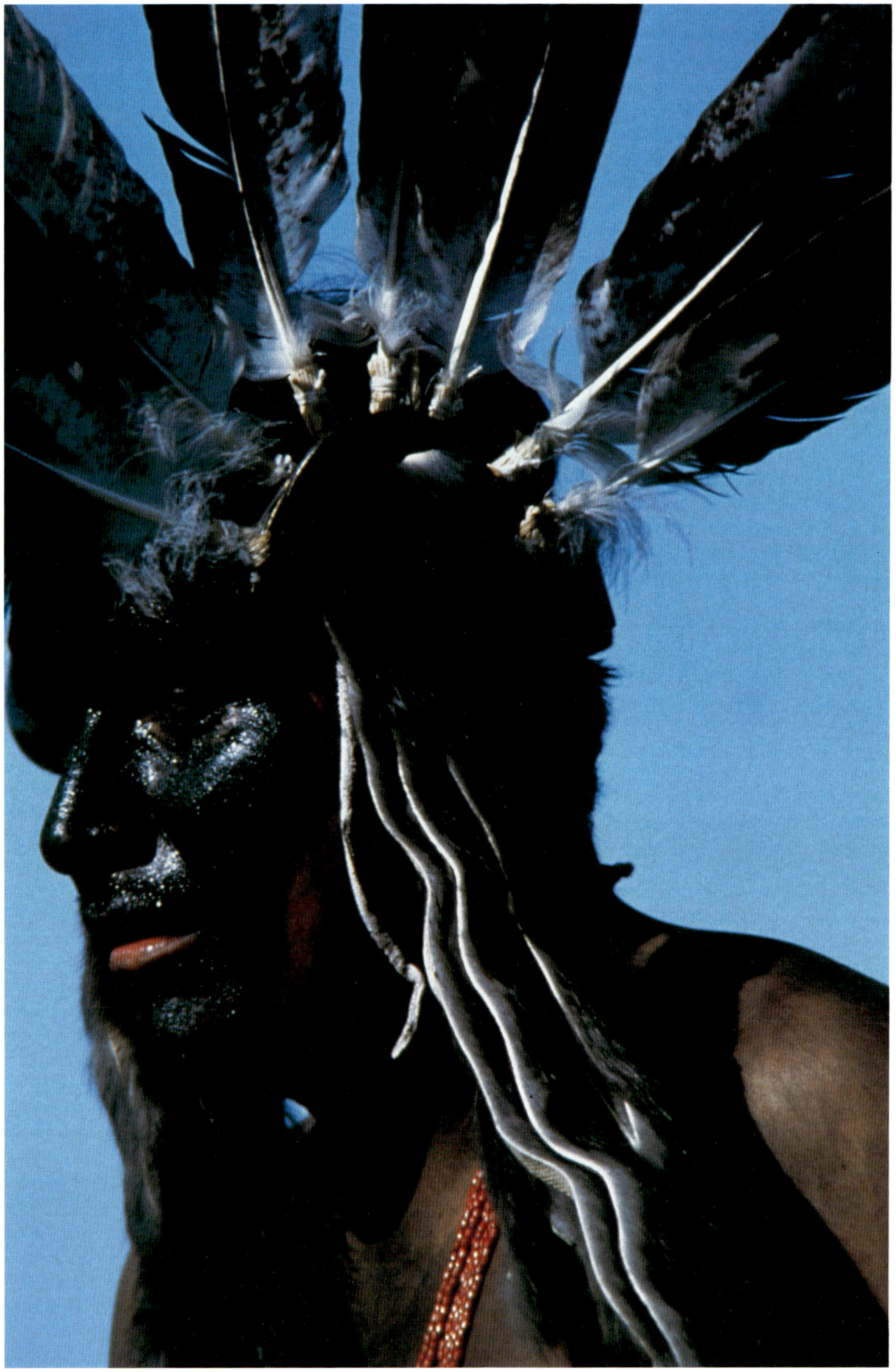

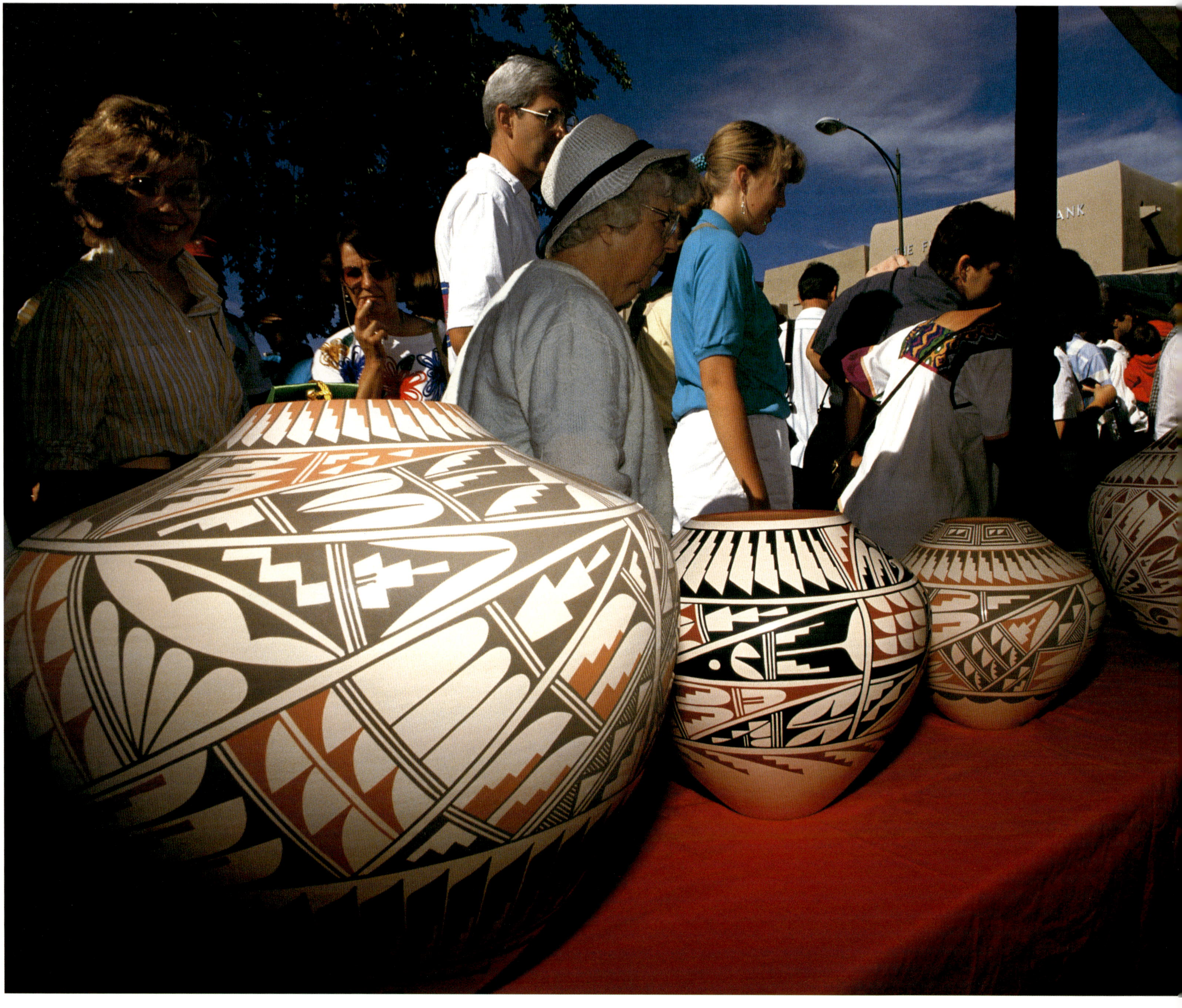

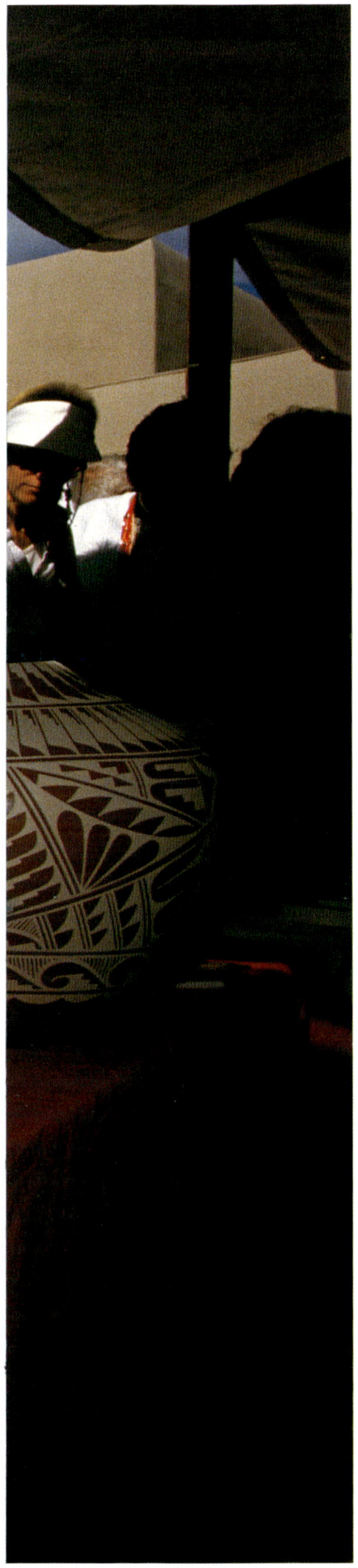

POTENTIAL BUYERS

PERUSE THE BEAUTIFULLY DESIGNED POTTERY ON DISPLAY AT THE ANNUAL SANTA FE INDIAN MARKET ON THE PLAZA. THE PRESTIGIOUS EVENT CELEBRATED ITS 75TH YEAR IN 1996, BOASTING 620 EXHIBIT BOOTHS PACKED WITH BOTH TRADITIONAL AND CONTEMPORARY NATIVE AMERICAN ART. INDIAN MARKET ORIGINALLY RAN IN CONJUNCTION WITH THE CENTURIES-OLD LA FIESTA DE SANTA FE EVERY SEPTEMBER, BUT IT EVENTUALLY WAS MOVED TO AUGUST AFTER IT BEGAN ATTRACTING SIZABLE CROWDS OF ITS OWN. TODAY, THE EVENT DRAWS NEARLY 70,000 VISITORS A YEAR. THE LATE MARÍA MARTÍNEZ, ONE OF THE MOST FAMOUS ARTISTS TO HAVE PARTICIPATED IN INDIAN MARKET, ONCE RECALLED SELLING ONE OF HER POTS AT THE EVENT'S INAUGURAL YEAR FOR A WHOPPING FIVE DOLLARS, WITH $3 BEING THE TOP PRICE PAID FOR A POT AT THE TIME. A PIECE OF MARÍA'S WORK (IF YOU'RE LUCKY ENOUGH TO FIND A PIECE FOR SALE) NOW IS WORTH SEVERAL THOUSAND DOLLARS.

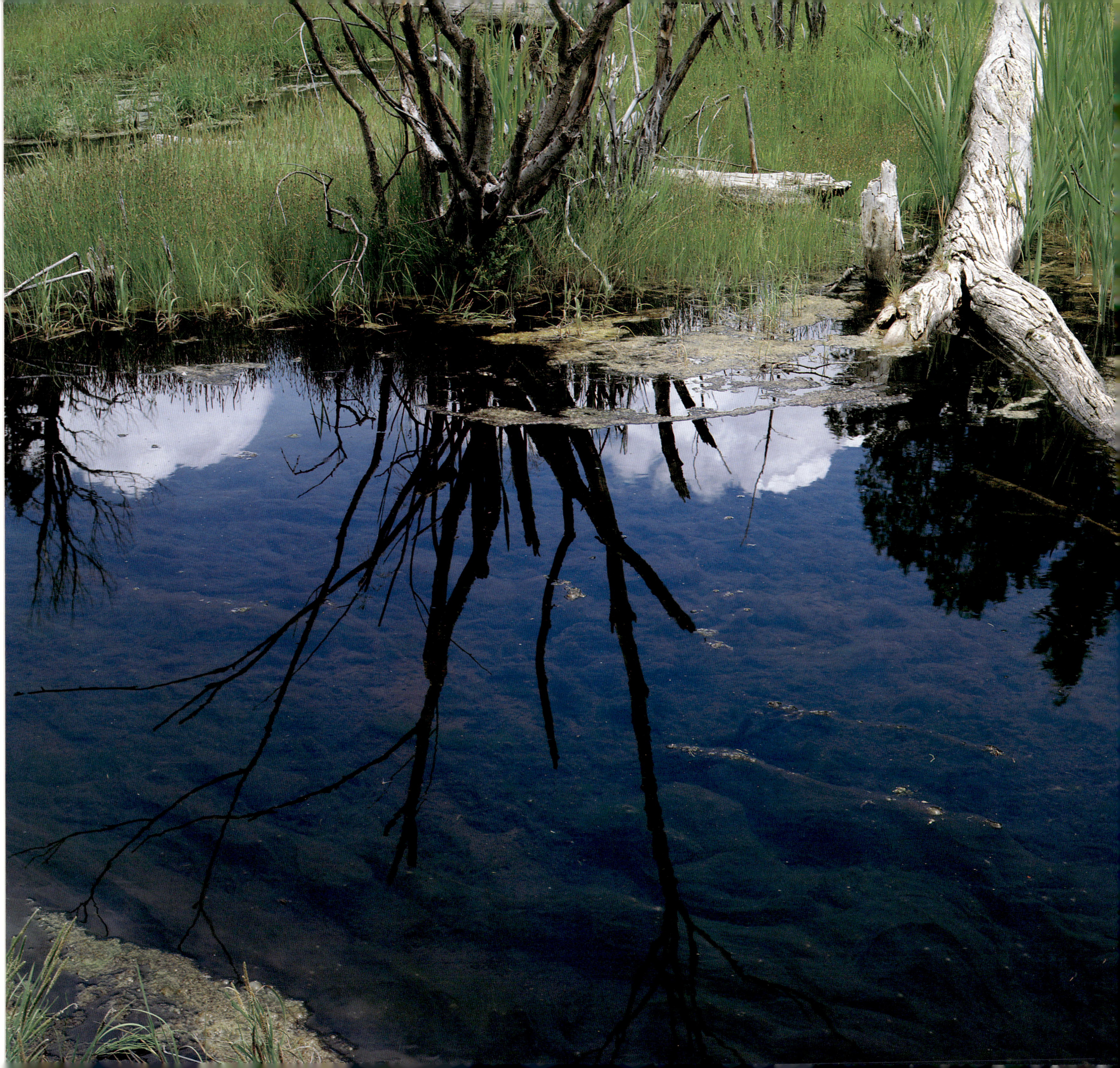

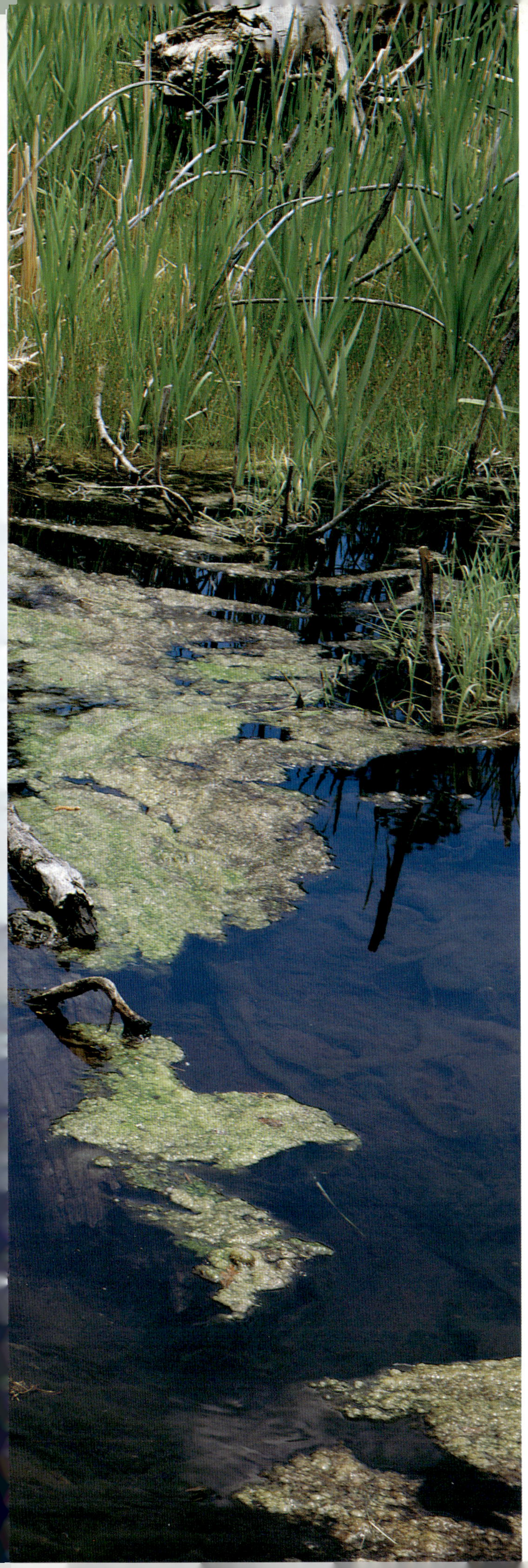

A dormant patch of water flanking a stream in the Valle Vidal unit of the Carson National Forest reflects its surroundings. The 100,000-acre preserve near the Colorado/New Mexico border north of Cimarron was donated to the U.S. Forest Service by the Pennzoil Corporation in 1982. Valle Vidal once was part of the 1.7 million-acre Maxwell Land Grant, deeded by the Mexican government in 1841 to a Mexican woman and her French-Canadian husband. The couple's daughter Luz and her husband, Lucien Maxwell, bought out other heirs to the land about 25 years later for $3,000. Maxwell eventually sold the grant to foreign investors in 1870 and a series of conflicts and court battles ensued between the new owners and homesteaders, whom the Supreme Court ruled against in 1887. Some of these conflicts resulted in the Colfax County War.

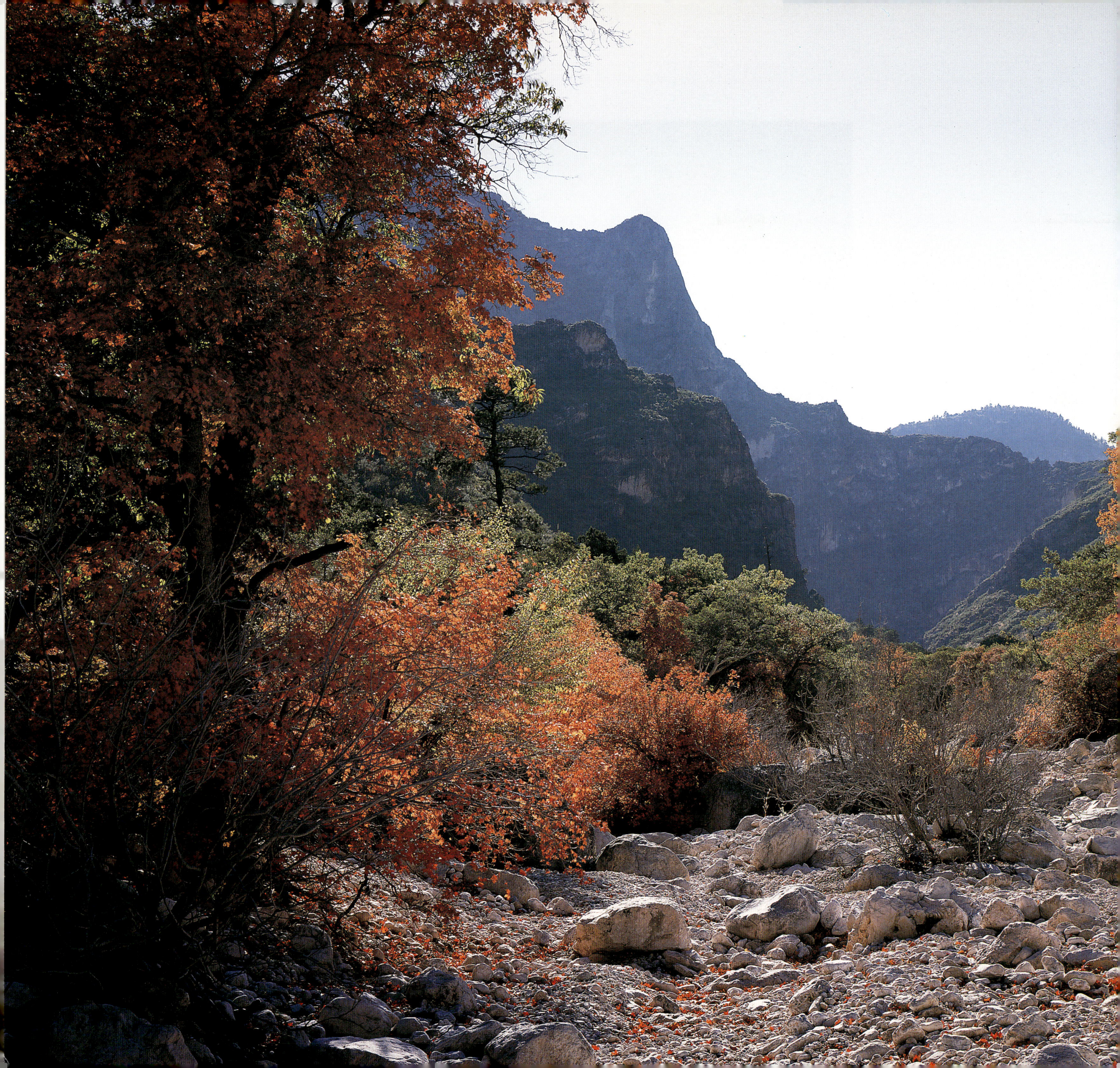

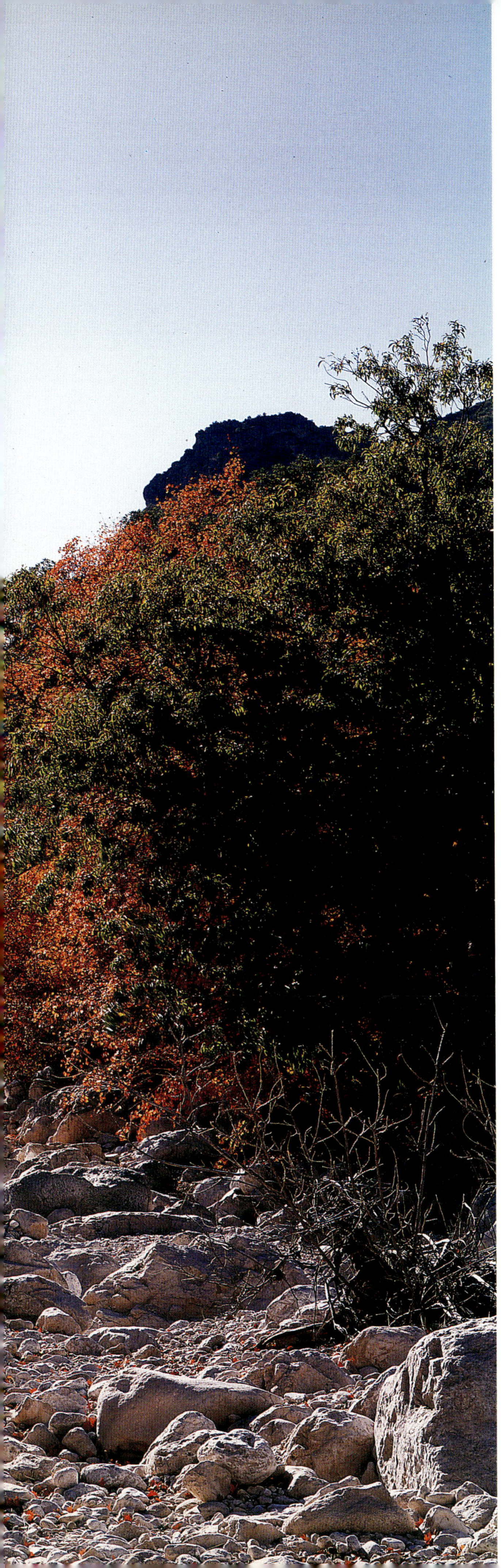

A dry riverbed in the Big Canyon area of the Guadalupe Mountains near the Texas/New Mexico border hosts a variety of changing trees and bushes. The mountains are impressive up close, but they do not possess enough mass or elevation to attract significant amounts of moisture from the sky.

Water that the area does receive, however, is quickly absorbed by porous layers of sediment that constitute the Chihuahuan Desert floor.

Scientists believe these mountains were once ancient reefs, created by coral and other marine life about 250 million years ago while southern New Mexico was submerged under a shallow portion of an ancient ocean.

Today, only a few varieties of cactus thrive in this harsh environment and most of the natural plant life comes in the form of hardy shrubs, including creosote bushes, mesquites, yuccas and ocotillo plants.

Army wagons loaded with heavy armaments in the latter 1800s caused these ruts near Fort Union National Monument. The fort was built in 1851 to establish a formidable military presence in the area after the United States claimed New Mexico as spoils for winning the Mexican War. It later became the largest military base in the Southwest with soldiers at the fort protecting caravans on the Santa Fe Trail from robbers and Indians. The coming of the railroad, less travelers on the trail and a decreased Indian threat eventually diminished the need for Fort Union, which was closed in 1891.

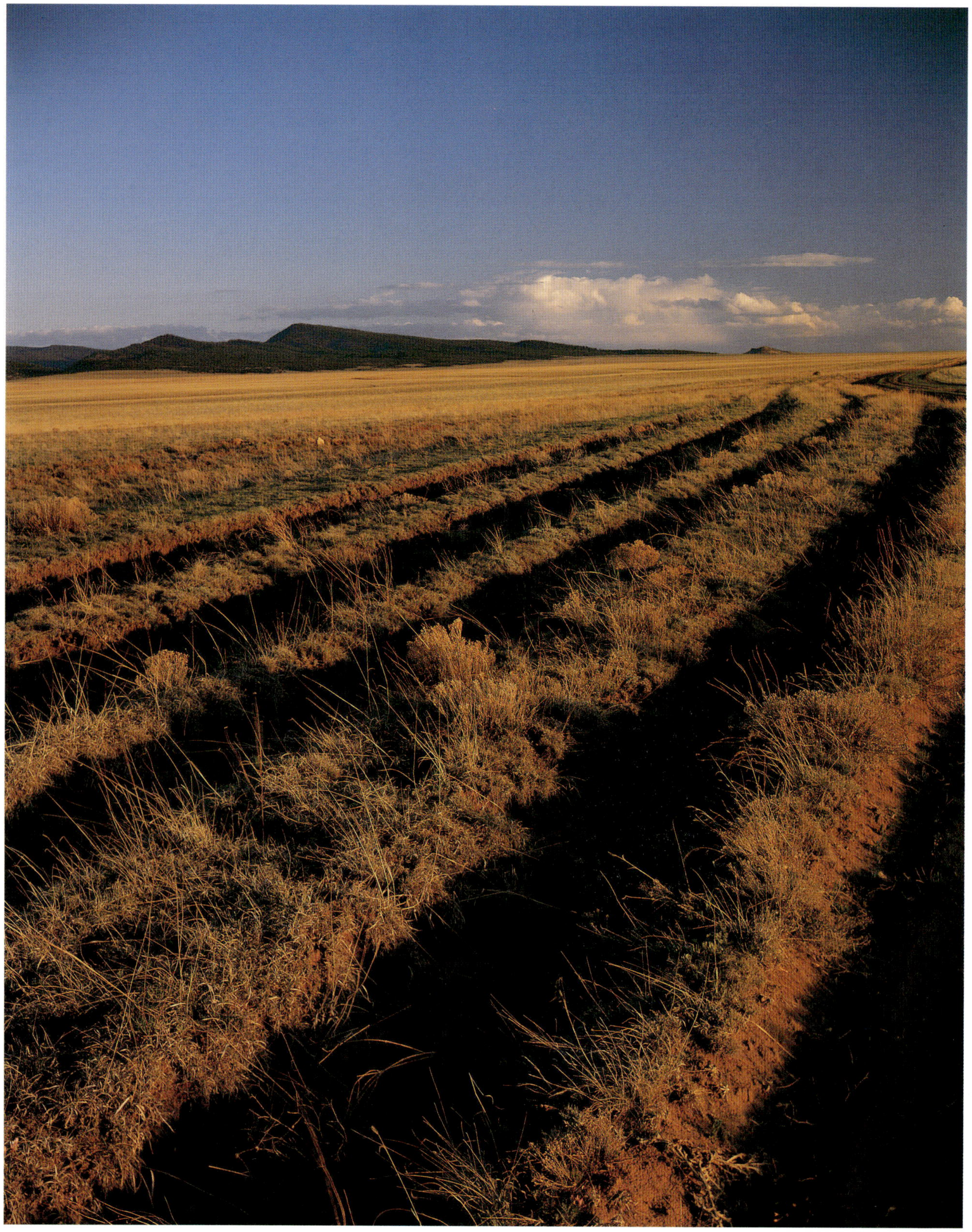

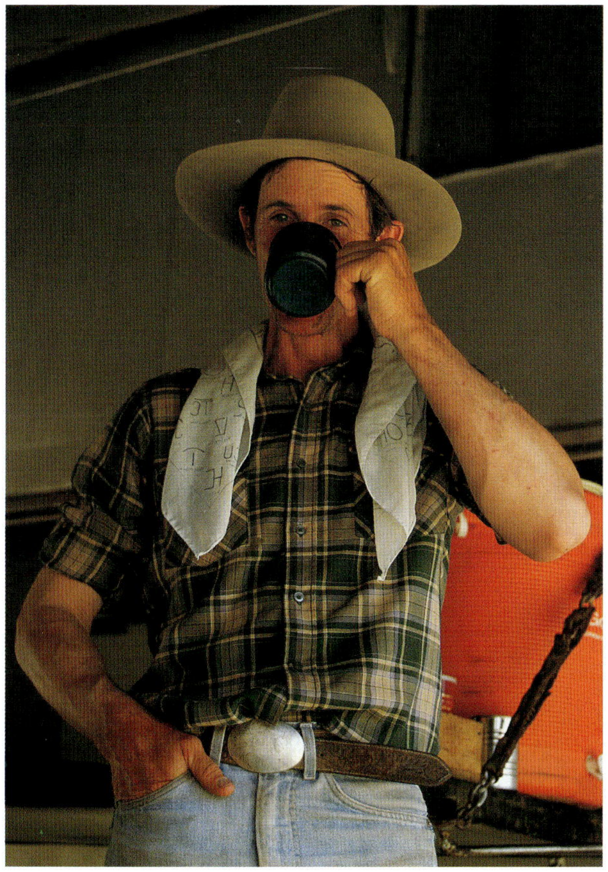

HARD WORK, LONELINESS AND LITTLE PAY ARE SOME CONSEQUENCES OF BEING A COWBOY IN TODAY'S AMERICA. BUT THAT ROMANTIC LIFESTYLE IS JUST FINE BY RICK TAYLOR, A RANCH HAND ON THE BELL RANCH IN NORTHEASTERN NEW MEXICO.

ROMANCING THE TRAIL:

A TRAVELER'S ADVENTURE ON THE WAY TO SANTA FE

by

Mark L. Gardner

From 1821 through the early 1880s, shortly after the coming of the railroad, the old Santa Fe Trail served as the main commercial highway between the eastern and the western reaches of what is now the continental United States. Many Easterners saw the trail as the gateway to fortune, health and romance in exotic and mysterious Santa Fe, the hub of northern Mexico and later the Territory of New Mexico. Here is a fictional account of what it might have been like to venture along the historic Santa Fe Trail.

Fort Union
New Mexico Territory
September 1, 1870

Dear Siss:

I suppose you think I've been killed by Indians or met with some unfortunate accident – sorry to disappoint you on that account. I've been such a vagabond the last few months in this western country that taking the time to put pen to paper has seemed rather a dull proposition.

I took the train as far as Kit Carson, and you should have seen all the commotion at that place when I arrived. Hundreds of "prairie schooners" and hordes of bullwhackers, oxen, mules and every other living thing you can imagine were crowded about the town. Especially busy were the forwarding and commission houses, where the New Mexican freighters receive their shipments.

I stopped in at a gunsmith shop run by a man named Zimmermann and purchased a pair of derringers for $17 (everyone out here carries a weapon of some kind) then set about finding some transportation *to New Mexico. I could have taken one of the stage-coaches, but that seemed too tame. So I hooked up with a Mexican mule train owned by a Mr. Perea. He charged me $10 for my passage, meals included.*

Our "dinners" were perhaps the most adventurous part of the trip: meat and cakes fried in a large pan, and these drowned in a gravy consisting mostly of red pepper or chile. My first taste of this latter reminded me of the time I backed up against the wood stove, only the pain was much more severe. This may strike you as odd, but I was fool enough to give the pepper gravy another chance, and I now actually fancy it at meals (it is a staple here in New Mexico).

The wagons of the Mexicans are quite large, holding about 6,000 pounds, and many of them are made in St. Louis. They are packed solid with barrels, crates and bundles, containing everything from sewing thread to parasols to window frames. The wagons are pulled by from six to eight mules, and the language of the teamsters is picturesque, to say the least. Some of their language I have been unable to find in the little Spanish primer you gave me, and I imagine that if translated into English, the words would be pretty scarce in Webster's, too.

At Trinidad, our route crossed a small spur of the mountains via a toll road over Ratón Pass. The gentleman who collects the toll at the top of the pass is an old mountaineer by the name of "Uncle" Dick Wootton. I dined with him the evening we were there, and he regaled me with many stories of his experiences, some of them true, no doubt. I asked him what he did if someone gave him trouble about the toll and he showed me his "toll collector" – an old shotgun.

I wish I could have sketched for you the scene as we dropped down out of the mountains. The shadows of the billowing white clouds glided over the distant plains and small peaks and buttes of the New Mexico Territory, making a very striking quilt of greens, blues, grays and browns that seemed to change every time you blinked your eyes. After we crossed the Canadian River, a small storm passed overhead, producing one of the most beautiful rainbows I can recall.

What I remember most about the trip, though, were the evenings in camp. Upon reaching the chosen site, the wagons were drawn up and a big fire was started for dinner. After the meal, and as the sun began to sink behind the distant mountains, two of the men pulled their violins from the wagons and began to scratch out an endless number of quick tunes while the others sang along and danced the fandango. As darkness settled in around us, the white canvas tops of the wagons took on a wonderful yellow glow. The distorted shadows of the men leapt around on these wagon covers, reminding me of our magic lantern shows back home.

The train halted for repairs at Las Vegas, which gave me time to visit the bath houses at the hot springs. These mineral waters, ranging from 80 to 120 degrees, are locally famous for their therapeutic powers, and I saw many health seekers there taking the cure. This was more of a pleasure excursion for me, though, as my health was already greatly improved by the time we reached New Mexico. The persistent cough that I left Missouri with is now entirely gone, and I feel quite strong and robust.

I left Mr. Perea's train at Santa Fe. This town is the capital of the territory, but I don't think that you would be impressed. Although it contains some two-story buildings around the Plaza, most are the flat-roofed mud structures common throughout this region,

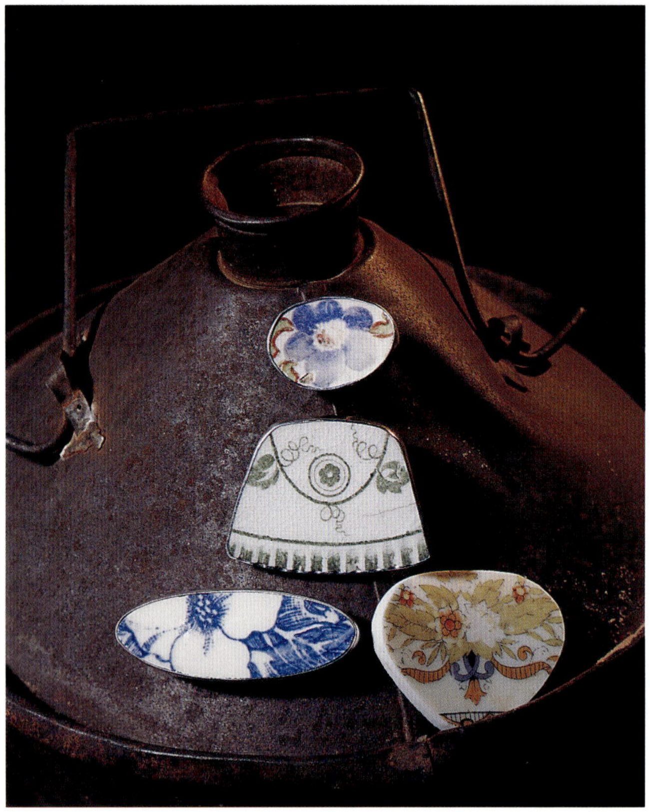

BEFORE THE ADVENT OF THE SANTA FE TRAIL IN 1821, MANUFACTURED GOODS AND OTHER FINE ITEMS, SUCH AS THESE PIECES OF CERAMIC FOUND ALONG ITS ROUTE, WERE RARE IN NEW MEXICO. THE OVERALL QUALITY OF LIFE IMPROVED FOR NEW MEXICANS AT THE TIME DUE TO THE NEW COMMERCIAL EXCHANGE BETWEEN MEXICO AND THE UNITED STATES.

which, from a distance, look like a bunch of brick kilns. The population is said to number about 6,000, but there are enough dry goods in town to satisfy the whole territory! The merchants are well supplied with assortments from St. Louis, Philadelphia, New York and Europe, although the prices are quite a bit higher here. They carry the latest fashions in bonnets and other items of female dress, yet some women continue to wear the Mexican reboso or scarf mysteriously wrapped around their head and face as of old.

I don't know how I escaped being run over by the many donkeys or burros that are driven into town every day overloaded with firewood, grass, wheat, fruit, meat, etc. Sometimes I thought the poor animals would snap underneath the heavy loads, but they never failed to deliver their mighty burdens. I also indulged my passion for billiards with some Army officers at the fonda or hotel. Occasionally we received news from the south of attacks by Apaches on small parties of men, who were usually being careless at the time. Don't worry yourself on my part, though, for I do not plan on getting myself in such a fix anytime soon.

On the invitation of some of my officer friends, I took the stage to Fort Union, which explains my presence at this place. The stage ride cannot be adequately described. Imagine being strapped to the paddle in Aunt Katie's butter churn during one of her fits of industry and you will get some idea of the experience. The driver actually seemed to relish our discomfort, urging his steeds on at every opportunity, so that I have only a faint idea of the scenery we passed. This matters little, though, as we took the same route out that our wagon train traveled to Santa Fe.

Fort Union is a very substantial and busy place.

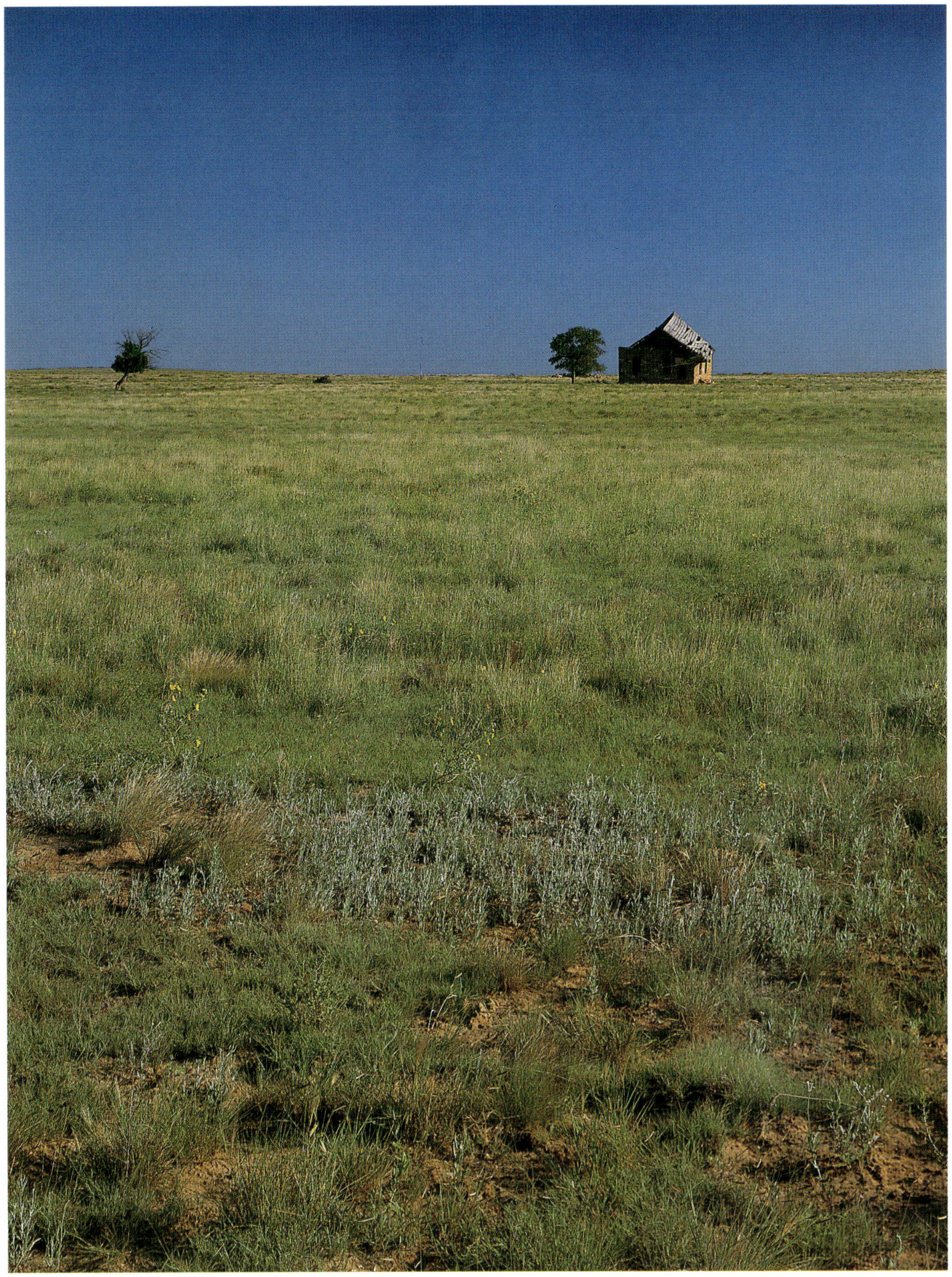

WEATHER AND TIME TAKE THEIR TOLL ON THIS ABANDONED HOMESTEAD ON THE NORTHEASTERN PLAINS. MANY HOMESTEADING FAMILIES WERE DEEMED "SQUATTERS" BY THE DUTCH BUYERS OF MUCH OF THE 1.7-MILLION-ACRE MAXWELL LAND GRANT IN THE 1870S. SUCH FAMILIES WERE FORCED FROM THEIR HOMES, SOMETIMES VIOLENTLY, CAUSING THE COLFAX COUNTY WAR.

It is situated in the middle of an extensive plain and is consequently much exposed to harsh winds. It has a nice row of officers quarters facing the west side of the parade ground. They are made of mud "adobes" like everything else, but recent plaster work and whitewashing have made them properly distinguished. And some of the officers' wives have done much with their furnishings to make the quarters very pleasant places to visit.

Fort Union is the supply depot for all the forts in the Southwest, and trains of mule and ox wagons are constantly arriving and departing amidst twirling clouds of dust and sand. The garrison here is made up of the Eighth Cavalry and the Fifteenth Infantry, and their officers are quite merry fellows. I have rented a room in the sutler's store for the duration of my stay, which is quite convenient, for it is a gathering place for the men of the post, and we often lounge about playing cards or billiards and reading the latest Harper's and other papers.

One Saturday evening I accompanied some enlisted men to Loma Parda, a small Mexican town some six miles from the post. There we had a grand fandango until late at night. The evening's entertainment ended somewhat abruptly, however, when a fight broke out between some of the soldiers who had sampled too much of the refreshments. The only serious casualty was Mr. Baca's violin, which I am afraid is beyond all hope.

During the last few days I have made several horseback excursions through the surrounding country. I have ridden into the Turkey Mountains a few miles from the fort and also have visited some of the nearby ranches that provide beef and forage for the post. This is perfect country for livestock, although the cattle here are a rather unattractive looking lot, most having been bred from Texan stock. Also raised here are large herds of sheep. Except for what little is used for weaving blankets here, most of the wool is shipped east by wagon to the railheads.

The Mexican horsemen are quite adept with their lassos, and at one ranch I got to witness some very interesting exhibitions of their skill. In a blur of movement, the vaquero can let loose his lasso, snaring it around his victim and pulling it snug in less time than it takes to read this. And the vaquero seldom fails to miss his target, even when it is running away!

Although the doctor ordered me to an arid climate for a six months duration, don't be surprised if I extend my stay here. This country has a charm all its own, and I am not willing to part with it just yet. I may take a job clerking in the sutler's store or else I will make a pleasure trip to Taos. Whatever I decide to do, I promise to write you again soon with another narrative of my adventures.

Please give my love to the folks and neighbors, and tell them that although my constitution has been restored, I have unfortunately fallen in with a band of horse thieves. Or tell them some lie of your own choosing.

Your affectionate brother,

William

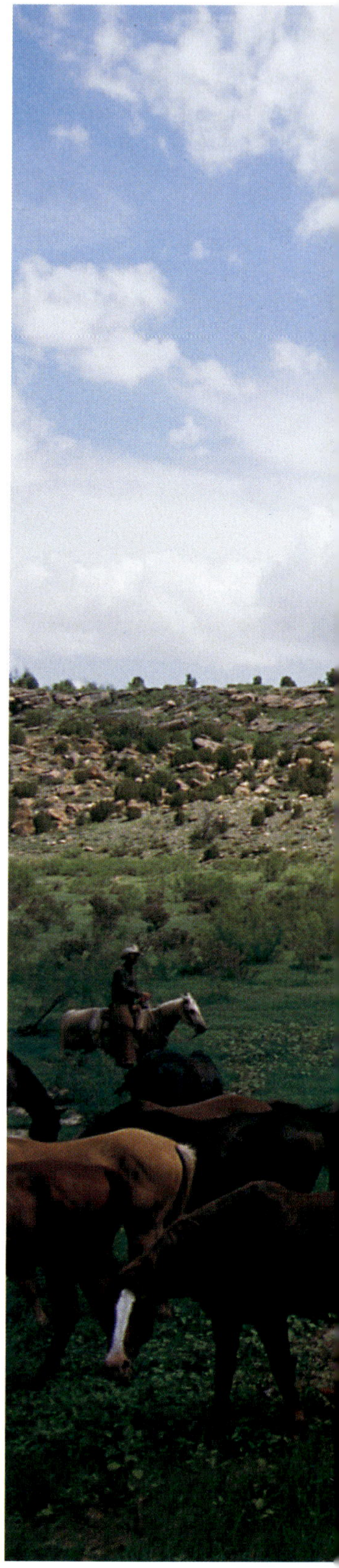

COWBOYS TEND TO A HERD OF HORSES GRAZING AND DRINKING ON A VERDANT PATCH NEAR A WINDMILL AND SPRING ON THE BELL RANCH IN NORTHEASTERN NEW MEXICO.

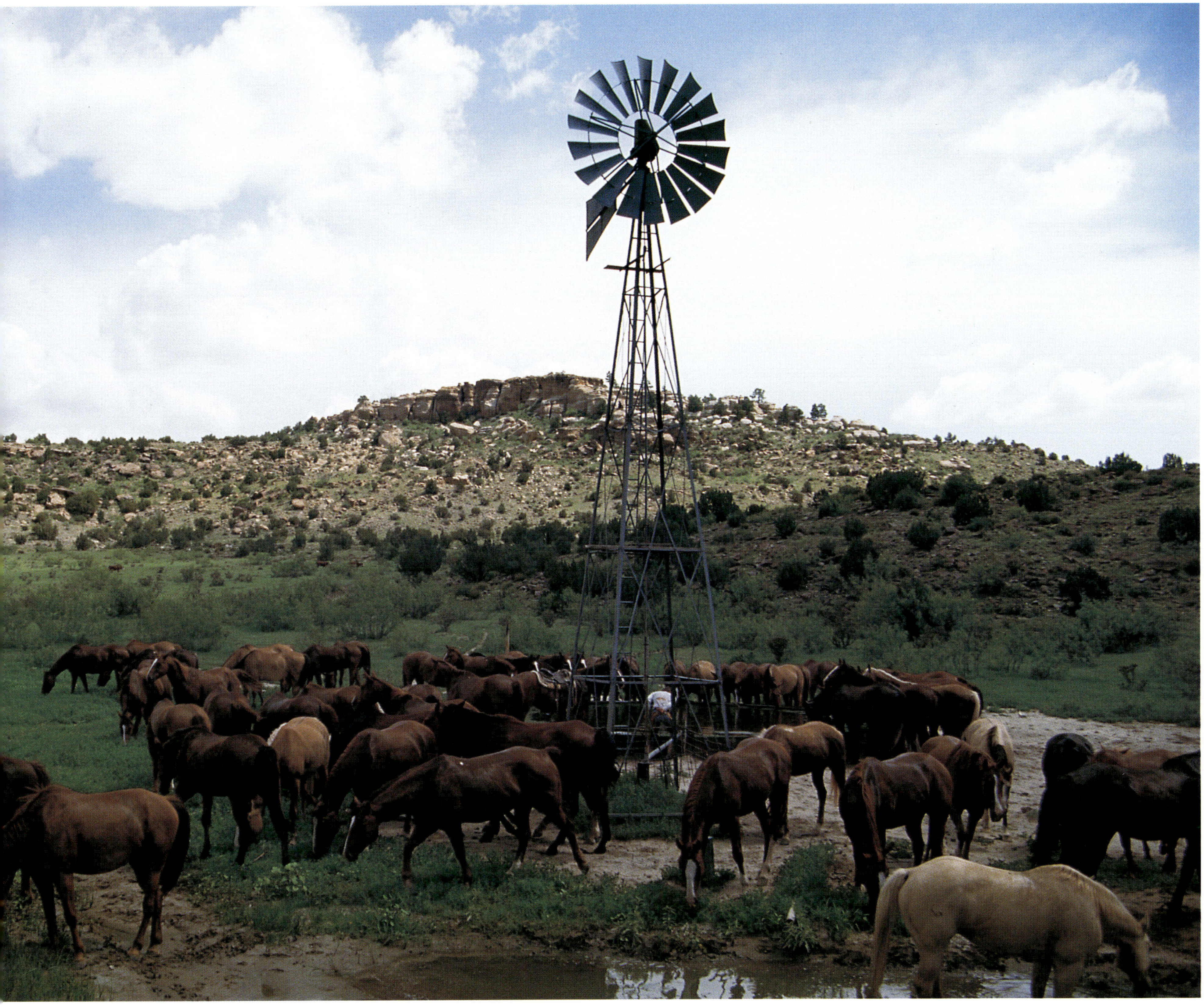

In the face of a brilliant setting sun, a windmill pumps water from the ground south of Santa Fe. The issue of water, historically complex in semi-arid New Mexico, is further being complicated by increased land development, especially in the larger cities. The demand for water is at an all-time high and the current trend is that the demand will increase. A lower than average snowfall in the winter of 1995-96 caused dismal surface and underground water levels the following spring and forced cities such as Santa Fe and Albuquerque to enact mandatory water-conservation measures throughout the summer months. These patterns of drought along with increasing demands for water have prompted many local governments to more closely scrutinize how proposed land-development projects will impact known water sources.

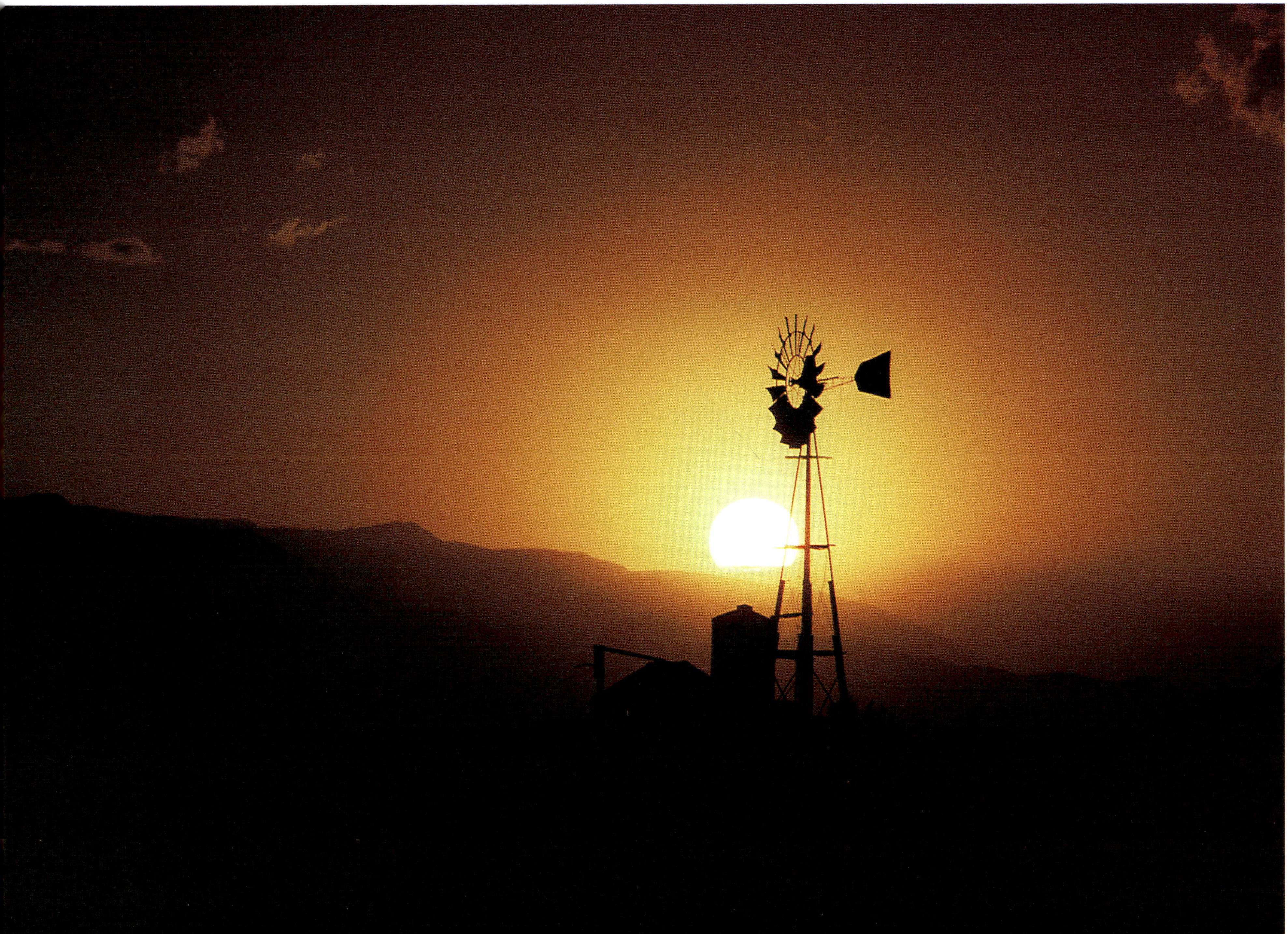

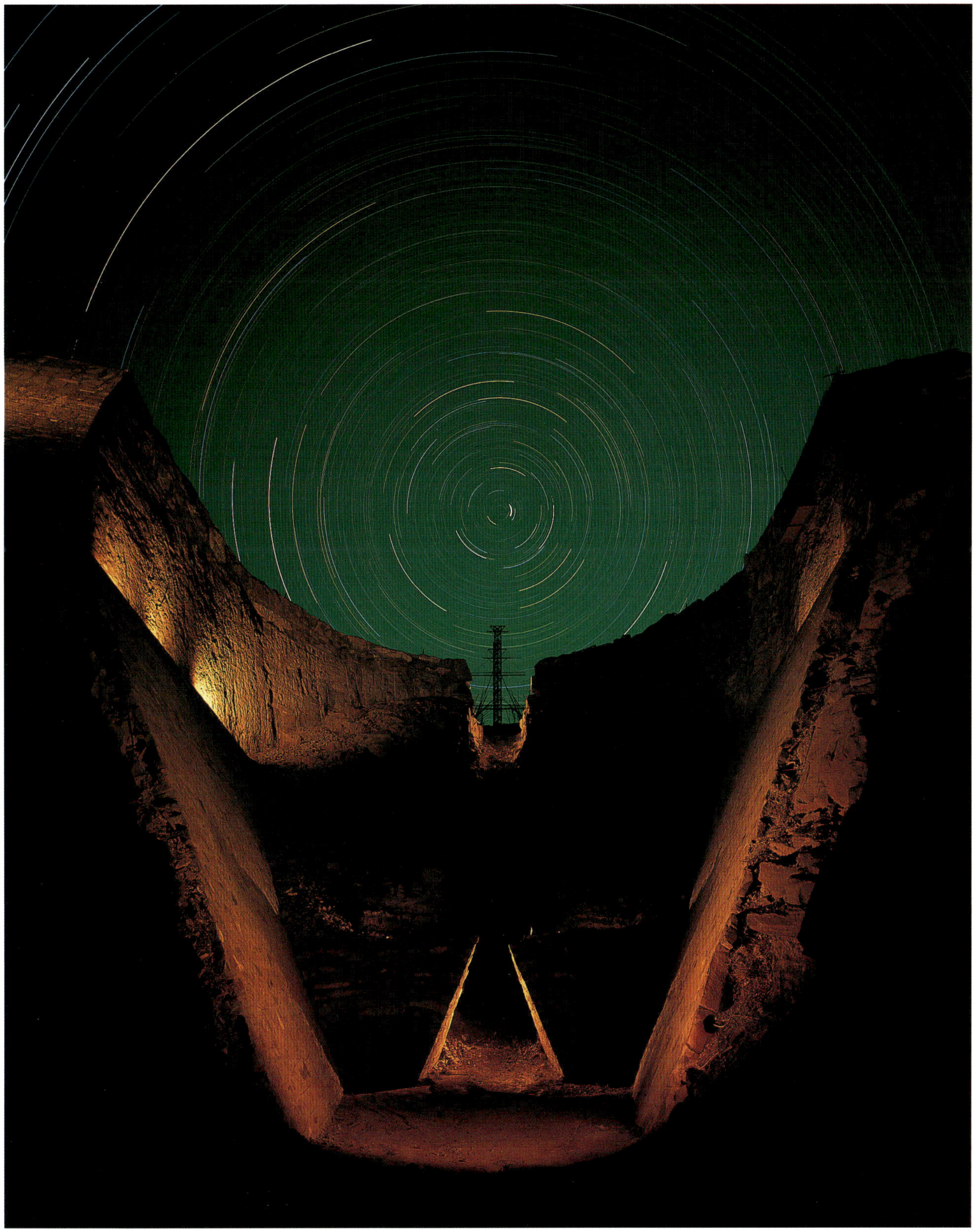

Artist Charles Ross' passion for the stars has driven him to spend more than 16 years cutting this 11-story tunnel into a granite and limestone mesa near Las Vegas to observe the heavens. The cut is aligned perfectly parallel to the Earth's axis to frame the north celestial pole.

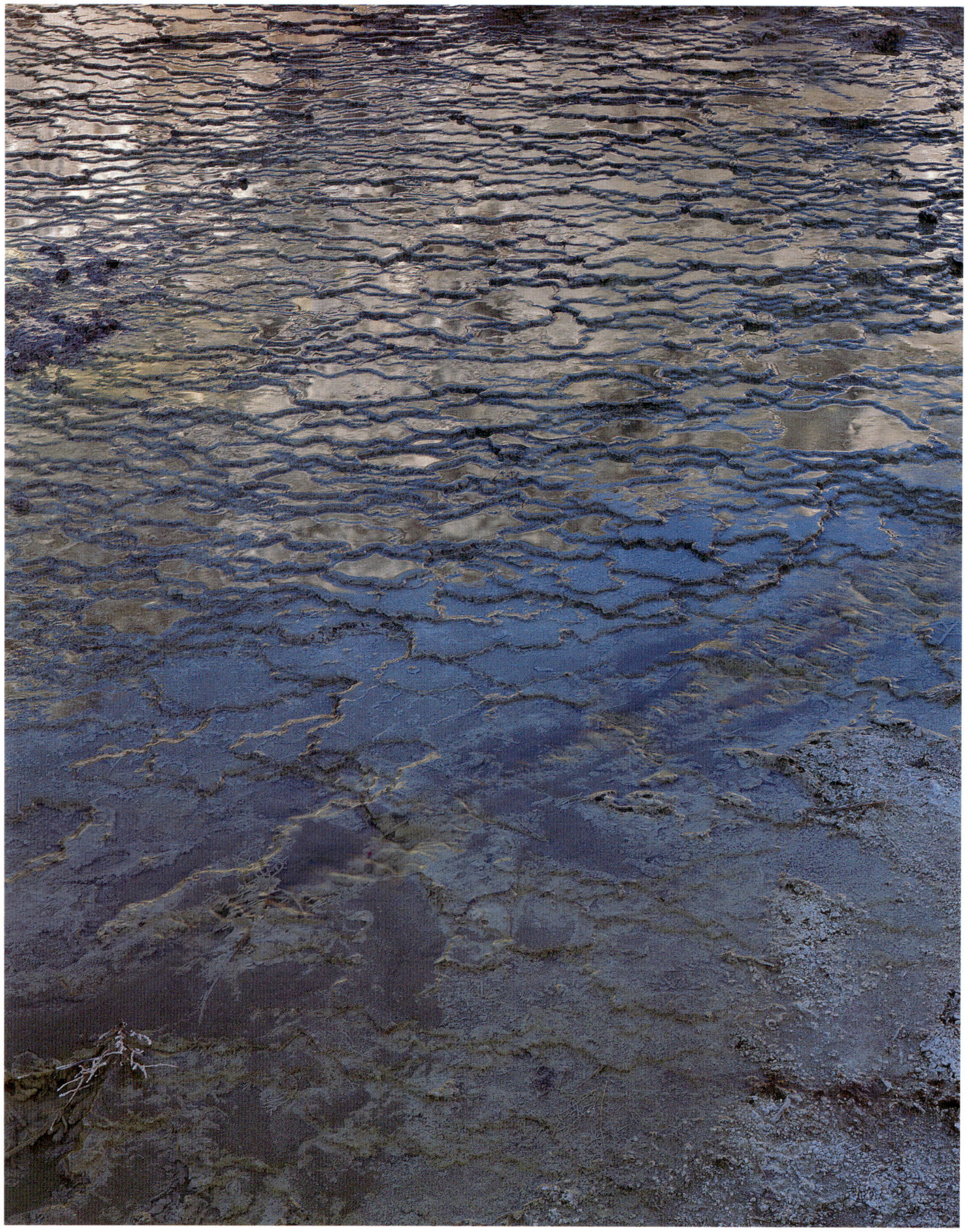

Flowing Texture

The free-flowing mineral waters of Soda Dam in the Jémez Mountains take on a frozen appearance in the soft afternoon light.

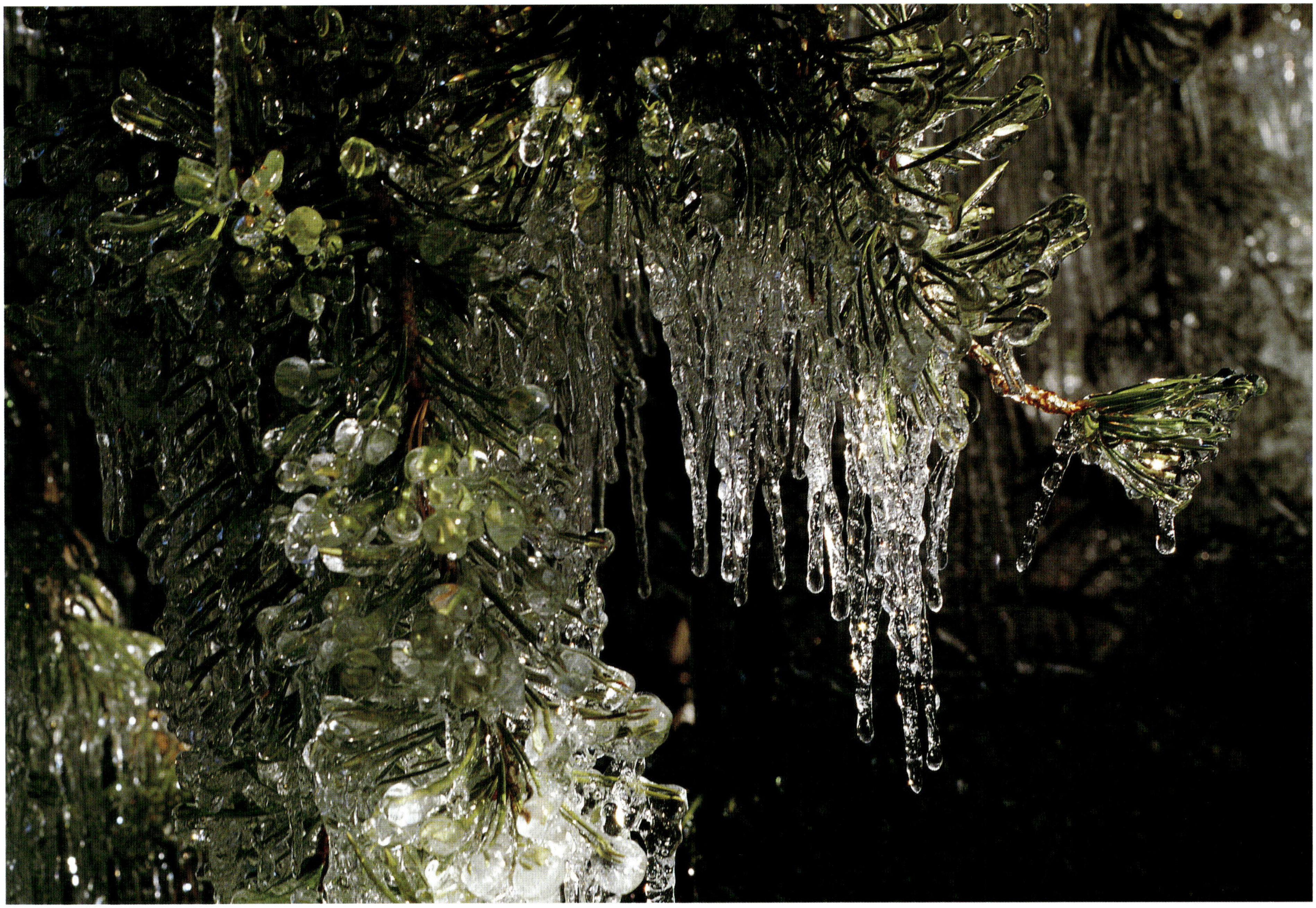

Signs of Spring

Warming sunlight from a bright, late-winter day melts festive decorations formed naturally overnight on the needles of a piñon tree.

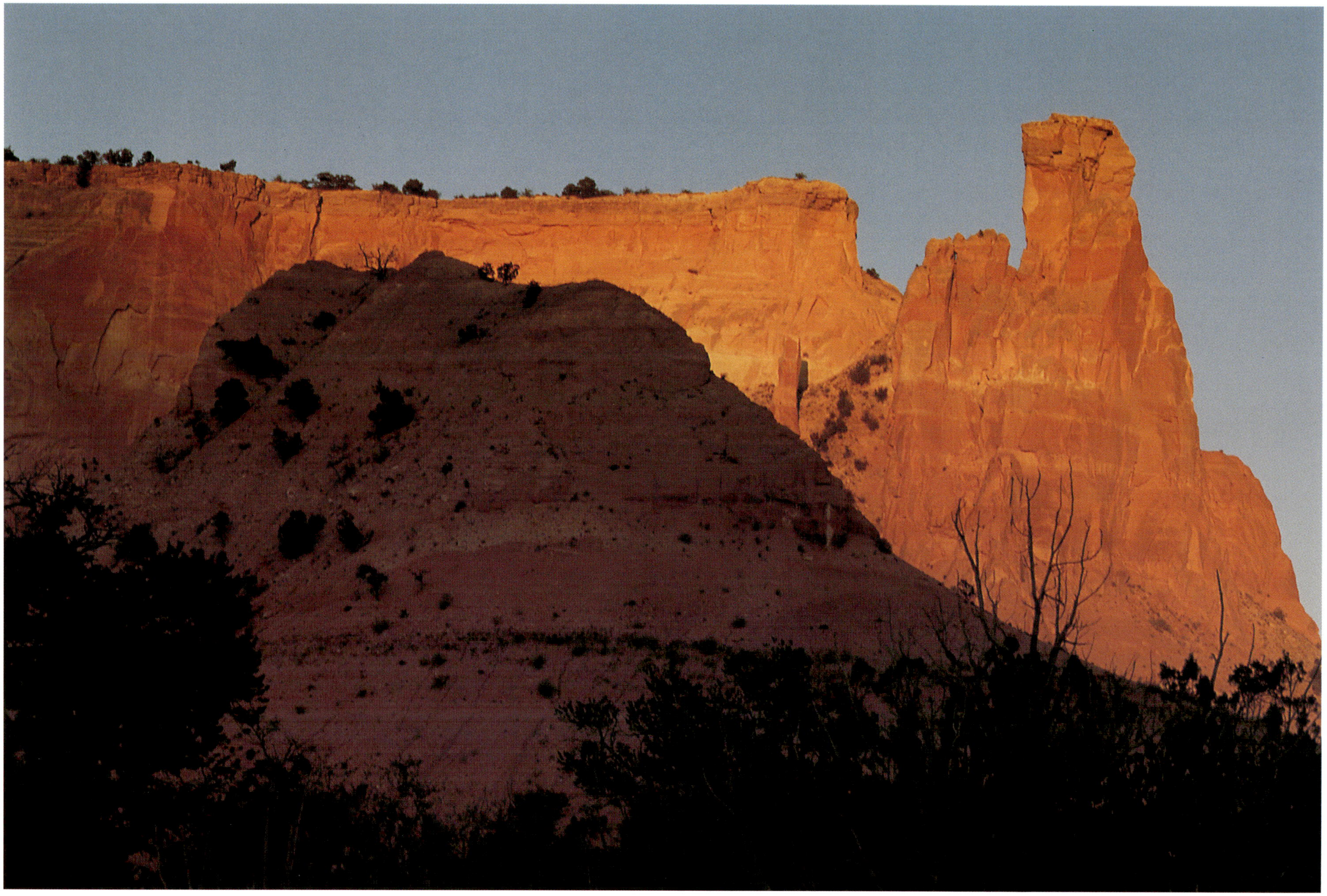

Fleeting Moments

Crisp light from a sunset reflects off the atmosphere to color the inner walls of this oft-photographed bluff at Ghost Ranch near Abiquiú.

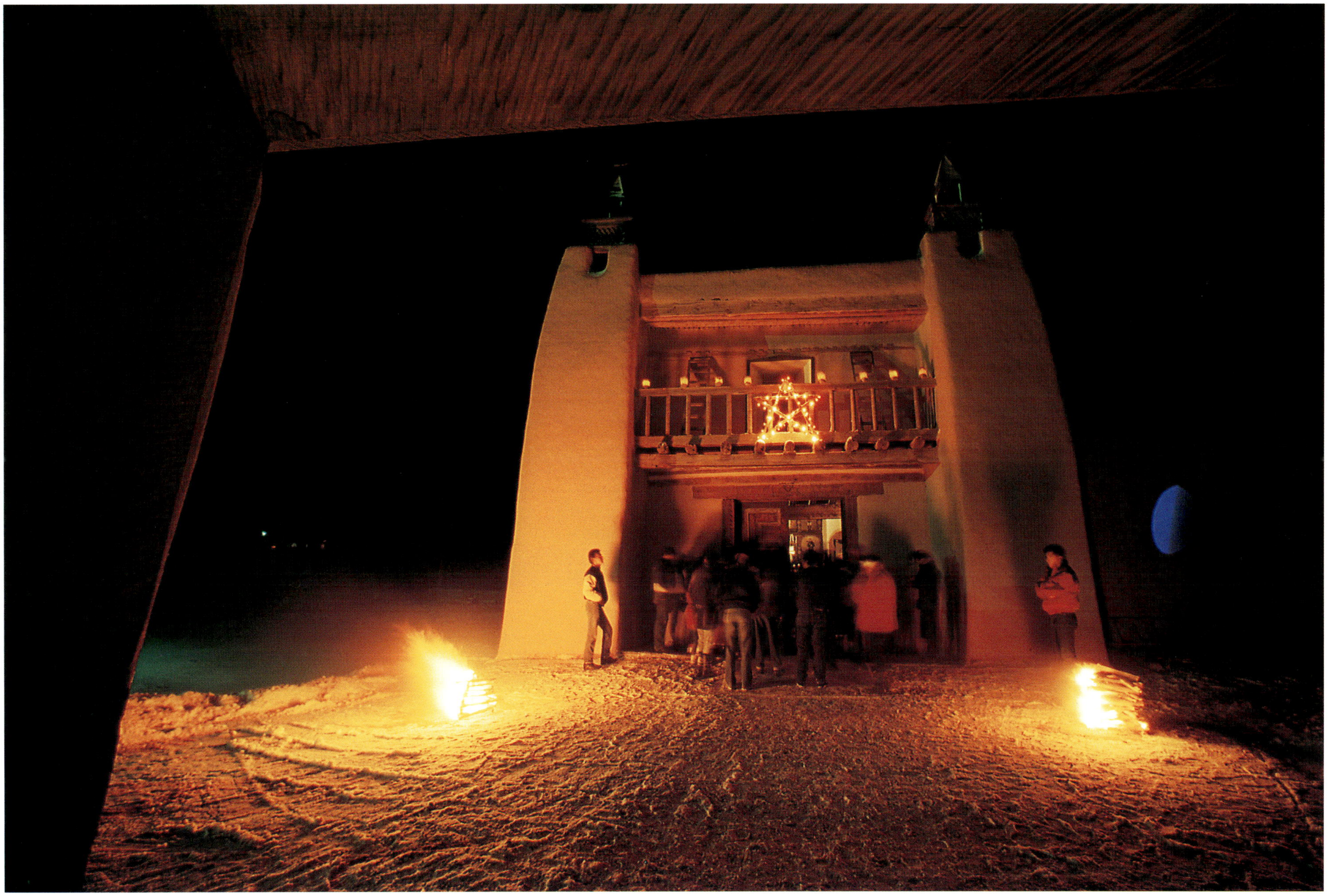

Grounded Tradition

While *luminarias* (small bonfires) roar outside the small historic church in the northern village of Las Trampas, locals pack inside for Christmas Eve festivities.

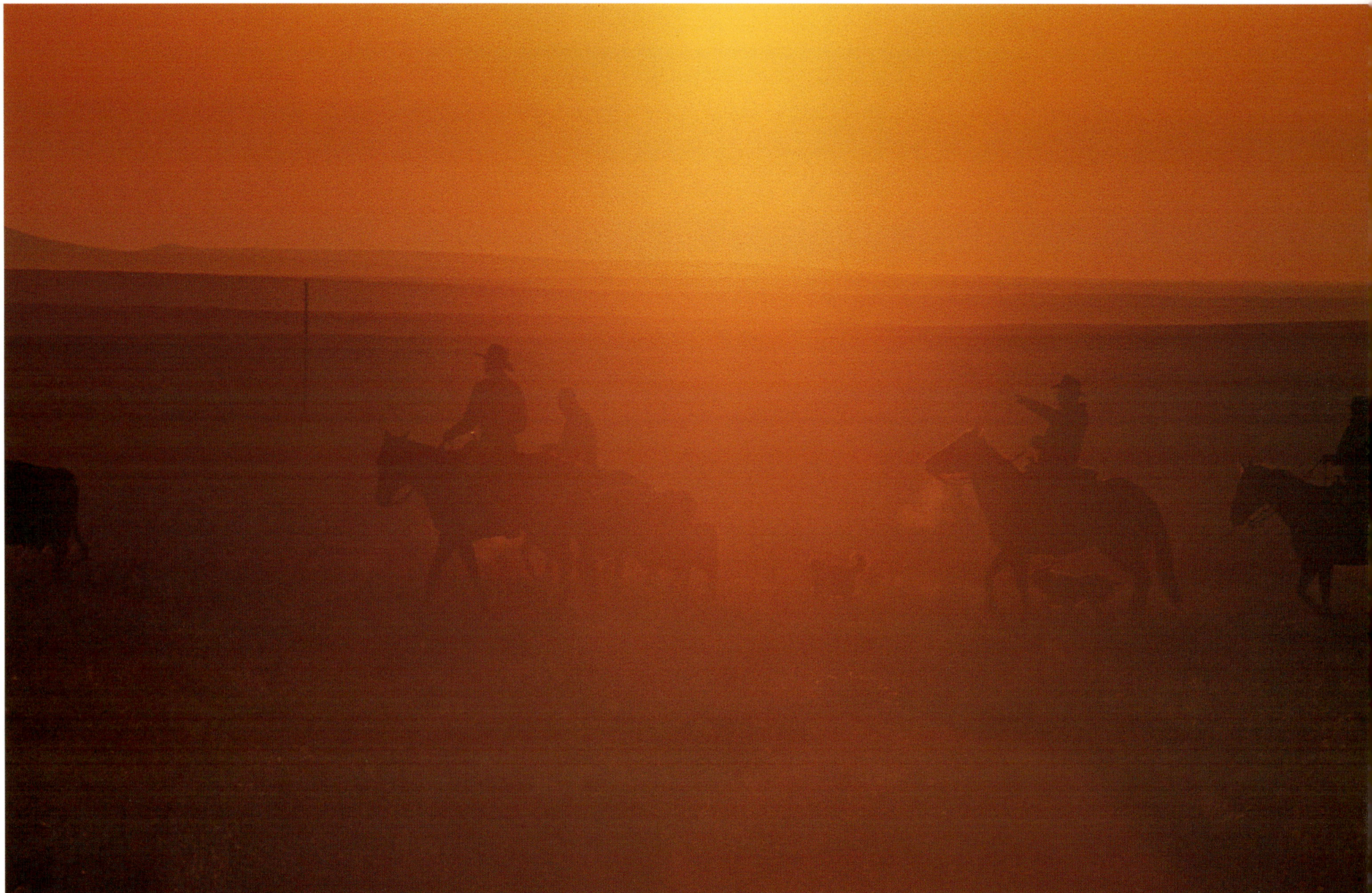

All the romance and nostalgia of the Old West is alive and well in many parts of New Mexico, especially in this dawn view of mounted cowboys riding the range with their attentive dogs on the Shaw Ranch near Springer. Horses have been an integral part of the state ever since the Spanish introduced them to the Southwest in the 1500s. The horse, as well as the burro, remain an ingrained cultural icon in New Mexico even though the invention of the internal-combustion engine has nearly rendered their original purpose obsolete.

The sight of horseback riders, whether their intention is recreational or functional, is common throughout the state, even in the urban areas. Although some cities have ordinances restricting horses within their limits, there is an unbridled fascination among most of the public for horses by the road.

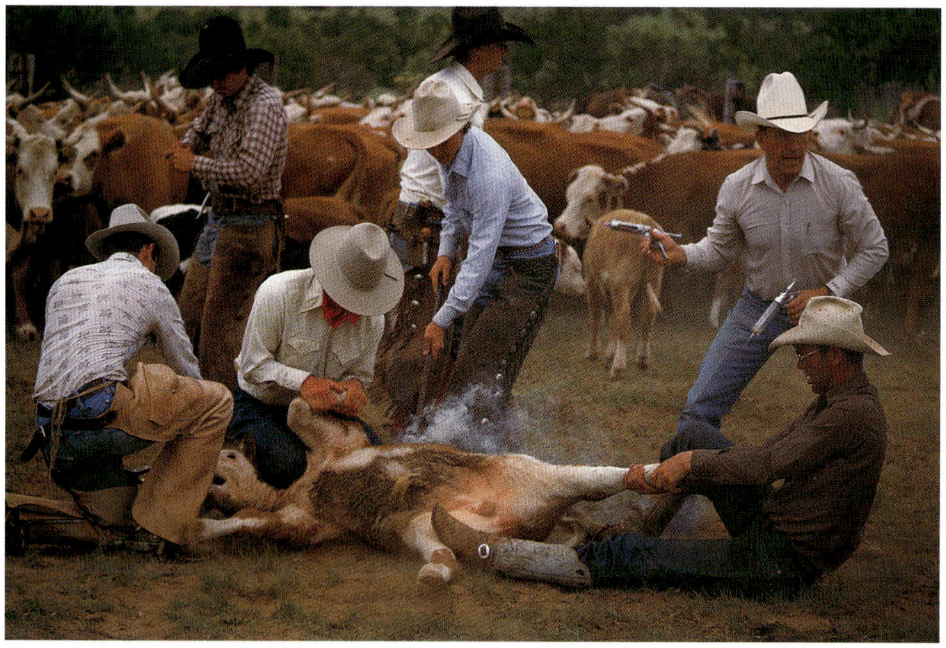

UPPER LEFT — OBLIVIOUS TO THE SMELL OF BURNING HAIR AND FLESH, COWBOYS HOLD DOWN A CALF WHILE MARKING IT WITH A SCATHING-HOT BRANDING IRON DURING ROUNDUP ON THE BELL RANCH. ROUNDUP, USUALLY CONDUCTED IN SPRING AND FALL, IS A BUSY TIME FOR COWBOYS WHO MUST CORRAL, CULL, BRAND AND VACCINATE CATTLE BEFORE THEY CAN BE EITHER BE TURNED LOOSE TO GRAZE AGAIN OR BE SHIPPED TO MARKET. EACH RANCH HAS ITS OWN DISTINCT BRAND TO MAKE IT READILY IDENTIFIABLE ON THE RANGE. THE BELL RANCH BRAND USES AS A DESIGN — YOU GUESSED IT — THE OUTLINE OF A BELL.

RIGHT — COWBOYS MUST DE-HORN COWS TO PREVENT THEM FROM INJURING THEMSELVES OR OTHERS DURING ROUNDUP AND SHIPMENT TO MARKET. MEAT BRUISED BY HORNS OR OTHERWISE IS UNSELLABLE.

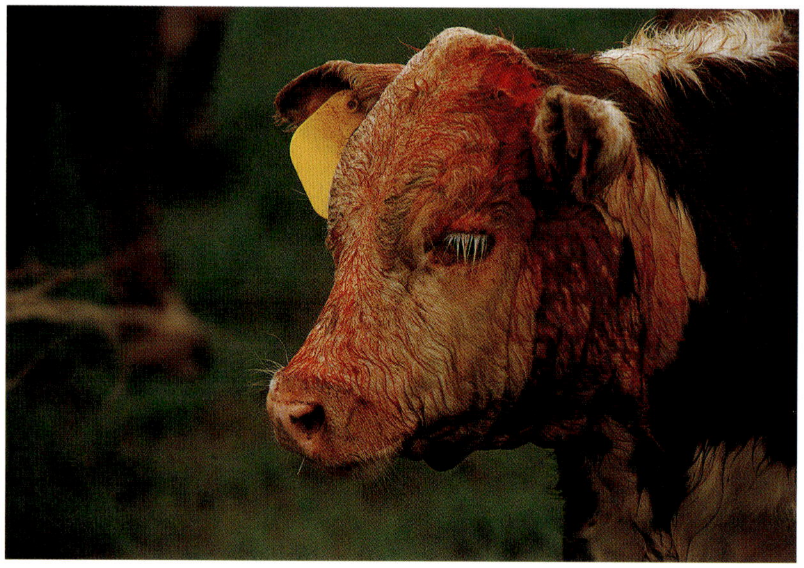

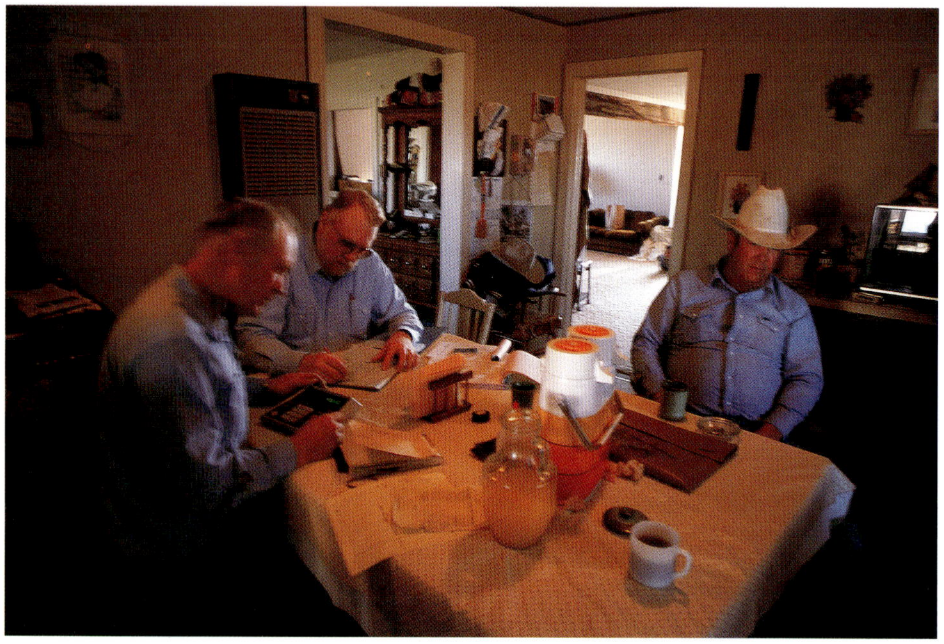

LOWER LEFT — PROVING THAT ALL COWBOYING DOESN'T TAKE PLACE ON THE RANGE, THESE RANCH FOREMEN ON THE SHAW RANCH NEAR THE CANADIAN RIVER CLOSE A DEAL AT HEADQUARTERS.

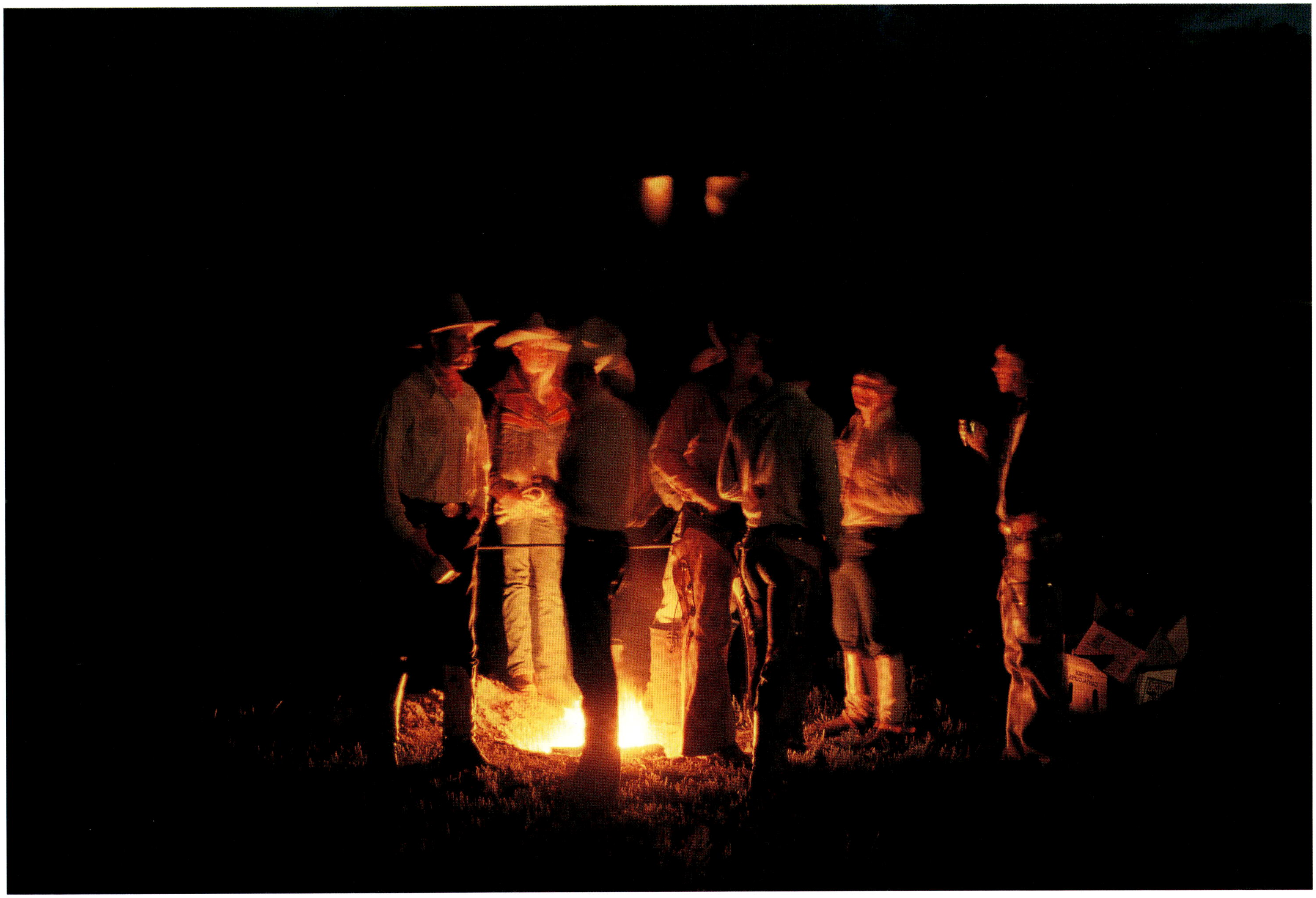

Cowboys at the Bell Ranch just northwest of Tucumcari warm themselves by a campfire before a long, hard-working day of roundup.

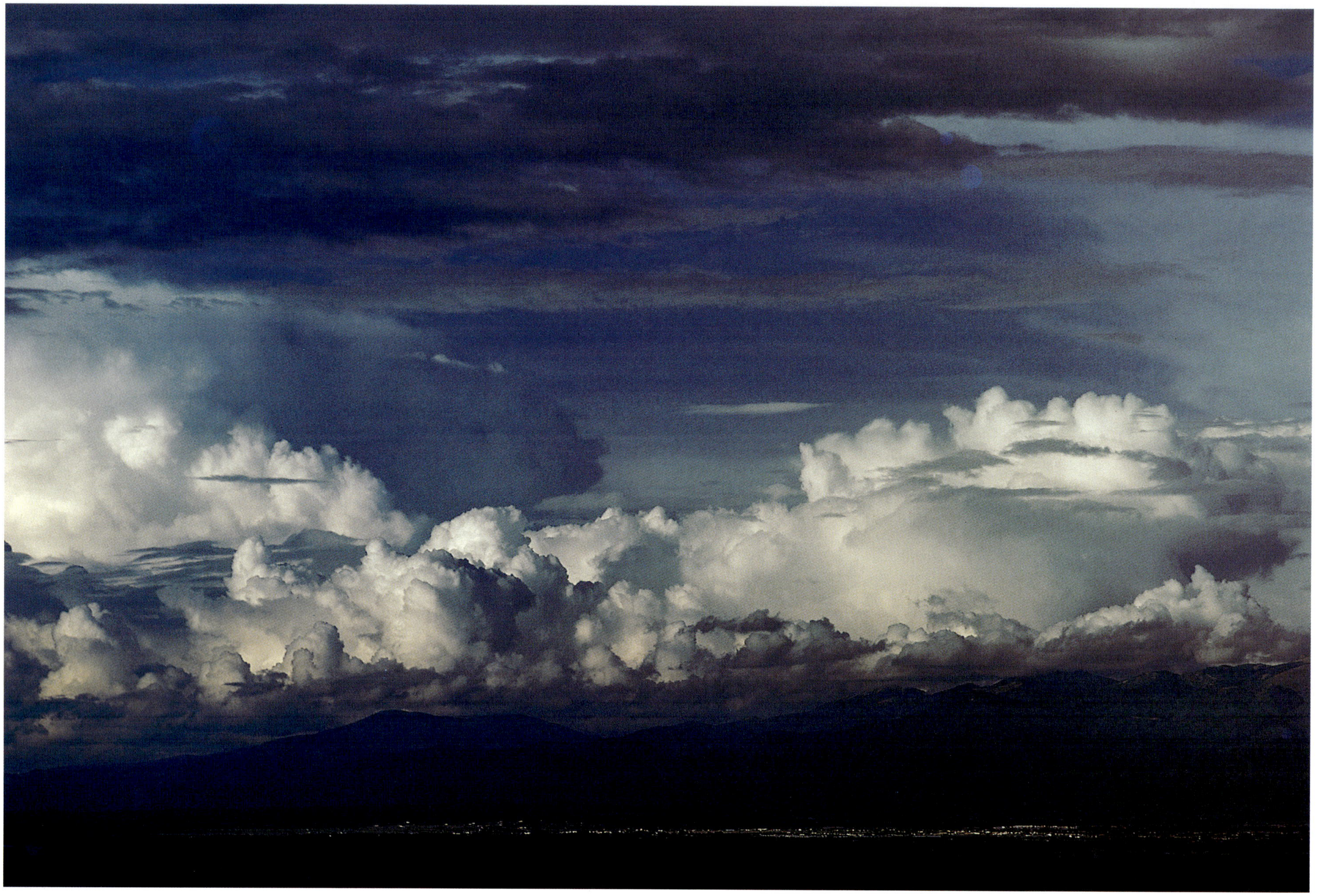

Magnitude of Nature

Dwarfed by high-forming clouds hovering over the Sangre de Cristo Mountains, the distinguishable city lights of Santa Fe begin to glow at dusk.

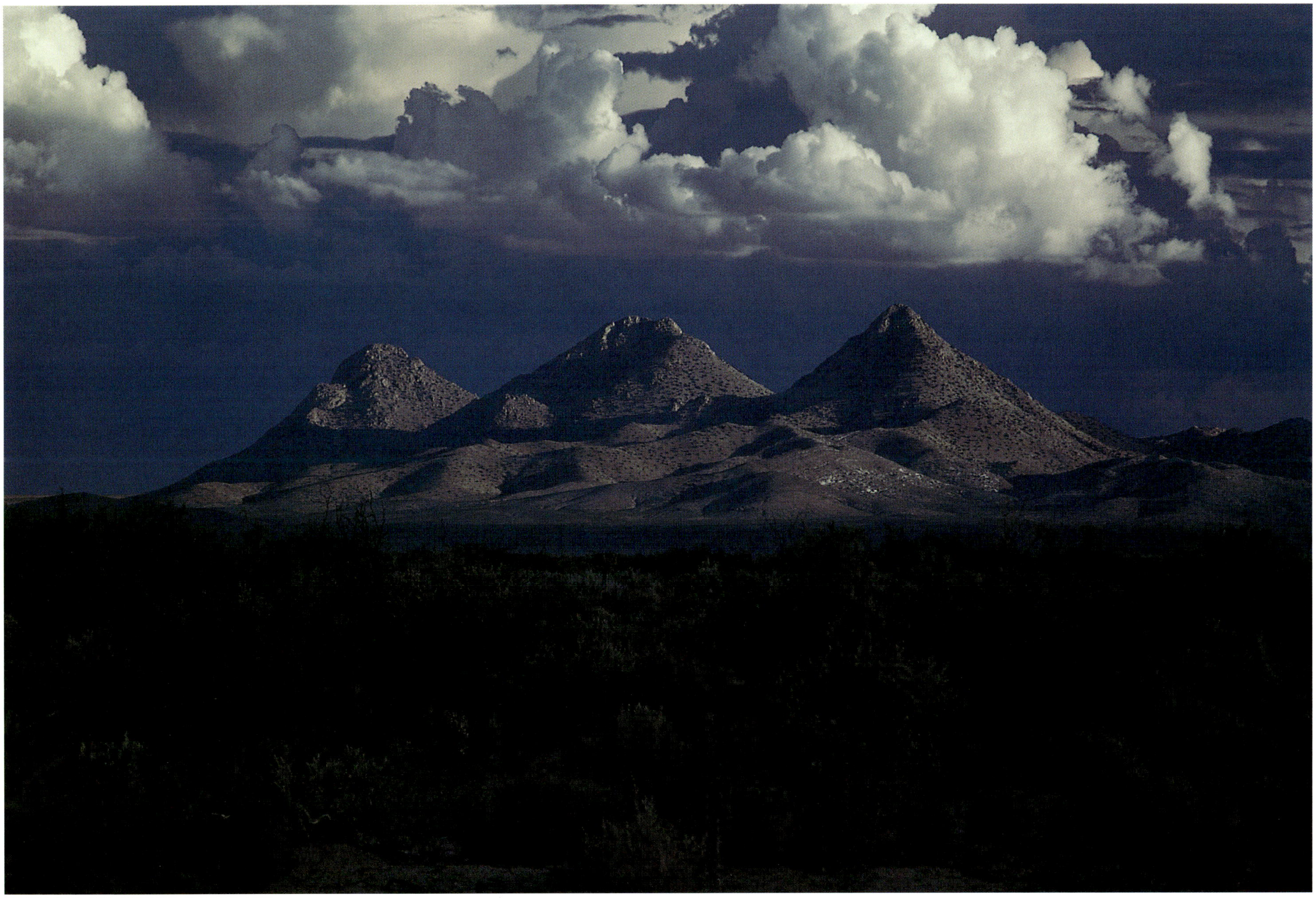

TRIPLE FARE

TRES HERMANAS PEAKS (THREE SISTERS) SOUTH OF DEMING COME ALIVE IN THE LATE AFTERNOON UNDER A PARTLY CLOUDY SKY IN THE CHIHUAHUAN DESERT.

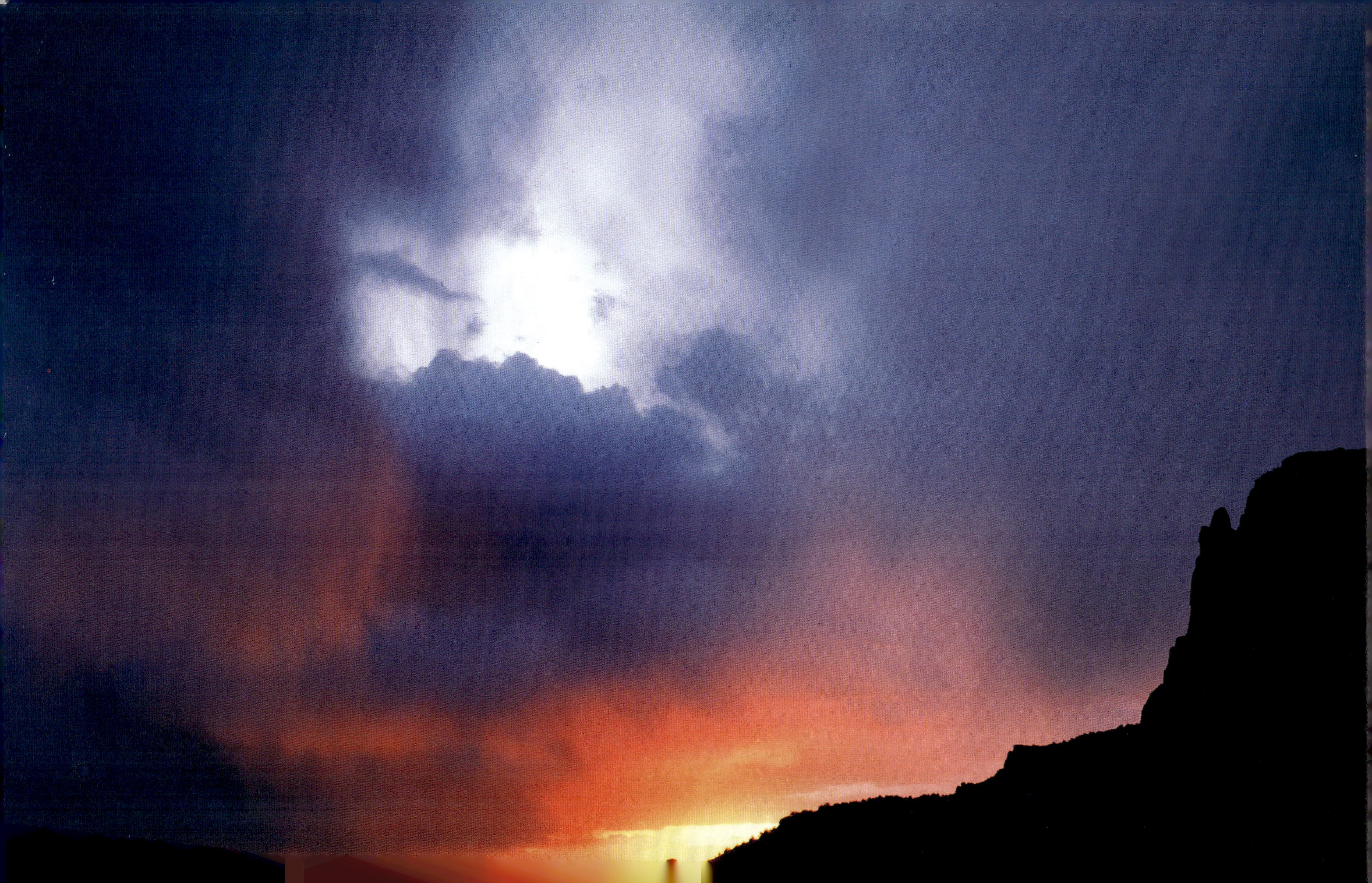

The skies over a mesa near Zuni Pueblo in western New Mexico light up in a blaze of burning glory at sundown. Many of the colorful natural formations in this area of the state, more popularly known as "Indian Country," hold sacred meaning to Native Americans, including members of the nearby Zuni, Navajo, Acoma and Laguna tribes.

The mineral-rich area also has held special meaning to the white man. In 1950, a Navajo sheepherder named Paddy Martínez unknowingly discovered a rich deposit of uranium ore near Grants, thus sprouting a prosperous mining boom that created many jobs. But the lessened demand for uranium in the last two decades has spelled bust for the mines and their operators.

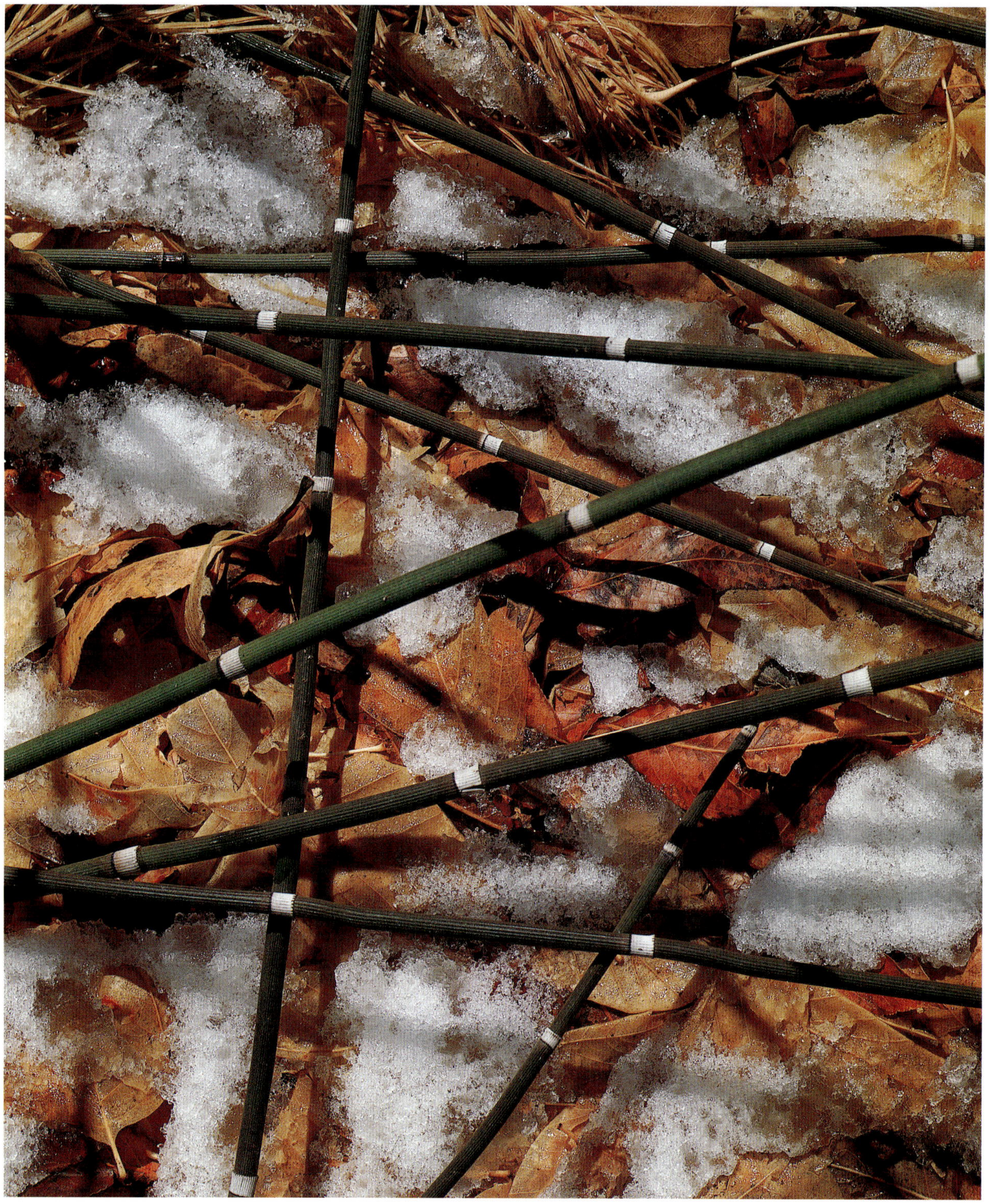

Seasonal Crossings

Fallen reeds and leaves previously blanketed by winter snowfall miraculously appear during the spring thaw at Bandelier National Monument.

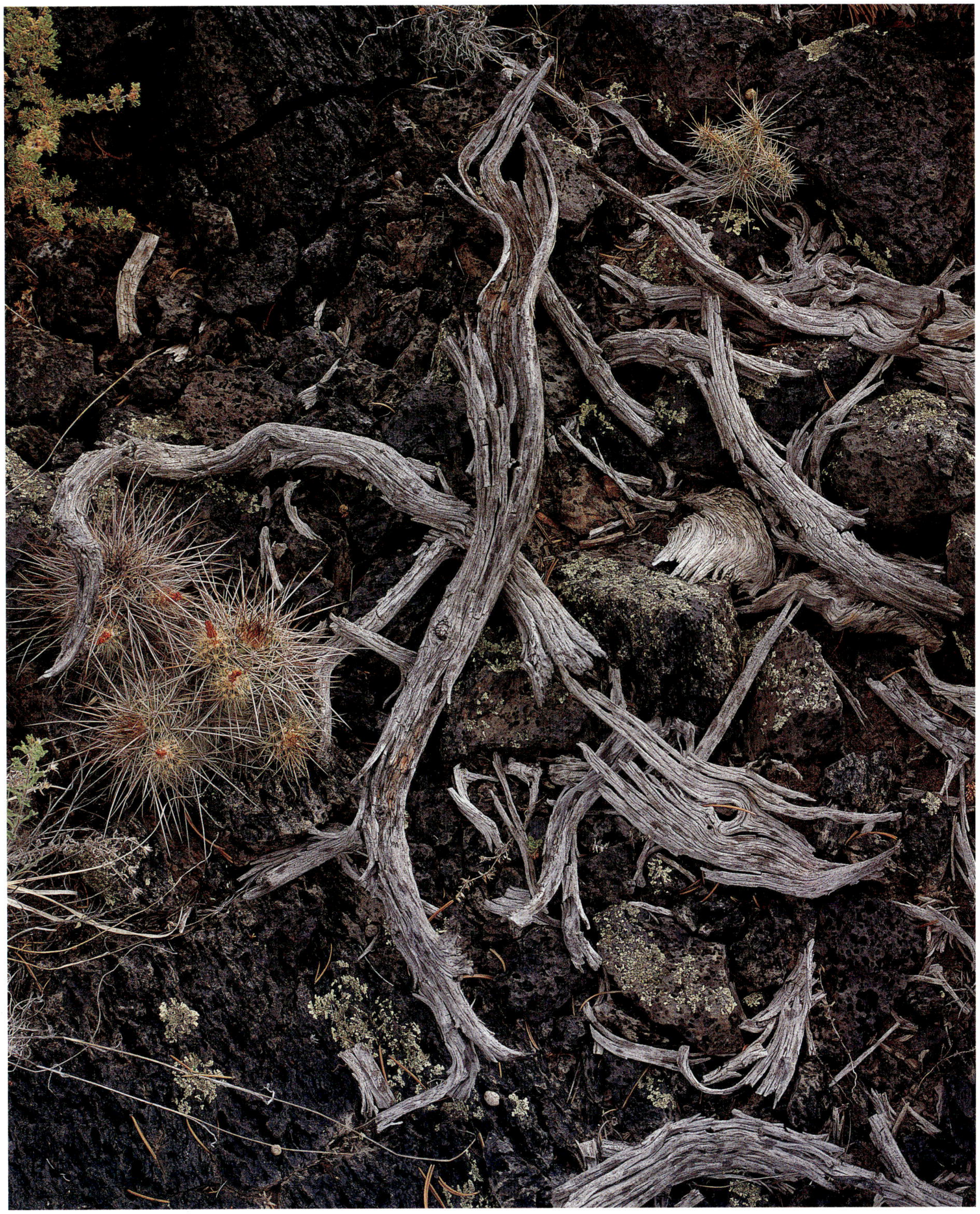

Badland Scatterings

Cactus plants and weathered branches cover a small section of the lava floor at

El Malpais National Monument near Grants.

The rising sun peeks through a crevice on Corn Mountain near Zuni Pueblo in western New Mexico. The Spanish first made contact with Zuni Indians in 1539 when Estéban the Moor and some Indians from Mexico visited their ancient Hawiku site to confirm the existence of the "Seven Golden Cities of Cíbola." Estéban, a black man, served as guide for Fray Marcos de Niza. He heard rumors of Cíbola years earlier while wandering throughout the Southwest with Cabeza de Baca after they were shipwrecked near Florida. The Zunis distrusted the Moor because he demanded women and wore a rattle with the depiction of an owl, causing them to think he was associated with evil. The wary Indians killed him. Fray Marcos de Niza told his superiors about the death and they kept secret the non-existence of Cíbola. Historians believe they did this so clergymen could safely accompany future armed explorations of New Mexico and Christianize as many natives as possible. Francisco Vázquez de Coronado's epic expedition in search of gold sought out Hawiku just a year after this incident.

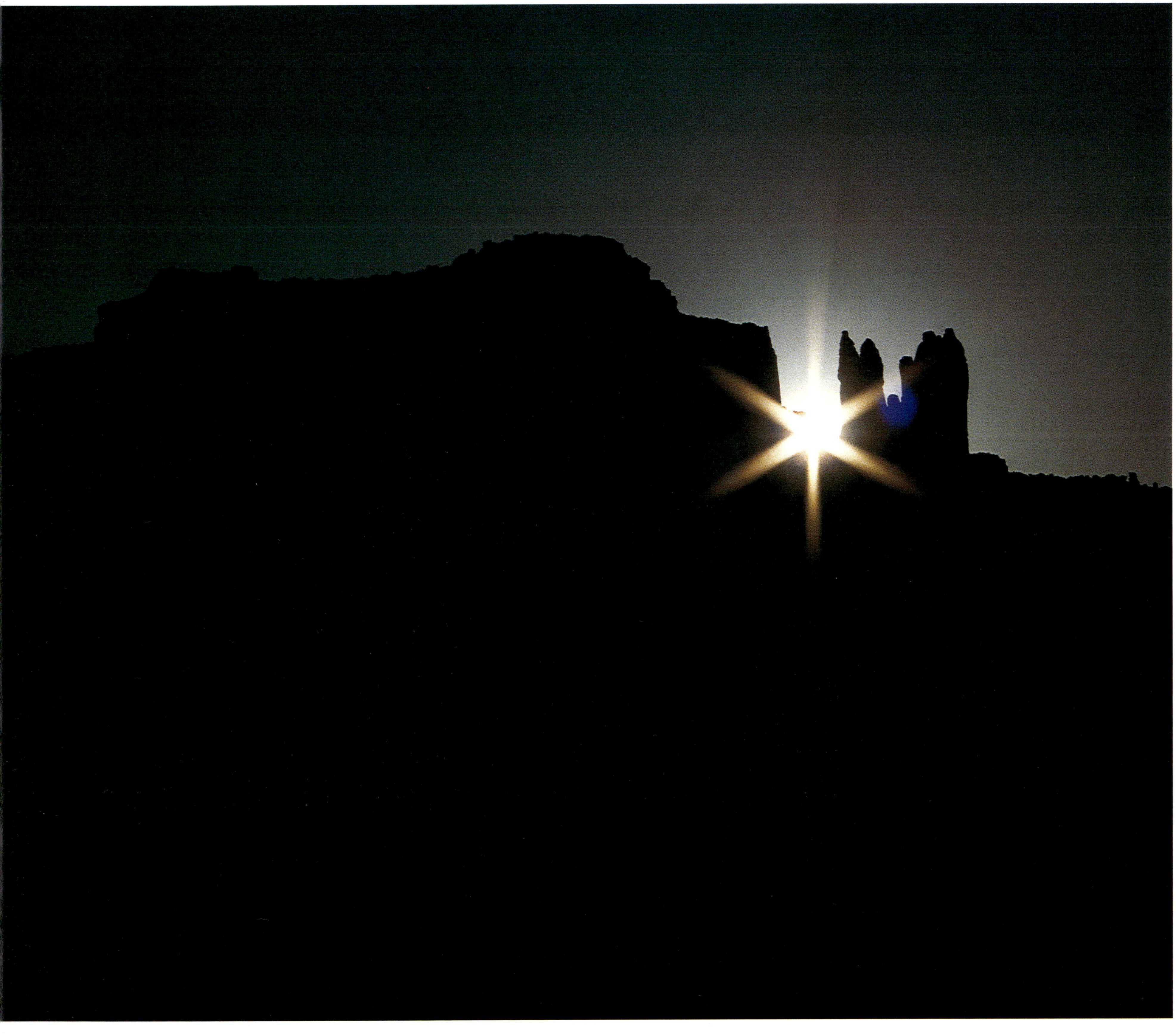

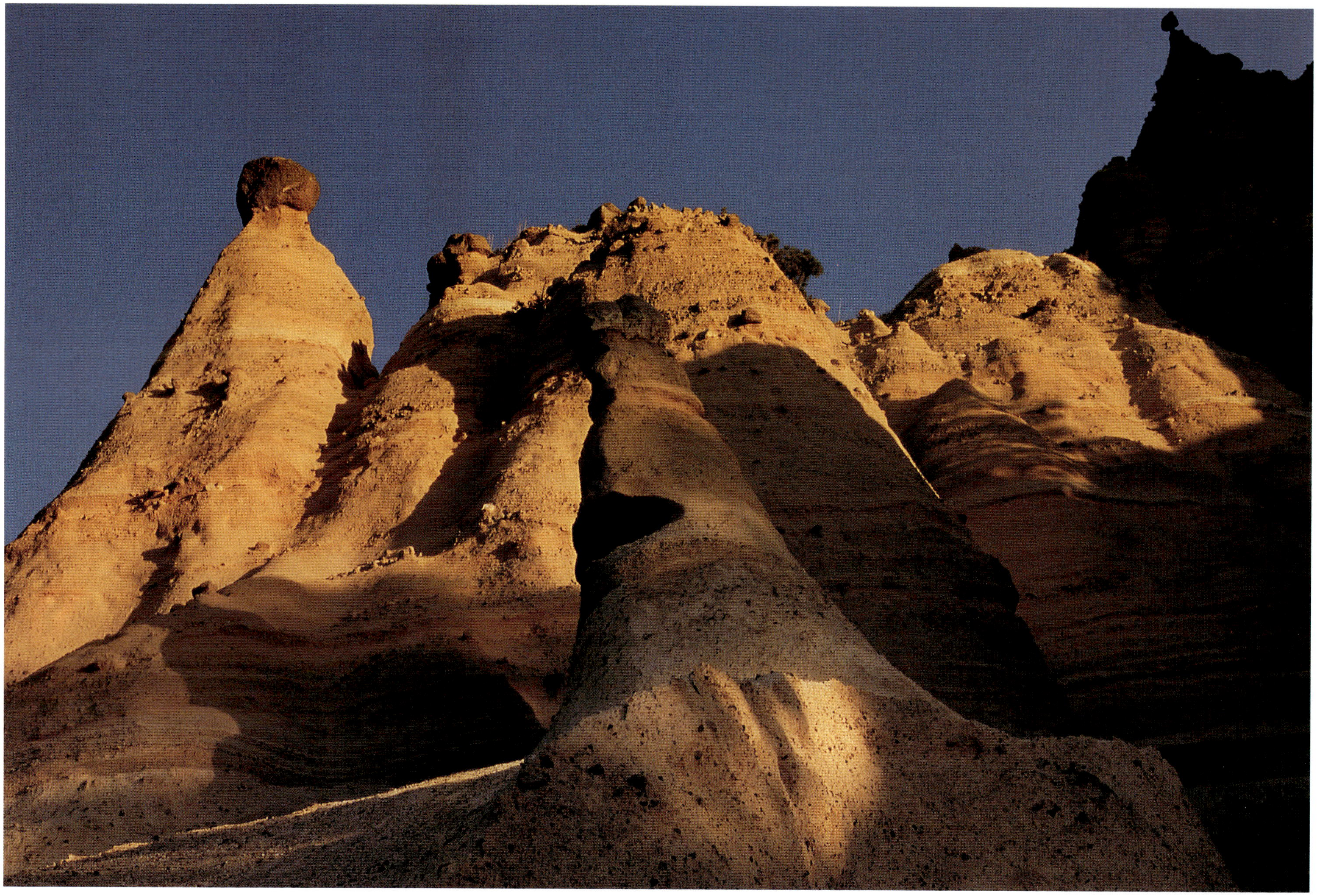

Rocks of Ages

Tent Rocks and the surrounding natural formations near Cóchití Pueblo
represent millions of years of dynamic geologic activity in New Mexico.

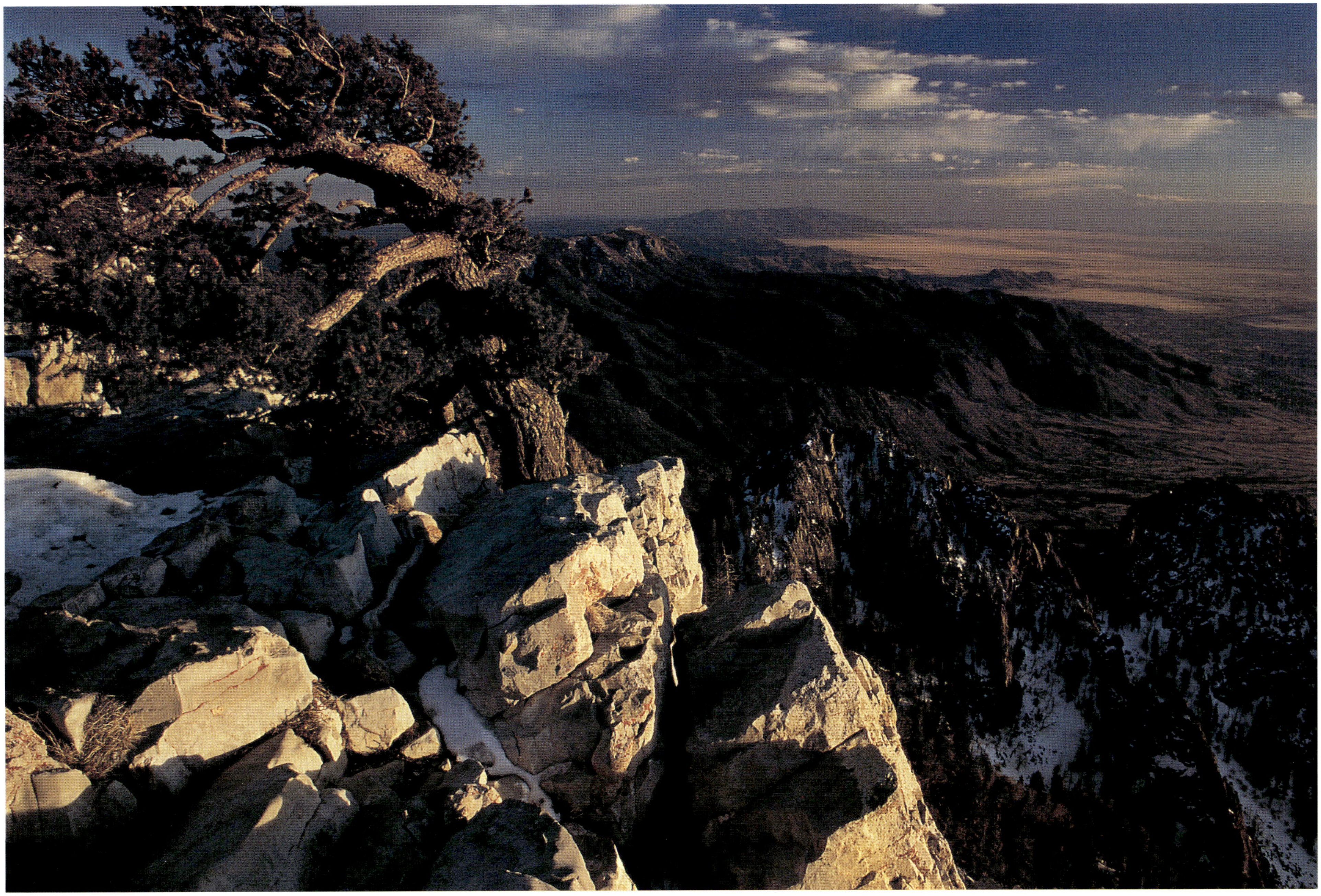

More Than Meets the Eye

A piñon tree atop Sandía Crest east of Albuquerque shows the effects of decades of high winds blowing over the scenic mountaintop. The Manzano Mountains stretch southward in the far background. There is an extensive, underground network of top-secret, U.S. military installations throughout the Manzano range.

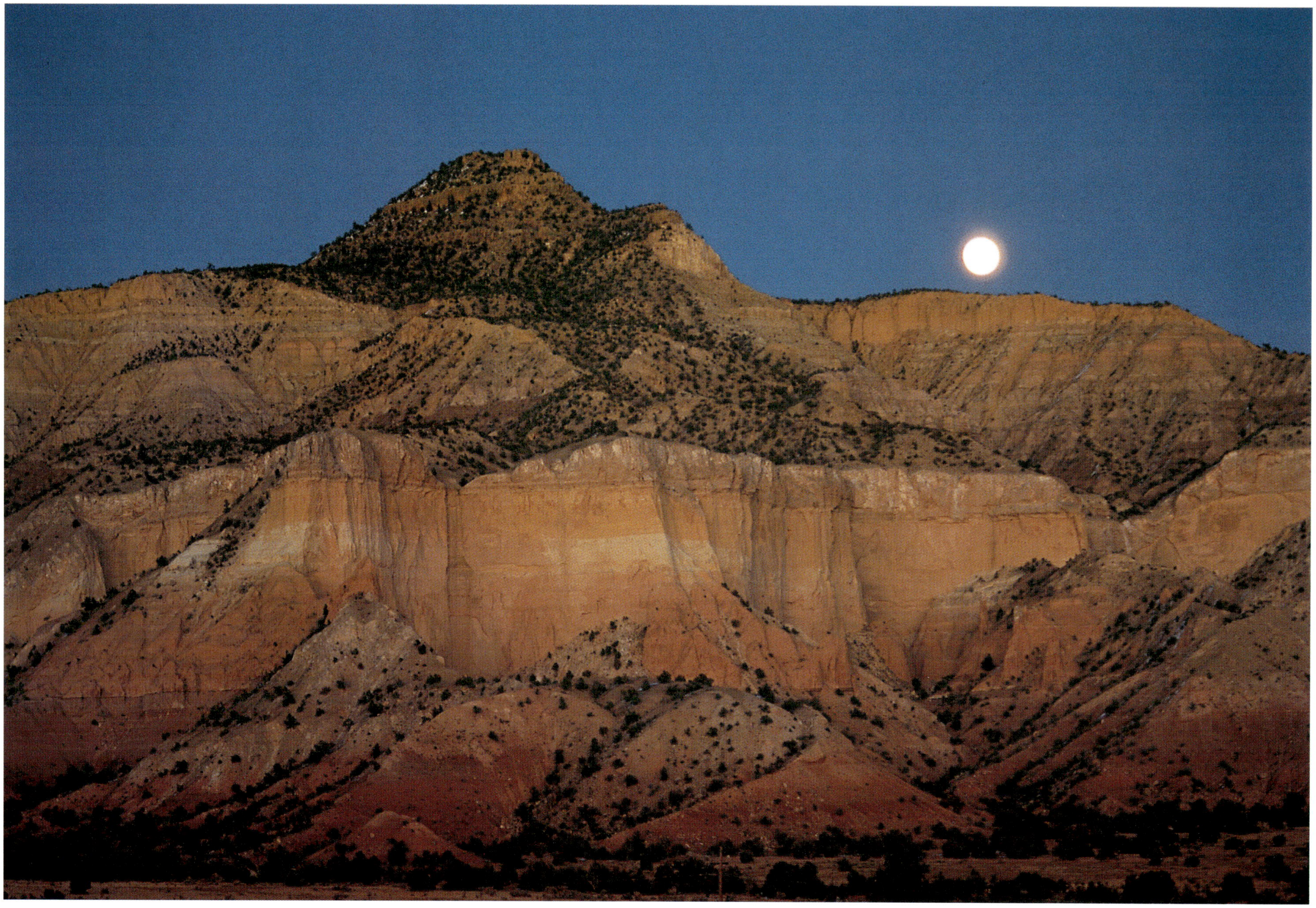

Upward Bound

The massive walls of Sombrero Peak near Abiquiú glow in the evening twilight while a full moon begins its nighttime trek across the darkening sky.

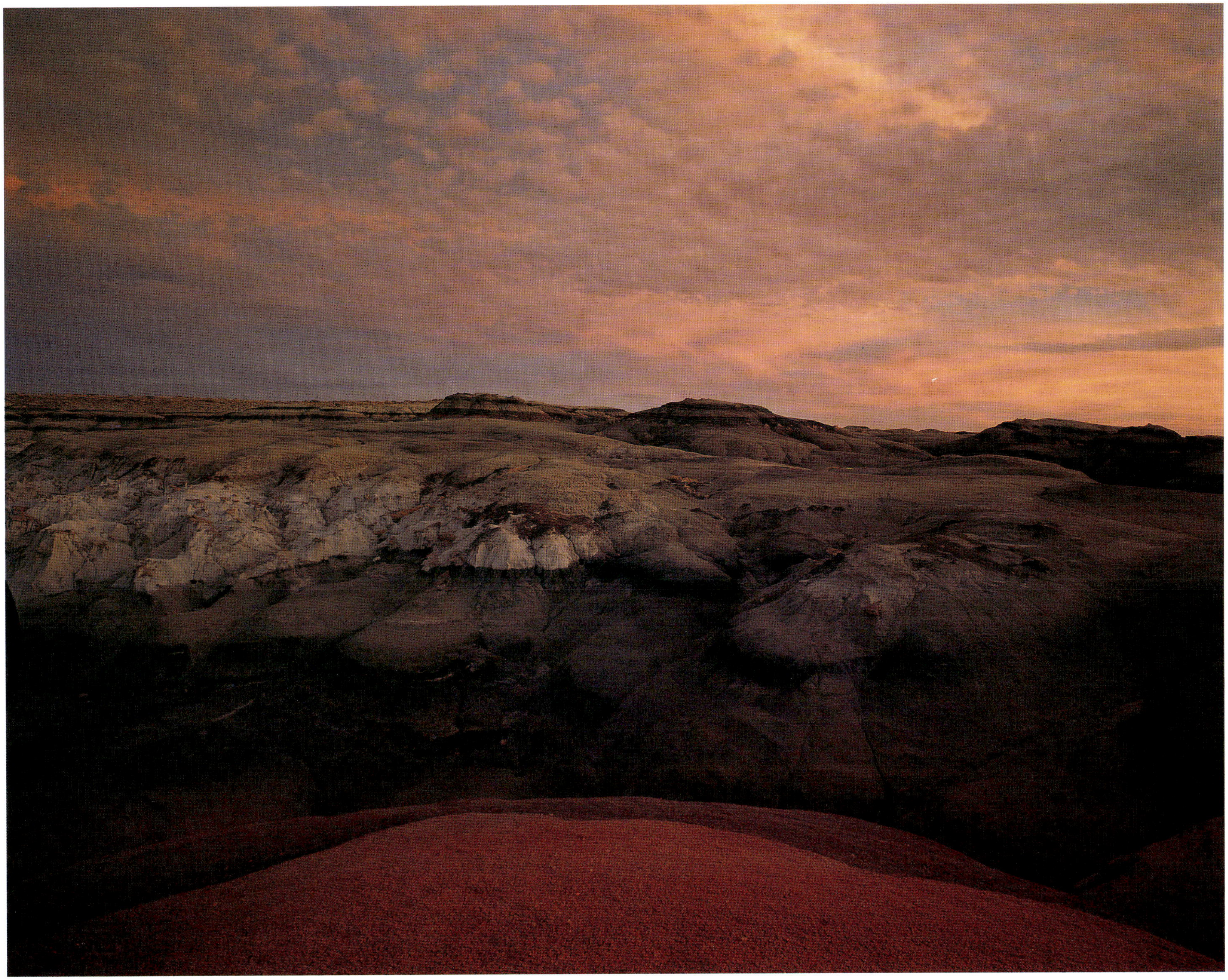

Evening Ovals

Looking like anything other than a landscape on planet Earth, the beauty of the Bisti Badlands Wilderness allures in the fading light of dusk.

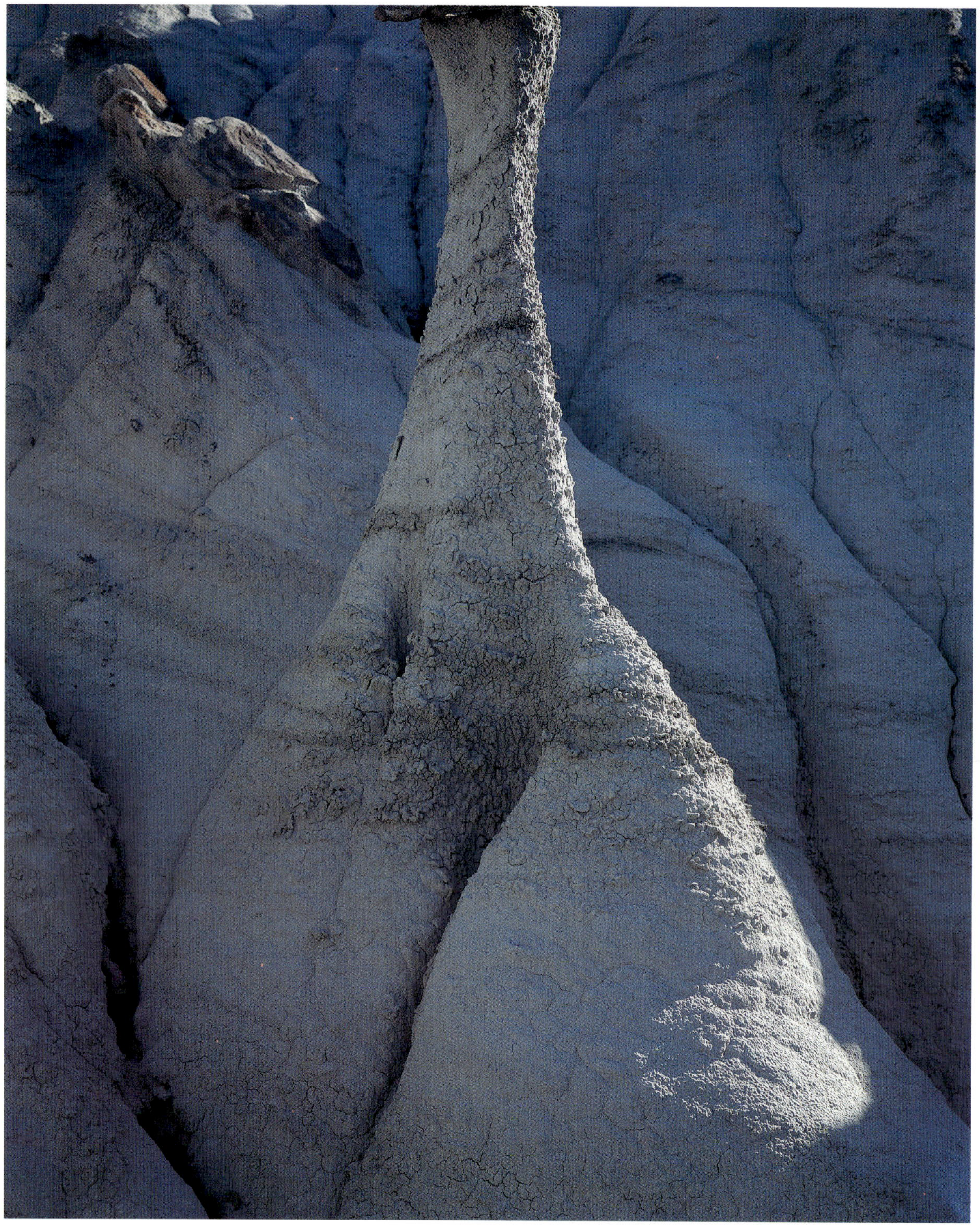

Bisti Figure

A fantastical column of rock, otherwise known as a hoodoo in western circles, contributes to the extraterrestrial appearance of the Bisti Badlands Wilderness.

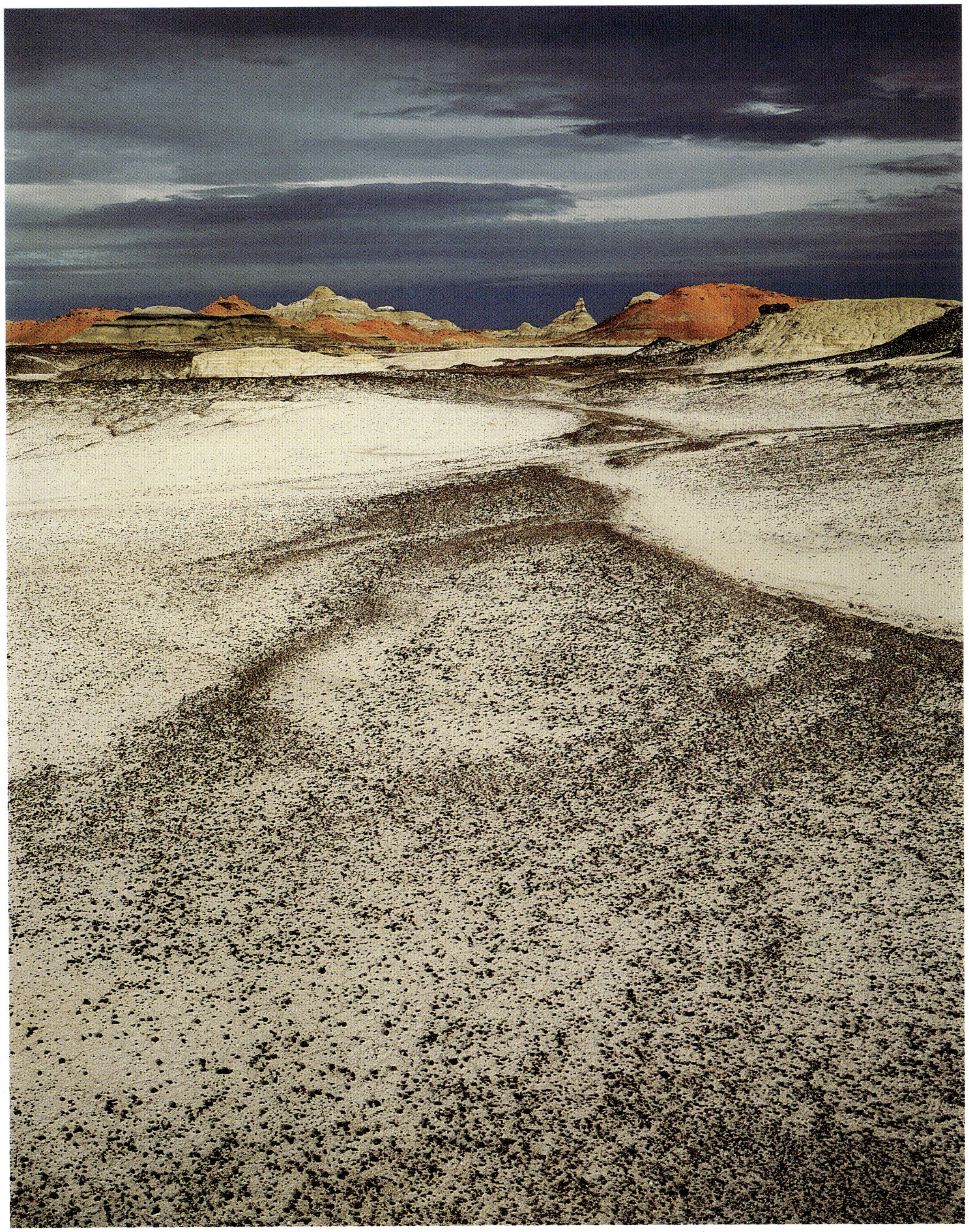

Early Dawn

The soft, subtle light emanating from a cloudy sky at dawn transforms the desolate landscape of Bisti Badlands Wilderness into an inviting surreal panorama.

My grandfather,
Frederick Albert Nohl,
born in Odell, Illinois in 1867, left
home at the age of 12, joined the
Santa Fe Railway and
followed the tracks to New Mexico in
1880 – I often marvel at the changes
he saw, not only in New Mexico, but in
the world as a whole. Spanning a life-
time from just after the Civil War to
space travel, he passed away in 1963
at the age of 96.

— Mark Nohl

Red Dawn Bisti Badlands
(Right)

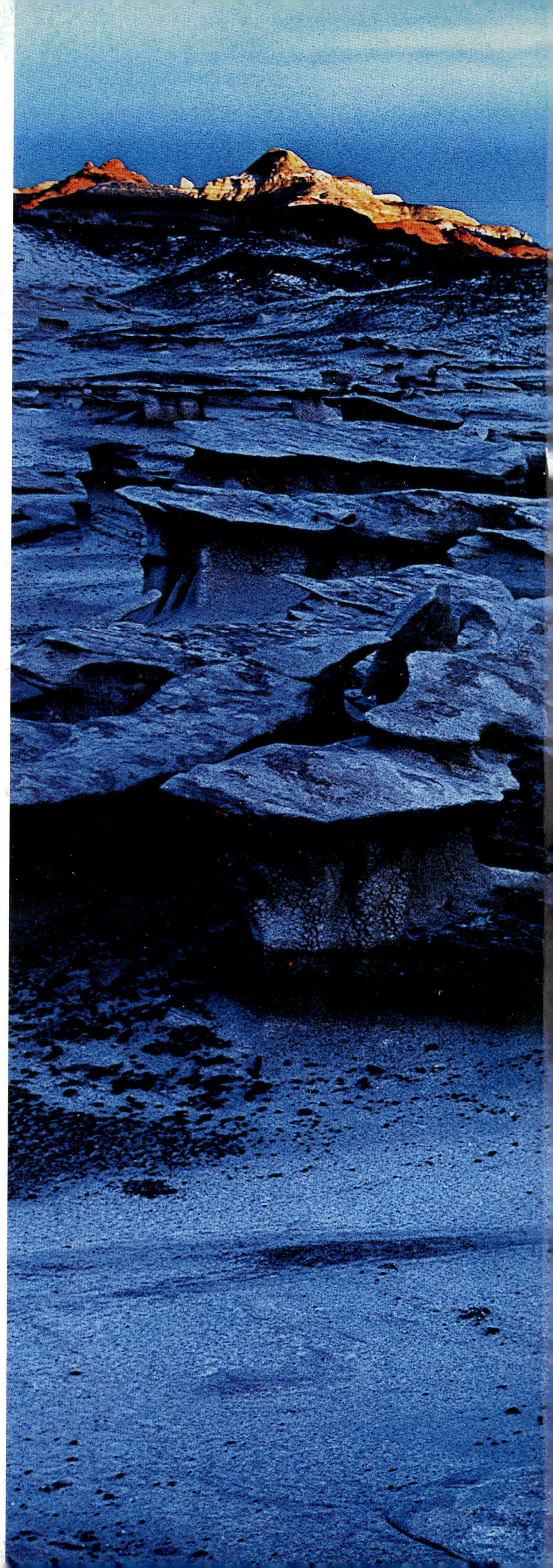

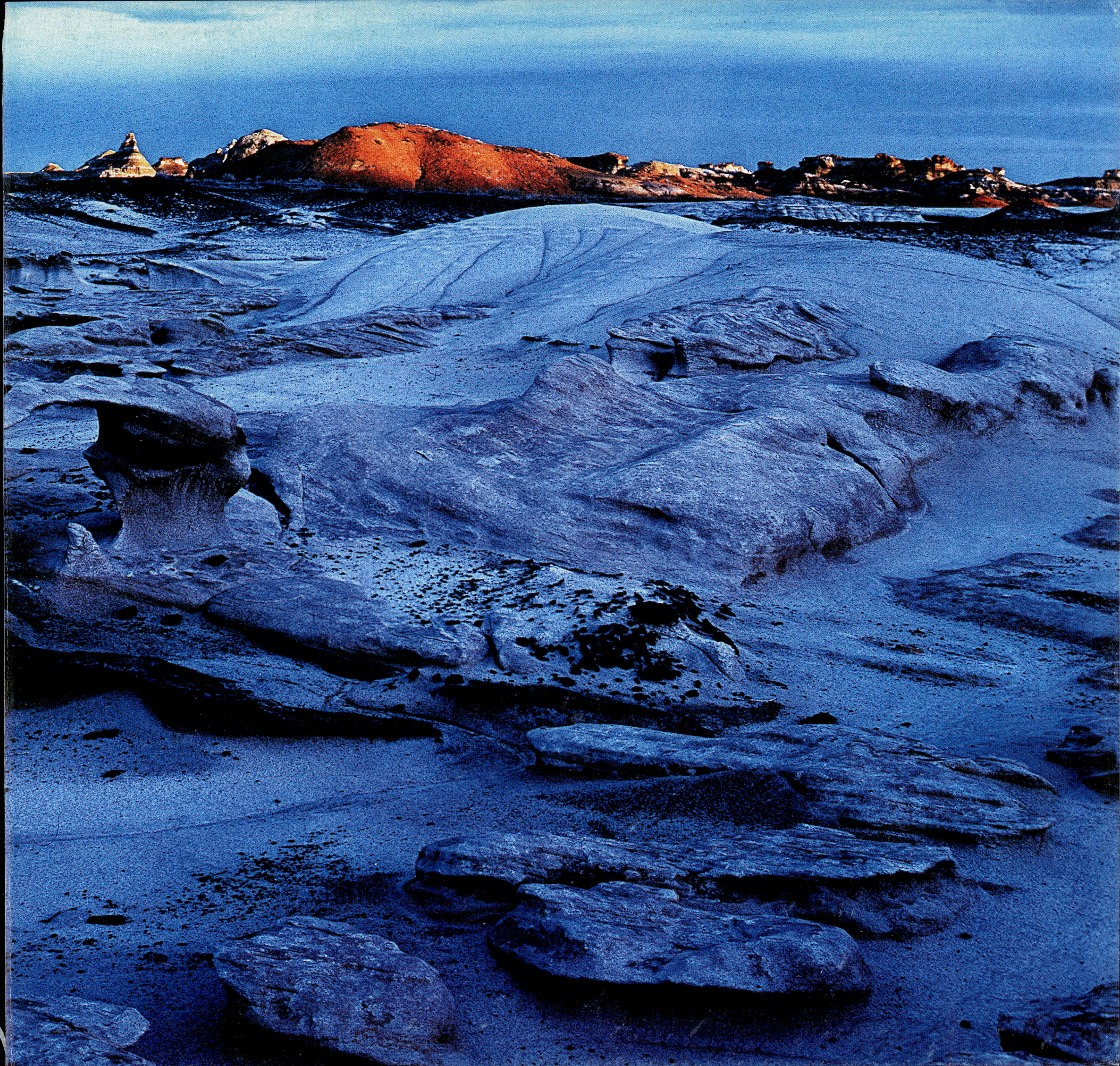

New Mexico Magazine
495 Old Santa Fe Trail
Santa Fe, New Mexico 87503

Printed and bound in Hong Kong
through Palace Press International.